THE ONLY BEGINNER FREEZE-DRYING BOOK YOU'LL EVER NEED

OTHER SELECTIONS

Coming Soon

Backpacking with Freeze-Dried Foods

Freeze-Dried Smoothies for Gut Health

Freeze-Dried Candy Making for Selling and Fun

COMPANION WORKBOOKS in Sizes X-L, L, M & S

GO.2MHE.COM

THE ONLY BEGINNER FREEZE-DRYING BOOK YOU'LL EVER NEED

LEARN THE SIMPLE PROCESS TO CREATE FOOD STORAGE FOR YOUR SURVIVAL PANTRY AND DISCOVER EASY RECIPES YOUR FAMILY WILL LOVE

MICRO-HOMESTEADING EDUCATION

For our children,
- you amaze us daily -
We are proud to see you understand the importance
and learning the knowledge of food preservation.

And
For the generations of parents
who continue the tradition of preserving food
for the sake of their family's health and well-being,
We adore you, support you, & encourage you to keep at it!

CONTENTS

INTRODUCTION

The cost of food is rising at an alarming rate. Natural disasters, pandemics, violence, and war are a few of the terrifying causes of shortages that leave grocery store shelves empty. Whispers of potential food shortages are coming from all over the place. The U.S. Department of Agriculture stated that 25 percent of households suffered from food insecurity in 2020. Now, with inflation, these numbers are expected to rise. At the same time, an average of 35 percent of the U.S. food supply goes in the garbage. Americans waste an average of 220 pounds of food per person per year, mostly through spoilage.

There are limitations on which foods can safely be preserved and in which manner. Canning, dehydrating, freezing, and culturing are important parts of preserving, and we will continue to utilize them all, but there is a new method available to us now.

Freeze-drying is so scientific it can be intimidating. Not gonna lie, my sister and I were a bit "scared" of using a freeze-dryer. We'd heard about "explosions," huge messes, and mistakes that ended up costing the owner big bucks to fix. We wondered how long it would take to learn how to use it and what hidden dangers there would be. We simply did not know how to use all the functions and buttons, so it was overwhelming at first.

After buying a freeze-dryer, we followed the rules, ran batch after batch, and learned that it's really quite easy! Once you know the tricks of the trade it's literally as simple as preparing the food, running a batch, and packaging the food.

We are at the point now where we can experiment and try new recipes and new ways of doing things. We found that the freeze-dryer is just another appliance that can be used to benefit us greatly. This morning, after my husband cleaned the chamber from yesterday's batch, he took some gallon bags of frozen banana peppers out of the freezer, spread them out on the trays, and popped them in the freeze-dryer, easy peasy. Just follow the steps and let the machine do its thing!

Freeze-drying allows you to create meals that can safely be eaten many years later. Your garden produce, your favorite treat, the food you got in a bulk buy, and even your leftovers! Foods low in fat, like vegetables or fruits, can be freeze-dried and stored for 25-30 years. Dairy can be stored for 10-15 years. And even full meals can be freeze-dried and stored for up to 5-10 years, depending on the ingredients. This means you can store up food for many, many years and protect yourself and your family from empty shelves when they arise.

Preservation Method of the Future

Freeze-drying is quite literally the preservation method of the future. It is the best way to preserve many different types of foods. Whatever your reasons may be for diving into the world of freeze-drying, I know two things for sure about you:

1. You want the freeze-drying process explained and streamlined.
2. You want freeze-drying recipes that make your taste buds happy.

This book will provide you with both these solutions and more, in a concise, fun, and easy-to-understand manner. You will not only learn what freeze-drying actually is, but also how to become more comfortable with operating a freeze-drying appliance and how to properly package freeze-dried foods for long-term storage. To simplify your life, printable batch logs, maintenance sheets, reference pages, and checklists are included.

This book was written because there is a need for quality freeze-drying information. It was quite difficult to source the facts about freeze-drying when I first started this journey. As a result, I made some mistakes that could have been avoided. There is no need for you to go through the same trial and error. I placed the knowledge I wish I'd had before I got started on this journey in these pages so you can achieve food stability and self-sustainability with as little fuss and hassle as possible.

Knowing where your food comes from, eating healthy, nutrient-rich foods, and watching your pantry grow from your own efforts are benefits you can glean from freeze-drying. Preparing for an uncertain future as our world is plunged deeper and deeper into chaos from sources we have no control over can bring great comfort. I want to share my 25-plus years of first-hand experience in food preservation to bring you this peace of mind.

This is an exciting journey. Turn the page to take that first step on this road of food preservation.

Using a freeze-dryer for your homesteading needs can be amazing! It is, however, an investment, so it's essential to be fully prepared. With our helpful checklist, you can rest assured that you're making an informed decision that aligns with your homesteading goals.

At Micro-Homesteading Education, we're passionate about homesteading and are committed to helping you achieve your goals. By providing you with the best possible resources and support, we can help you live a fulfilling and sustainable life on the homestead.

We hope you find our checklist useful in your homesteading journey! If you have any questions, please don't hesitate to reach out to us. We're always happy to hear from fellow homesteaders.

Scan the QR code for a checklist or visit: BFDC.2MHE.COM

1

LEARNING ABOUT FREEZE-DRYING

Y ou are about to go on an adventure in food preservation! You will learn new things and experiment with this cool scientific process. You will undoubtedly have fun with food if you embrace the learning curve and give it a shot!

Freeze-drying is the process of removing water by combining freezing, lowering the pressure, and applying heat. During the freezing phase, the chamber can reach temperatures as low as -40°F and works to freeze the foods rapidly. Then the vacuum pump turns on and lowers the pressure inside the chamber. At this point, sublimation occurs, and the majority of the water begins to change directly from a solid state into a gas. The shelves start to heat up, and the warmth facilitates the final removal of water from the food.

You might also hear the freeze-drying process by other names like lyophilization and cryodesiccation. No matter what you call it, the basic process remains the same: food is preserved by being dried at low temperatures and in low-pressure conditions and then having heat applied.

I can't tell you how happy I am when I see my strawberries retain their original shape after being freeze-dried. That is only possible because the strawberries were dried under low temperatures. This "low and slow" approach removes approximately 95 percent of water. It also means your foods go from frozen to dry without becoming a soggy wet mess! This process creates a final product with remarkable quality.

The methodology of freeze-drying has a long history, even though it has only been a popular term as of late. The technique was invented in 1906 in Paris by Jacques-Arsene d'Arsonval. However, its use was not immediately advocated for food preservation. Instead, freeze-drying was primarily used to preserve blood serum during World War II. But it didn't take long to catch on to what an asset freeze-drying would be in maintaining the freshness of food.

The commercialization of freeze-dried foods started in the 1950s. Commercial applications by pharmaceutical companies and corporations were the main uses for freeze-drying technology. Freeze-drying machines have only recently been on the market for everyday people to use at home. Harvest Right™ has been in business since 2014 and makes freeze-drying appliances for home use.

My aunt Michelle bought a home freeze-dryer in 2014, the first year it came out. Her family has been using it almost exclusively to create lightweight backpacking meals. They regularly go backpacking in remote areas and need the benefit of easy meals that don't weigh much at all. They can add water and have a homemade meal in minutes!

When I started researching home freeze-dryers, Harvest Right was the only American-made company I could find that sold freeze-dryers for home use. While there may be others out there, it is without a doubt true that no other company has the experience or comparable quality of Harvest Right. The quality of the freeze-dried final product is highly dependent on the quality of the machine you use. Harvest Right has a long-standing reputation for making great quality products. So, take the time to find the best machine for your needs. This book covers the experience gained from using Harvest Right™ freeze-dryers.

Despite the complicated processes inside the freeze-dryer, there is nothing to it for the user. All you have to do is follow five steps:

Five Steps to Freeze-Drying

1. Prepare cooked or raw food
2. Pre-freeze the food
3. Place in freeze-dryer and run batch
4. Check weight until dry
5. Package the final product

How Freeze-Drying Stacks Up Against Other Methods

While freeze-dryers are a bit up there in cost, it's still cheaper to buy a machine and freeze-dry your home-cooked meals than it is to purchase pre-packaged freeze-dried food for a year's supply for your family. After experiencing 25 years of preserving food by various means, I can confidently say that freeze-drying does indeed beat all other forms of food preservation. It's utterly amazing technology.

To be clear: I promote all forms of food preservation. There are so many good ways to preserve food, and there are benefits to being able to do them all. In addition, there will always be foods you'll like best when preserved in a certain way. I plan to continue canning jam, making pickles, dehydrating beef jerky, and pre-freezing everything before placing it in the freeze-dryer.

So, I am definitely not suggesting that you ditch other food preservation techniques and start freeze-drying exclusively. Instead, I'm advocating that freeze-drying is a worthy addition to your repertoire for food stability.

Freeze-drying is one of the best ways to preserve food long-term, and it gives a high level of quality when done right. Many people are turning to this food preservation method because the benefits cannot be matched.

Canning

The food preservation method of canning uses heat and pressure to seal jars with wet contents. The sealed contents do not come into contact with air, so they last longer. There are several ways to go about canning food, including water bath canning, pressure canning, and atmospheric steam canning.

Even fermented foods (those preserved using acidic substances like vinegar to give them improved nutritional value, new flavor, and, at times, a unique texture and appearance) can be canned.

Unfortunately, the heat used during canning damages the nutrients in such food. Only about 40 percent of the food's nutrition can be saved. Freeze-drying has the leg up in this case as it keeps the nutrients intact.

The foods are kept in a liquid like oil, water, or broth while sealed. Therefore, the texture of canned food is often mushy, whereas Freeze-dried food has a firm texture and rehydrates well.

It is often recommended to use up any home-canned goods within a year, but there really is no set date. As long as the seal remains intact, the food should be safe to eat, though the nutrient value will diminish with time. It's generally best to consume them within five years.

People who do canning are celebrated because canning requires skill. You can't just enter your kitchen one day and be an experienced canner. The techniques must be learned and practiced. Freeze-drying is push-button easy, on the other hand. All you have to do is prep the food beforehand. Canning takes less time to process (a few hours, depending on the type of food). Lower temperatures in the freeze-dryer mean it takes longer to process.

After acquiring the tools and mastering the art of canning, you'll need to ensure you have the storage supplies, such as glass jars, lids, and rings. Filled jars need to be stored on racks or shelves in a cool, dark space to ensure you gain maximum value in shelf life.

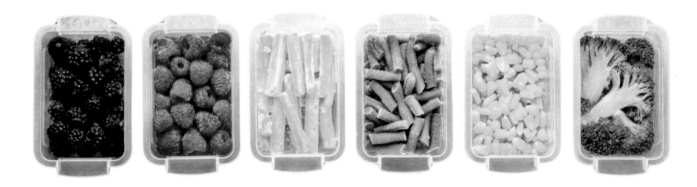

Freezing

Freezing works best for large food items, such as a roast. Freeze-dried foods must be prepared in smaller-sized pieces or slices for proper drying. Unlike canning, which requires skill, anyone can use their freezer to preserve food.

The challenge with freezing is ensuring the food is packaged correctly to avoid freezer burn. Freezer burn happens when frozen foods are exposed to air, leading to dehydration and possibly forming large ice crystals. This changes the quality and texture of foods.

Freezing is fast and easy, but it is a short-term solution for food preservation. Most foods can only be stored for a few months in the freezer, with the maximum recommended time being one to two years. Freezers can get filled up and become cluttered quickly. Additionally, storage size is limited, and a freezer requires continuous power.

Dehydrating

Dehydrating and freeze-drying are often mistaken to be the same, but they have very different end products. It is cheaper to run a dehydrator than a freeze-dryer, making dehydrating the less expensive drying method. Let's compare the two processes side by side:

Shelf life: Dehydrated foods have a shorter shelf life (5-15 yrs) than freeze-dried foods (5-25 yrs). But dehydration is still an excellent method for those that choose it, resulting in food storage with a good shelf life.

Physical Change: Dehydrating changes the shape, size, color, and flavor of the food. Freeze-dried foods change little physically, maintaining their shape, size, color, flavor, and nutrients.

Nutritional Value: Dehydration uses higher temperatures and is known to cause a degradation of nutrients. Sixty percent of the nutrition in dehydrated foods remains. Freeze-dried foods retain 97 percent of their nutritional value.

Texture: Dehydrated foods are chewy. Freeze-dried foods are crunchy.

Rehydration: It's easier to rehydrate freeze-dried foods because they absorb water quickly, especially compared to dehydrated foods, which must be soaked for a while.

Dehydration lengthens the shelf life of food by removing water from the food using heat to cause evaporation. It is a more rapid process of heating and drying compared to the heating during the latter phase of freeze-drying. Higher temperatures are used in dehydration, and most foods take eight to ten hours to dry. On the other hand, the heating stage of freeze-drying can take as long as four days, though it typically takes less than two.

Shelf Life of Preserved Foods

For the best nutrients and flavor, it is recommended that you consume preserved foods within a specified period or before the "expiration date." Most foods are still edible for many years after their "Use by" date. The nutrients will begin to diminish, the flavor may change, and the color may be off. Be sure to give it a sniff test before tasting any expired food.

> Frozen food: 1 to 2 years
> Canned food: 3 to 5 years
> Dehydrated food: 5 to 15 years
> Freeze-dried food: 5 to 25 years

The above figures are averages; some foods may last a shorter span (especially if not stored under optimal conditions) or extend past these times. I have eaten home-canned cherries that were 25 years old. It is important to note that these average dates are because the food begins to degrade after this point. Just like the "Best by" date quotes on the packaging of food bought in the store is helpful, but does not mean the food isn't edible. However, the quality goes down the more you pass this time. No matter what, always do a peek-and-sniff test before eating.

The Shelf-Life of Freeze-dried Foods

When appropriately freeze-dried and stored in the proper packaging with oxygen absorbers, most foods have a long-term shelf life of between 15 and 30 years. There is no need to do anything additional to extend the shelf life. After freeze-dried food is opened, it must be consumed before it spoils. Some freeze-dried foods will begin absorbing moisture and become more like a chewy dehydrated snack, but they may still be good. Keep freeze-dried food in an airtight container after opening for best results. The general rule for freeze-dried foods is to consume them between 6 and 12 months after opening the sealed package.

Freeze-Drying Advantages and Disadvantages

The freeze-drying process creates foods that are more nutritious and in better condition than any other preservation method. With freeze-drying, produce can be selected when it is ripe, at its nutritional peak, and preserved with all its healthy goodness.

Dairy foods are lovely to freeze-dry, too, and they retain their probiotic cultures. Freeze-dried yogurt has the same probiotic benefits as fresh yogurt (lower the Dry temp to 90°F).

Freeze-dried foods also do not rely on chemical preservatives to achieve their incredibly long shelf lives. Freeze-drying can generate pure, complete, and nutrient-dense foods with a significantly extended shelf life, enhancing the adaptability, accessibility, and convenience of food items. Let's break down the benefits of freeze-drying food:

The Advantages

Having the ability to process whole, nutritious food ingredients which have a significantly extended shelf life is an incredible thing! I absolutely love this about freeze-drying. It makes food items practical and versatile.

Food Quality Control & Nutritional value maintained

When you are choosing which foods to freeze-dry and therefore, which foods to store, you become the gatekeeper of nutrition. You can select which types of foods your family will eat. You can control the variety. You can use your own recipes. On top of that, 97 percent of the nutritional value of freeze-dried foods is retained. This is a lot higher than other drying-based food preservation techniques.

Little to no physical changes to food

Freeze-dried foods retain their shape, texture, natural flavor, and color because the process does not affect the physical structure of the food. This gives you a product that looks, tastes, and feels like the original when water is reintroduced to the food.

Remember, it will be rehydrated back to how the thawed food would be. In other words, fresh strawberries will undergo freezing temperatures and the sublimation process to become freeze-dried strawberries. When water is added back to the strawberries, they will behave like frozen, thawed strawberries, not fresh strawberries.

25+ Years!

No refrigeration needed for 25+ years of food storage

At any time, a disaster can prevent us from accessing foods in the ways we are used to, such as in restaurants and supermarkets. It is recommended that every household has at least two weeks' worth of food per person saved up for this possibility. Freeze-drying allows you to be prepared no matter what without constantly restocking foods that might expire soon. No need to refrigerate or freeze; just keep the food in a cool, dry, clean environment.

Rehydration is fast and easy

Most freeze-dried food absorbs water quickly (via rehydration or reconstitution) and can be eaten shortly after. Cooked meals, cooked meats, fruits, veggies, and dairy can all be eaten without any additional cooking. Make your own freeze-dried meals, and easy dinner options will be available whenever needed. All you have to do is add hot water and wait 5-10 minutes! (Some foods, such as bread, require more delicate care when rehydrating.) And some foods, such as those that are raw, must be handled more carefully.

> - Raw eggs: To reconstitute, add 2 Tablespoons powder to 2 Tablespoons cold water. Stir and allow it to sit. Use as you would a raw egg.
>
> - Raw meat: To rehydrate, place the meat in a bowl of cold water and refrigerate overnight. Treat it as you would raw meat and thoroughly cook it. All packages of raw meat should be clearly marked.

Fun, convenient, and healthy snacks

Despite its bad reputation, snacking is part of a balanced diet as it allows you to fuel up between the main meals of breakfast, lunch, and dinner. However, that benefit can only be achieved with healthy options to snack on. Freeze-drying allows you to have easy-to-access options at your fingertips so that you do not reach for fat-, sugar-, and salt-laden snacks that are so readily available.

Kids love the crunchiness of freeze-dried food. Freeze-dried corn is often described as "candy" because the sugar content is concentrated. Surprisingly, freeze-dried cauliflower is another kid favorite, especially when you prep BBQ Cauliflower Bites.

Your family will not need unhealthy snacks to satisfy their crunch craving when they can munch on freeze-dried mango slices, a handful of freeze-dried peas, or some yogurt bites.

Custom recipes for Just-Add-Water meals

Just-Add-Water meals make life easy. You can freeze-dry your family recipes, and then when you need it, add water to make an instant delicious meal! This method is similar to the MRE, which stands for Meal-Ready-to-Eat, the self-contained, individual field rations eaten by military personnel.

Ingredient/Allergy Awareness

You control the healthy ingredients used in freeze-dried items. Therefore, you do not have to worry about ingredients that risk your family's health.

Lightweight for Easy Transportation

Most of the water content is removed from freeze-dried foods, making them lightweight and easy to carry.

And now,

The Disadvantages

Even in the fantastic world of freeze-drying, you will encounter a few disadvantages that are good to be aware of:

Water is required to rehydrate

Needing water doesn't seem like a disadvantage since we all need water daily anyway. But this can be inconvenient if you have to eat freeze-dried food on the go and need help finding water or if you are in a place where water is either not readily available or needs to be purified first.

Airtight containers are required

No matter how well the freeze-drying process goes, if the stored food is exposed to air, it will spoil. Thus, there is a necessary investment in obtaining airtight containers. Whether you use Mylar bags, canning jars, or #10 cans is up to you.

Storage space is required

The containers you choose to use will take up space. Your storage space must be adequately prepared to ensure the foods remain as fresh as possible for as long as possible. You can place Mylar bags in totes (to prevent rodent damage) and stack them to the ceiling because they are so lightweight. You can place canning jars or #10 cans on shelves or in crates and stack them relatively high because weight isn't a factor.

Production costs

On average, a brand-new home freeze-dryer costs between $2,500 and $5,000. This price depends on the size of the freeze-dryer and the type of pump installed. In addition, recurring expenses include power consumption, machine maintenance, and storage materials. Harvest RightTM has a fantastic layaway program that makes saving for a freeze-dryer hassle-free. Pay a downpayment ($250+ depending on model), pay what you can when you can at 0% interest, and it's shipped after your final payment!

Time Use

Each batch takes time, and we must be patient while it completes the cycle. The average time to complete a batch is 24-60 hours. Some full-moisture items will take longer; we have no choice but to wait until it's done.

Noise pollution

The appliance itself purrs similarly to a clothes dryer, and the pump is a loud hum that can bother some people.

Learning Curve

While anyone can use a freeze-dryer, learning the best practices will always give you the best products. You'll need to learn how to prepare foods beforehand, run the machine, and package freeze-dried foods properly. And these are steps you can learn!

Knowing which Foods to Freeze-Dry

There is a large variety of food items that can be freeze-dried. There will be a more extensive list in chapter 5 (and in Appendix 3,) but the basic categories of foods that can be freeze-dried are below.

Foods you CAN freeze-dry

- Fruits
- Vegetables
- Lean Meats
- Dairy
- Eggs
- Full meals
- Leftovers
- Herbs
- Spices
- Snacks
- Desserts
- Candy
- Drinks
- Edible Flowers

DON'T TRY THESE AT HOME!

While the list of what you can freeze-dry is rather extensive, some food items do not freeze-dry well and can cause problems or messes.

Oily foods, fatty foods, some high-sugar foods, and syrupy foods do not freeze-dry well for the most part. Any foods with oil or fat in the ingredients (such as a cheesy hamburger casserole) should be used within 1-5 years due to the nature of fats, which go rancid over time. The following list of items will make a mess or could damage your freeze-dryer. More detail about this is in chapter 5 and Appendix 3.

Foods you CANNOT freeze-dry

- Fats
- Butter
- Nuts
- Syrups
- Preserves
- Chocolate
- Vinegar
- Alcohol

A Variety of Uses for Freeze-Dried Foods

You can use your freeze-dried ingredients in your regular recipes. You can also use your everyday recipes in the freeze-dryer to create healthy meals for later. That is quite the time-saver! You can make camping meals and wholesome snacks, assemble the ideal emergency food supply, and preserve your garden produce. In contrast to other food preservation techniques, freeze-drying keeps the food's flavor, color, and nutritional value. Some of the best uses of freeze-dried foods are:

Having food always ready to go

Having everyday, healthy meals available anytime–simply by adding water–is a game changer! Now you can have a powdered smoothie ready to mix up in the morning before school. You can take nutritious meals to work and have a hot, delicious lunch easily just by adding hot water. You can rehydrate a complete meal by adding water and popping the casserole dish into the oven. That sure makes making dinner a cinch.

With your freeze-dryer, you can save your leftovers, avoid food waste, and have another meal at another time. You can have camping meals and wholesome snacks with no sweat. The best part is that the food's flavor, color, and nutritional value remain intact. At the same time, you easily avoid allergens or foods your family won't eat because you know the ingredients in your meals.

Garden and orchard preservation

Gardening is a relaxing activity that often provides an abundance of food. This is how free zucchini ends up on all the neighborhood porches. Sometimes we can't possibly consume all the produce before it spoils. Save the bounty of your garden by freeze-drying your harvests.

When you get a large harvest, you can prepare and freeze it in Ziplock bags until you can put it in the freeze-dryer. Freeze-drying maintains the appearance and, most importantly, the nutritional value of foods better than any other method. Preserving your garden harvest also saves you money because the food you grow will last for decades.

Emergencies, food storage, and survival prepping

We can unexpectedly find ourselves in a variety of emergency situations. We can prepare ahead of time for natural disasters, job loss, and food shortages. Have peace of mind by having food stored up for more challenging times.

Save yourself time, energy, and money by stocking freeze-dried items that last years and years. Put your freeze-dried Just-Add-Water packages in your 72-hour kits, bug-out bags, short-term food supply, and long-term storage. Knowing your food storage has a long shelf life means you will no longer worry so much about these uncertain times. And as a bonus, you'll save a ton of money compared to purchasing freeze-dried foods from a store.

Starter cultures for yogurts, sourdough bread, kefir, etc.

Freezing is often the go-to method for preserving yogurt. The live bacteria (called probiotics) promote good gut health so it's a great food to have around. Bacteria can handle freezing temperatures for at least 2 months before the colonies begin to slowly diminish. Freezing halts the growth and puts these bacteria into a dormant stage which revive and begin to multiply when the proper temperatures return.

This is applicable for other foods that contain live cultures, like sourdough bread, kefir, and kombucha. Freeze-drying maintains the population of these live bacteria and when the food is rehydrated, the bacteria "wake up" and work just as well as before. Set your Dry temperature on the Customize screen to 90°F. Store live cultures in your food storage and always keep probiotics available for your family.

Be ready for traveling, backpacking, camping, and hunting

Freeze-dried foods in pouches are easy to rehydrate and eat. You just add water, and you're all set. Add to that freeze-dried foods are lightweight and easy to carry, and you can take them anywhere. You can take munchies on road trips and pack full meals to eat when you stop at your destination. Just tuck them in your bag, and you're good to go.

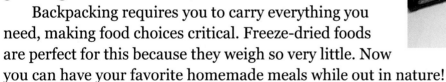

Backpacking requires you to carry everything you need, making food choices critical. Freeze-dried foods are perfect for this because they weigh so very little. Now you can have your favorite homemade meals while out in nature!

You can also use your freeze-dryer to preserve the game meat and fish you bring home, raw or cooked, so it's ready when you are.

Pet food preservation

Pets are members of the family, and they deserve healthy meals, too. Pet food can easily be stored for emergencies after being freeze-dried. The same rules apply—keep it within the size and weight limits and use up fattier foods within 1-5 years.

Freeze-Drying Non-food Items

As I alluded to earlier, edible items are not the only products that can be freeze-dried. Freeze-drying can be used to preserve the quality of things you do not eat as well, like decorative flowers.

Why would you want to preserve flowers? Many people want to keep memories of special occasions like weddings and memorials fresh in their minds, and preserving the flowers used on that day is a way to do just that. Freeze-drying also increases the lifespan of flowers we love and visually enjoy. Some flowers freeze-dry better than others. Handle freeze-dried flowers carefully, as they will be very delicate. Some flowers that freeze-dry well include: Amaranthus, Aster, Begonia, Bird of Paradise, Calla Lily, Calendula, Carnation, Cornflower, Daffodil, Dahlia, Dianthus, Freesia, Gardenia, Hyacinth, Hydrangea, Iris, Lavender, Lily of the Valley, Narcissus, Pansy, Peony, Rose, Snapdragon, and Viola.

Water-damaged paperwork is another non-food item that can be preserved with freeze-drying. When paper is water damaged, it sticks together and will be permanently ruined if allowed to dry out. If the wet (or frozen) paper is put in the freeze-dryer, all the water will be removed, and the paperwork can be restored. We had a house fire a few years ago, and quite a bit of paperwork (soaked by the firehose water) was put into the freezer. Once we had the time to run it through the freeze-dryer, we could open the books and look at the pages again.

Working smarter, not harder, is the name of the game. Therefore, getting the right tools to make your freeze-drying efforts as fruitful as possible is necessary. Next, we will look at choosing the best freeze-dryer to suit your needs and explore various available accessories.

2

PLANNING FOR A FREEZE-DRYER

Your freeze-dryer will be an appliance you will use like a workhorse and care for like a Mustang. The right one for your needs makes your life simpler. Harvest Right™ has been manufacturing home freeze-dryer appliances since 2014, and they make good machines. If you already have your freeze-dryer set up in your home, you can skip forward to chapter 4.

Selecting a Freeze-Dryer

You can choose from four sizes of home freeze-dryers. They range from a 3-tray Small to a 6-tray X-Large. How do you decide which freeze-dryer is for you? There are a few criteria that could make a difference for you.

Size

Do you plan on using this appliance a lot or a little? Will you be making larger batches of food or smaller ones? For how many people are you storing food? How much food do you want to freeze-dry per year? Do you want stainless steel or a color? The answer to these questions determines the size of the freeze-dryer best suited for you and your needs.

You can obtain more information about the four options from the Harvest Right™ website at this link: FDHR.2MHE.com. Here are the specifications unique to each size that can be obtained from Harvest Right™:

Specifications		Small	Medium	Large	X-Large
Current Price	Color Stainless Steel	$2,495 $2,695	$3,195 $3,395	$3,895 $4,095	$5,095
Size	Width Depth Height	17.4" W x 21.5" D x 26.8" H	19" W x 25" D x 29" H	21.3" W x 27.5" D x 31.3" H	24.3" W x 37.4" D x 35.6" H
FD Weight		61 lbs SS 80 lbs	112 lbs SS 133 lbs	138 lbs SS 161 lbs	265 lbs
Premier Vacuum Pump Weight		32 lbs	32 lbs	32 lbs	33 lbs
Shipping Weight		139 lbs SS 150 lbs	212 lbs SS 221 lbs	253 lbs SS 274 lbs	370 lbs
Average Power Draw		9-10 amps/hr. Spikes to 16.	10-11 amps/hr. Spikes to 16.	10-12 amps/hr. Spikes to 16.	12-14 amps/hr. Spikes to 16.
Power Needs		110 Volt Outlet. Dedicated 20 amp circuit recommended. No GFCI.		110 Volt Outlet NEMA 5-20. Dedicated 20 amp circuit REQUIRED. No GFCI.	

Food Information		Small	Medium	Large	X-Large
Number of Trays		3	4	5	6
Tray Size	Width Length Height	7.75" W x 14" L x 0.75" H	7.5" W x 18" L x 0.75" H	9" W x 20.5" L x 0.75" H	10.9" W x 29.5" L x 0.75" H
Max Fresh per Tray	Cups Ounces Liters Pounds Kilograms	3 c 24 oz 0.8 L 2.3 lbs 1 kg	4 c 32 oz 1 L 2.5 lbs 1.1 kg	5.5 c 44 oz 1.4 L 3.2 lbs 1.5 kg	10 c 80 oz 2.5 L 5.8 lbs 2.6 kg
Max Fresh per Batch	Cups Ounces Liters Pounds Kilograms	9 c 72 oz 2.4 L 7 lbs 3 kg	16 c 128 oz 4 L 10 lbs 4.5 kg	27.5 c 220 oz 7 L 16 lbs 7.5 kg	60 c 480 oz 16 L 35 lbs 15.8 kg
Freeze-dried per Batch	Gallons	1-1.5 gal	1.5-2.5 gal	1-3.5 gal	8-10 gal
Average Annual Batches		200+	200+	200+	200+
Average Pounds		4.2 lbs	7.25 lbs	12.5 lbs	25 lbs
Average Annual Fresh		840 lbs	1,450 lbs	2,500 lbs	5,000 lbs
Average Annual Freeze-dried		195 gal	312 gal	546 gal	1200 gal

Location

Space Needed

Regardless of which size you choose, this is a large appliance that needs to be elevated. You'll need a countertop, tabletop, or heavy-duty cart to set it on with a dedicated outlet nearby. Whatever type of elevated space you choose will need to have the following minimum dimensions available for the different-sized Harvest Right™ Freeze-dryers:

> - Small - 18" Wide x 22" Deep
> - Medium - 19" Wide x 25" Deep
> - Large - 22" Wide x 28" Deep
> - X-Large - 25" Wide x 38" Deep

The pump needs to be plugged into the back of the freeze-dryer and placed next to it on the table or just below it on a shelf. Make sure you factor in the space you will need for the pump. The freeze-dryer needs to drain into a bucket. It leaves the factory draining from the left but could be adjusted to drain to the right. Just make sure that space is allocated for this as well.

Ventilation & Temperatures

Your freeze-dryer needs to be set up in an open and well-ventilated room. The appliance will create heat. Having your freeze-dryer in a temperature-controlled or air-conditioned location will help immensely. Some people have found that a window A/C unit in the room where the freeze-dryer is located helps with temperature control issues.

The freeze-dryer works best in rooms kept between 45°F and 75°F. It is safe, however, to use your freeze-dryer in rooms with temperatures between 35°F and 90°F. Do not operate the freeze-dryer below 35°F. The external freezing temperatures will damage the unit. The freeze-dryer will not work efficiently in temperatures higher than 90°F.

The vacuum pump runs hot, so it generates a lot of heat. It can get up to 160°F during regular operation. This heat helps to dissipate moisture, so it is beneficial.Ensure children and pets do not touch the pump. Fans are an easy solution to keeping your pump cooler but are unnecessary unless the temperature gets over 160°F. The oil-free pump gets hotter than the oil pumps and may need a fan, maybe even an exhaust fan. Many people put a fan on their pump to keep it cool regardless of indoor temperature.

If the environment gets too warm, the freeze-dryer will give a warning message on the interface screen. This usually happens when the room reaches 80°F. The warning lets you know you need to immediately lower the temperature in the room or expect the batch time to increase by as much as double. The freeze-dryer battles with the external heat as it works to get the internal temperature of the chamber down to the extreme cold required.

If you choose to use the freeze-dryer in temperatures over 80°F, you must use fans to help it run more efficiently. You can station a fan to pull the warm air out of the right side or have a fan blowing on the left side of the appliance to help keep it cool. Our freeze-dryer is in a 70°F basement, and we still use fans every time. We have a fan blowing on the pump and one blowing towards the openings on the left side of the freeze-dryer. I recommend using fans in any room that isn't holding a low temperature of 65°F.

Rarely the demister on the premier pump can create an oily vapor or mist. This is usually caused by overloading the pump with oil. This mist can be contained (so you don't breathe it in) by putting a piece of fabric over the demister. I've heard of people using a sock, so keep that in mind if you need a good substitute. Covering the demister is more critical if the pump is located in a room that is lived in, like a bedroom or kitchen. We've never seen the demister do this, so keep your pump appropriately filled, and you should be perfectly fine.

Other Considerations

Associated noises

When the freeze-dryer is running, it will cycle through different phases. The sounds are slightly different for each phase, but the noise is like a refrigerator or clothes dryer hum. It is also normal to hear popping sounds. When the freeze-dryer is defrosting, it can have crackling and popping noises as the ice melts. This can happen naturally with the door open or with the Defrost phase.

The pump is the noisiest part, and the premier pump is the quietest. The standard pump is the loudest. There is nothing quiet about vacuum pumps, so make sure you've chosen a good location. I have gotten used to my freeze-dryer's sounds. They eventually become background noise, just like the hum of any of my other appliances.

The Pillow

Older freeze-dryer models had a "pillow" that rested between the shelf rack and the door. The manufacturer no longer includes a pillow for the front of the freeze-dryer. It has been found to be unnecessary and gets in the way of seeing your food! Some people love using their pillow, and you can purchase custom-made pillows!

Moisture

There will be some condensation around the gasket. Large amounts of ice forming on the outside is not normal and will need customer service assistance. But, typically, there will be a little frost or some moisture. The front of the unit (just below the gasket) may drip or dribble water as the ice melts during the batch runs. Have a towel to catch and clean up the excess moisture.

Power Requirements

A dedicated 20 amp circuit for the 110 volt NEMA 5/20 outlet is required to operate the large and X-large Harvest Right™ freeze-dryers. But it is also recommended for both the medium and small machines due to peak power consumption (freeze-dryers can spike up to 16 amps.) The large and X-large freeze-dryers come with a NEMA 5-20 plug that only works with a NEMA 5/20 outlet. This type of outlet has 12 gauge wire to a 20 amp breaker and can handle the heavy load of these larger appliances. You may need a qualified electrician to put in one of

these outlets. Never use an adapter to run a 20 amp appliance on a 15 amp circuit. You can cause a breaker to explode or even risk a house fire. Do not use surge protectors, extension cords, or GFCI (Ground Fault Circuit Interrupter) outlets. The freeze-dryer power cord is only 6', so prepare your space, table, and outlet accordingly.

Let's run through a list of the most frequently asked questions about the power needs of the Harvest Right™ freeze-dryer.

How much power does a freeze-dryer use?

All four sizes can spike to 16 amps, so an outlet with a dedicated 20 amp circuit is recommended for all freeze-dryers. Freeze-dryers use an average of about 10-12 amps per hour. To be more exact, the average number of amps used per hour looks like this for each size:

> - Small: 9 to 10 amps
> - Medium: 10 to 11 amps
> - Large: 10 to 12 amps
> - X-Large: 12 to 14 amps

What is the power cost to run a freeze-dryer?

The cost to run your freeze-dryer will vary depending on the price of electricity, the size of the freeze-dryer, and hours of usage. A typical batch takes 24-60 hrs and averages about $2-$5 per day.

What if there is a power outage?

When the power goes out, don't worry. Your freeze-dryer will remember where it left off and return to that function when the power is restored. The appliance will hold its cold temperature for quite some time, just like a freezer. But if a prolonged period of time has passed, you may want to move the food to the freezer. If your area happens to have a lot of power outages, you may consider a permanent solution, such as getting a whole-house generator or even a whole-house surge protector. (This is NOT a surge protector you plug your cord into; do not use one of those.)

Any safety concerns if I go on vacation?

It is wise to unplug the freeze-dryer when it is not in use. Occasionally, after a power outage, the freeze-dryer will turn on. It is a safety mechanism that lessens the chances of a surge damaging the sensitive machine. Keep it unplugged unless you're running it.

All the information about the power consumption and requirements can be found in the manual, which is also located at this link: https://harvestright.com/wp-content/uploads/2020/08/Owners-Manual-072020-DIGITAL.pdf

Freeze-Drying Stuff

Necessary Items for Freeze-Drying

You will get everything you need to get started in the package that comes with your freeze-dryer. Here is a list of the **standard items** that come with your purchase from Harvest Right™:

> - Freeze-dryer: Small, Medium, Large, or X-Large
> - Shelving unit, 6' power cord, and drain line tubing
> - Vacuum pump and hose (I recommend the Premier Pump)
> - Stainless steel trays (three, four, five, or six)
> - Impulse sealer 12", 5mm width, 13 pounds
> - Vacuum pump oil and oil filter (unless oil-free pump).
> - 50-pack Mylar bags & 50-pack oxygen absorbers

The mylar bags, oxygen absorbers, and pump oil will need to be replenished as they are used up. I recommend using Harvest Right's or Wallaby's. You can also use canning jars or metal cans - if you have the equipment. Below are our recommended freeze-drying accessories, kitchen equipment, and other useful items. We only recommend what we use and love.

Recommended Accessories

Additional Items Available From Harvest Right™

There is some convenient equipment you can get from Harvest Right™. Quick Link: FDHR.2MHE.COM. The ones I recommend are below:

Stainless Steel Trays

The standard purchase comes with one set of stainless steel trays. However, having an extra set of stainless steel trays is quite helpful as it will save you time when working with multiple batches. You can run a batch while also pre-freezing the next batch.

Lids

The lids fit nicely by snapping directly onto the trays, which makes stacking the trays in the freezer much easier when pre-freezing food. Harvest Right™ lids can withstand the freeze-dryer's extreme temperatures, so they can also be used as 3-partition trays placed directly on the shelves.

Silicone Mats

The silicone mats are both heat- and cold-resistant. Food doesn't stick to them, so cleanup is easy. The mats are perfect for juicy fruits and an excellent choice to avoid parchment paper waste. (I regularly use both.)

Silicone Cube Molds

These are 1" x 1" cubes with 60 sections per tray. Like the silicone mats, they are heat- and cold-resistant so they can go in the freeze-dryer. Put soft-textured foods like yogurt, smoothies, jello, and pudding in the molds while sitting on a tray and place them in the freeze-dryer. The mold can also be used as a mold in the freezer and then emptied onto a tray to go into the freeze-dryer.

Filter Replacement Cartridges

Replace your cartridge when it can no longer create clear oil. Keep extras on hand, so you're not in a pickle when they are needed.

Vacuum Pump Oil

Having extra oil on hand is essential. Your hard-working machine needs regular maintenance. Ensure you stock up, so it always has the clean oil it needs.

Resealable 7-mil Mylar bags

7-mil Mylar bags are for long-term storage and are a sturdy and useful kind of bag. They often have a zip closure that comes in handy after opening. Because it is thick Mylar, there is a lessened chance of a puncture. You can also get Mylar bags from other suppliers, so feel free to shop around. The same philosophy applies to the next accessory we will discuss—oxygen absorbers. They can be sourced from other suppliers as well.

Oxygen Absorbers

Oxygen absorbers must be put in every Mylar bag or canning jar you store food in for the long term. 300cc is needed per gallon bag, while 100cc is needed per quart jar. Oxygen absorbers must be stored in a sealed container to keep them working. After opening the oxygen absorber package, remove what is needed immediately and reseal the package. Then place the oxygen absorbers in the bags or jars that have already been packed with food, and seal them.

Accessories from Freeze-Drying Supplies

As mentioned before, there are other suppliers to choose from for some accessories. One such supplier is Freeze-drying Supplies, and the link to their website is https://www.freezedryingsupplies.com/collections/all. Items I recommend for consideration from Freeze-drying Supplies include:

Tray Dividers

The tray dividers can go in the freeze-dryer with your food. These are great for separating portions or individual items on each tray. They are especially great for keeping taffy and other candies from sticking together. I love that they can be arranged for different-sized portions. As many as 40 small sections can be created, and as few as 4 large sections per tray.

Corner Tray Stackers

The stackers allow you to stack the trays on top of each other to save space. They can be stacked on the counter while preparing foods or placed in the freezer for your pre-freeze.

Food Funnel

The 10" food funnel is very helpful when filling many Mylar bags simultaneously. It fits both 8x12 and 10x14 and can also fit a wide-mouth jar opening. It helps minimize spills and frees up your hands to multitask.

Pre-Cut Parchment

This parchment paper comes in packs of 100 that are already cut to the size of your tray. These come in handy when doing sticky foods. I have found that candies do best on parchment. If you run out, you can use regular kitchen parchment and cut it to size yourself.

No Suck Kit (Anti Siphon Drain Hose Fix) - Two ⅜" Y fittings

These Y fittings can be purchased much cheaper at your local hardware store, and I recommend getting them there. The two ⅜" Y fittings should be attached to the drain hose near the top to prevent the dreaded dirty water suction, which can destroy entire batches by spraying contaminated water back onto the completed product. This happens if the drain hose is sitting in a bucket of waste water when the valve is opened at the end of a run. By having these simple Y fittings in line, air will always be available when the machine needs it, and it won't be able to suck up any nasty water.

Accessories available from Frozen Right

Frozen Right is another accessories supplier I recommend. The link to the website is: https://frozenright.com/shop/. Items that are worth considering include:

Tray Scoop

This stainless steel scoop is 6" x 6" with a flat lip. It works exceptionally well with small things like corn or Skittles. The tray scoop is one of my favorite tools. After trying out spatulas and a big ol' ice scoop, I finally found this beauty, and I loved it so much I bought a second one.

Tray Trowel

This tool helps you level the food in your trays to be either ⅜" or ½." I have found this tool helpful with spreads, such as sour cream.

Tray Dividers

The tray dividers are 100% FDA-approved silicone. These make it possible to put smaller servings of food on a single tray. Excellent for preparing camping meals or using up leftovers.

Roller Berry

This tool makes puncturing berries easy! Blueberries, ground cherries, gooseberries, and other thick-skinned foods must be pierced before freeze-drying to release moisture from within. This thing makes me feel like I'm holding a Medieval weapon! And it works so well.

Bag Racks

You can use the bag rack to keep your Mylar bags upright when packed with goods. No more spilling food and struggling to balance them on a slick countertop when putting food or oxygen absorbers into your bag before closing. Your surfaces are protected by soft rubber feet.

Ice Guard & Rails

The ice guard and rails help prevent the overflowing of ice. This prevents the ice from touching the shelf and melting, thus starting the sublimation process over again. My husband went to our local hardware store and got a section of 1" aluminum angle iron for $8. He cut it to the length of our shelves, placed it between the chamber and shelves on both sides, and it's been working flawlessly. (The open part of the V should be against the shelves.)

Kitchen Equipment

Many of the items listed below you may already have. While they are common kitchen finds, they make your freeze-drying adventure all the easier. This list includes:

Kitchen Scale

A kitchen scale is an absolute must. The scale will be used before and after the trays go into the freeze-dryer. We always weigh using grams. Weighing your trays prior will help ensure the trays are not overloaded. Too much weight means the machine will have to work harder and, therefore, longer than usual. This places additional strain that wears down your freeze-dryer faster. After the freeze dryer has completed its cycle, it's time to do the Two Hour Weight Check.

Two-Hour Weight Check

The two hour check is a very important step. When the batch goes into extra dry time, hit Cancel and weigh all the trays. Then you put them back in and after two hours, re-weigh all the trays. If the weight changes, then repeat. If it stays the same, the food is dry and ready to be packaged. By weighing afterward, you will also know the weight of the water removed. This allows for easy rehydration if you keep track of it. Water weighs 237 grams per cup. Get yourself a decent kitchen scale that measures accurately by grams.

Blender

You can use your blender to make smooth sauces, which can go into your silicone molds or directly on the trays. You can also use your blender to powder the dried product afterward. Our Vitamix blender has a wet and a dry pitcher, and both work very well.

Food Processor

A food processor is an excellent tool for preparing food for freeze-drying. It can be used to chop and purée fruits and vegetables, grind meat, and combine sauce and marinade components. It can save you a lot of time and work by processing large amounts of food swiftly and efficiently.

Mandoline

A nice, sharp mandoline will make cutting up produce easy, whether fresh or frozen. It will create clean-cut and uniform pieces, essential to gaining the highest quality final product. We got ours from Pampered Chef, and it has become my husband's favorite kitchen tool. You can adjust your thicknesses, and it saves so much time because it slices so quickly.

Jar Sealer

We have a FoodSaver® Vacuum Sealer with the jar sealer accessories, and it works fantastically. You will need a jar sealer to store freeze-dried food in canning jars. The FoodSaver® Vacuum Sealer can help you store things for the short term (up to five years.) You can use the jar attachments to seal glass canning jars and the clear bags with the FoodSaver® machine to vacuum and seal fresh, refrigerated storage. While many vacuum seal machines are on the market, this is the one I prefer. Instead of the electric FoodSaver® vacuum sealer, you could get the Pump-N-Seal, a manual pump that uses Tab-check tape valves, or the FoodSaver® jar sealer accessories to seal canning Jars.

Pressure Cooker

A pressure cooker is an excellent tool for quickly and efficiently cooking food for freeze-drying. It can be used to cook meats, poultry, and vegetables fast and to produce soups and stews. The pressure cooking procedure preserves the nutrients and flavors of the food, making it an excellent choice for freeze-drying.

Peeler, Corer, Slicer

These three pieces of equipment can be extremely helpful when preparing fruits and vegetables for freeze-drying. A peeler is useful for removing the skin from fruits and vegetables, a corer helps remove the cores from apples and pears, and a slicer is terrific for cutting fruits and vegetables into uniform pieces. There is a device that does all three for apples from Pampered Chef that I love!

Knives, Shears, Herb Scissors, and Cutting Boards

Sharp knives are required for freeze-drying food preparation. They are used for chopping, slicing, and mincing fruits, vegetables, and meats. Kitchen shears and herb scissors can also be helpful. Cutting boards will also be required to protect your surfaces and facilitate food preparation.

Colanders and Strainers

When preparing food for freeze-drying, colanders and strainers are invaluable. They can be used to rinse and drain fruits and vegetables and remove extra water from cooked dishes. They come in a variety of sizes and forms that can be beneficial for a variety of foods.

Tray Grids for Trays

Use food-grade plastic or silicone grids to add layers to your trays. Place a layer of bananas on the silicone mat, lay down a few grids on top, and place a second layer of bananas on the same tray! Just make sure you give them plenty of space and watch the weight of each tray. We got our tray grids from Sophos Survival. You can also layer parchment paper that has slits cut into it.

Silicone Molds

You can use any shape silicone mold to pre-freeze foods before popping them out onto the trays. Simply keep the frozen pieces in a zip-sealed bag in your freezer until you have enough for a tray.

Stainless Steel Trays

You can use any stainless steel trays in your freeze-dryer. You can pre-freeze in these trays (or other small containers) and then pop them out onto your trays. Otherwise, you can put stainless steel trays directly in the freeze-dryer. Stainless steel trays can also go in the oven.

Other Items Needed

There are a few additional items that are important to have. Most of these can be found around the house.

Bucket

Your freeze-dryer will have a drain line that needs a place into which it can empty. A bucket will work well for this task. Make sure it is big enough, so water doesn't overflow. Also, make sure the vinyl tubing is not ever sitting in water. We used a 5-gallon bucket we already had. Keep your bucket empty and clean it regularly.

Oil Funnel

You will need a dedicated oil funnel to get the oil into your pump. It is very helpful in avoiding messy spills and makes refilling easy and clean.

Fans

Your freeze-dryer wants to feel the breeze of fans! Fans are vital if your freeze-dryer is in a warm room (over 65°F.) It is highly recommended that you direct a blowing fan on the left side of the appliance every time you run a batch.

Sharpies

You will need a permanent marker to write the item name, date, and expected expiration on your Mylar bags. The bag should be itemized so there is no mistaking the content. The dates are also required so that the best-by date for consumption is known. Fingernail polish remover will take off the marker so you can easily re-label the bag.

Bread

You will also need a loaf of cheap bread. This is for a test run on your first attempt using the machine. This bread will absorb the "new car" smell and make sure the appliance runs correctly. The freeze-dried slices of bread should be thrown out when the batch is complete.

For a list of recommended equipment with links to find them, scan the QR code or visit: FDR.2MHE.COM.

Now that you've chosen the necessary equipment and tools, you're ready to learn how to set up your freeze dryer! Running your freeze-dryer correctly and cleaning it regularly are key to ensuring its longevity. The next chapter gives you the scoop on setting up the appliance correctly so it is as efficient as possible.

3

SETTING UP YOUR FREEZE-DRYER

Getting your Harvest Right™ freeze-dryer set up is fairly simple. This chapter walks you through the process so you give yourself the greatest opportunity to get the most out of this machine. **Grab your Getting Started Checklist in Appendix 3** and let's discuss what to do at the beginning – the day your freeze-dryer gets to your home.

When Your Machine Arrives

Your freeze-dryer will be delivered by freight on a semi-trailer right up to your driveway. Prior to delivery, you will be called by the freight company to schedule a time for delivery. You must be home at that time to inspect and approve the delivery.

Approving your Shipment

The driver is obligated to allow you 15 minutes to inspect your order, so take the time to do it right. Any shipping wear or damage on the outside of the boxes warrants a much closer look at the freeze-dryer once unpacked.

Always inspect the unit whether there is obvious damage to the box or not. Remove the freeze-dryer from the packaging and look it over for scratches, dents, or other damage. Do NOT accept a damaged unit, or you will be held responsible for any expenses to fix the damage.

Refuse a damaged unit and have it returned to Harvest Right™. Freight damage is not uncommon so Harvest Right™ is prepared for these types of things and should have another one shipped to you within a week or two.

Have the Harvest Right™ phone number (801-386-8960) ready in the unlikely chance there is a problem. Open all the boxes and ensure all items ordered are present and in perfect condition.

What Is Included With Your Freeze-Dryer

Once you are confident that all's right with the condition of your freeze-dryer, you can move on to ticking off the list of items included in your order.

- Harvest Right™ Freeze-dryer
- Shelving unit (inside the appliance)
- 6' power cord (black)
- Drain line tubing (clear)
- Vacuum pump
- Vacuum hose (black)
- Vacuum pump oil (unless oil-free)
- Oil filter (unless oil-free)
- Impulse sealer
- Stainless steel trays (Small: 3, Medium: 4, Large: 5, X-Large: 6)
- Package of Mylar bags
- Package of oxygen absorbers (OA)
- Harvest Right™ owner's manual
- Harvest Right™ Guide to Freeze-drying Booklet
- Additional accessories that you purchased, which may include lids, silicone mats, silicone molds, extra trays, extra oil filter cartridges, extra pump oil, extra Mylar bags, and extra oxygen absorbers.

Once all is deemed good, sign the Shipper's Bill, and rejoice! You now have a freeze-dryer!

Positioning Your Machine

A freeze-dryer is a large appliance, and it is very heavy. It's not just the weight but the bulky, boxy size that makes it hard to move around. The stainless steel freeze-dryers are a bit heavier than the colored ones. A quick reminder:

- The Small weighs 61 lbs (SS 80 lbs)
- The Medium weighs 112 lbs (SS 133 lbs)
- The Large weighs 138 lbs (SS 161)
- The X-Large weighs 265 lbs

The stainless steel units add between 20 and 30 additional pounds. Moving will be difficult and awkward, so make sure you know where you're going before you start. Please get the help of some friends and family, or at least a dolly, to move it. We had two adults and two teenagers carrying a large, and we were sweating it as we carried it down the basement stairs. Don't try to move this by yourself.

Do your best to avoid tilting the freeze-dryer as you move it. Be cautious around twists and turns, corners, and stairs as you carefully maneuver the appliance to its final destination. The location should have been prepared beforehand and, thus, have a level, stable surface in a cool, dry, and clean environment for the best performance. The proper electrical outlet should also be ready at your destination (see chapter 2.)

Keep in mind:

- A warm room will cause the freeze-dryer to take longer to process the food. This can cause batch times to almost double.
- A dusty room will cause dirty vents, clogged cooling fins, and reduce the efficiency and life of the freeze-dryer.
- To ensure proper airflow while in operation, be sure the side vents on the freeze-dryer are not blocked and have adequate open space.

It starts getting exciting when you see your freeze-dryer in position! There are a few more things to do, beginning with waiting. The refrigerant in the freeze-dryer has to balance out due to its bumpy ride on the freight truck. Don't plug it in, and don't turn it on.

Allow the freeze-dryer to sit for 24 hours to stabilize the refrigerant. Keep in mind that if you move the freeze-dryer at a later time, you will need to allow it to sit for 24 hours again. Start your countdown clock and continue with the manual setup.

Getting Started Tasks

While waiting, tick off the tasks on the checklist. Here are the details of the activities on the Getting Started Checklist in Appendix 3 to complete:

- Open the door and ensure the shelving unit is connected and positioned correctly. They often get flipped upside down during shipping. The stainless steel trays will sit on the stainless steel shelves, so the orange heating mats should appear to be above the trays.

- Inspect the rubber gasket and the acrylic door and ensure they are clean. Use warm water and a cotton cloth to wipe down the gasket and door. Don't use detergent.
- Attach the drain hose to the fitting on the side of the appliance. It comes with the fitting on the left but can also be switched to drain from the right.
- Allow the vinyl hose to fall into a 5-gallon bucket while hanging loosely.
- Add the ⅜" Y fittings (purchased separately) to your tubing. Place them in line near the top by cutting the tubing and pushing the ends onto the fitting. One of each of the Y ends will be open to the air. This allows the freeze-dryer to always have air available and avoids accidental suction of wastewater from the bucket back into the appliance. If you do not have the Y fittings, be extra cautious when running the freeze-dryer. Make sure the end of the vinyl tubing is above the water level in the bucket. These little fittings will save you heartache!
- Attach the power cord, but do not plug it in until the 24 hours have passed.
- Position the pump on the right side or below the freeze-dryer. If it is the oil-free version, it should be to the right or above the freeze-dryer.
- Using a funnel, add the included oil to your pump up to just above the centerline (unless oil-free). The premier pump has a black demister that removes excess water vapor. Unscrew the demister to access the oil inlet.
- Attach the vacuum hose to the fitting on the right side of the freeze-dryer and attach the other end to the pump. Do not over-tighten this. Do not use Teflon tape or adhesive, as this will obstruct the O-ring and cause a vacuum leak.
- Plug the pump into the receptacle on the back of the freeze-dryer. This allows the freeze-dryer to turn the pump on when the freeze-dryer calls for vacuum pump operation, at will. Do NOT plug it into a wall outlet, or your freeze-dryer will not work.
- Flip the pump switch to the ON position. Don't worry; the pump won't turn on until the freeze-dryer signals for it to do so.
- To view the breakdown of the steps to set up your freeze-dryer and pump in the first 24 hours, look in your owner's manual. Or go to this link: https://harvestright.com/wp-content/uploads/2020/08/Owners-Manual-072020-DIGITAL.pdf
- Place a fan so that when the freeze-dryer is running, it will blow directly on the left side of the appliance. You only need to place a fan blowing on the vacuum pump if it is hotter than 160°F.
- Find locations for your equipment: impulse sealer, food funnel, FoodSaver®, etc. We keep our impulse sealer permanently on the far end of a countertop so we can use it easily. Our food funnel and FoodSaver® also have permanent places on the counter because we use them all the time.
- Find a good storage place for your packaging materials like Mylar bags, oxygen absorbers, and any freeze-drying accessories you purchased, like silicone mats, silicone molds, pre-cut parchment, corner stackers, dividers, and more. We placed our freeze-dryer on a countertop, so we use the drawers and cupboards below to store items specific to freeze-drying.

After the 24 hours have passed

Woohoo! The time is up, and the excitement is building. Now it is safe to finish the physical setup of your freeze-dryer.

- First things first: plug your freeze-dryer into your prepared outlet. (Remember: it is recommended that all freeze-dryers use a dedicated 20 amp circuit because of the power draw, but it is required for the large and X-large sized freeze-dryers. Like other household appliances, these freeze-dryers have a plug that only fits in a dedicated 110-volt NEMA outlet.)
- Make sure the drain valve on the side of the freeze-dryer is closed. The small, black handle needs to be perpendicular to the drain tubing, and the end of the tubing should be dangling in a bucket.
- Close the acrylic door in two quarter-turn stages. After the second turn, examine the seal between the door and the rubber gasket. There should be a thin line from the pressure of the door against the gasket. This seal is critical for the vacuum to work. Sometimes the gasket needs to be reseated to get this seal. I've found pulling the gasket out just a bit helps it to seal well every time.
- And finally, flip the power switch on the back of the freeze-dryer to the ON position. Your freeze-dryer interface screen will start up in 3-5 seconds.

You are now at the point where it's time to test the freeze-dryer appliance to ensure it will work correctly. We start with Functional testing. Touch the leaf icon in the upper left corner, and it will take you to the Functional Testing screen. From there, you need to test two things: the capacity to freeze and the ability to vacuum.

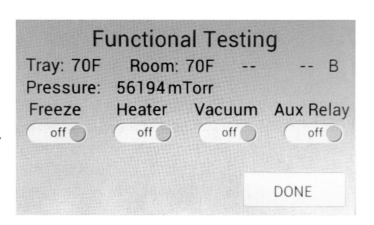

1. Test the Freeze function

Touch the OFF button underneath the word Freeze to turn it on. The condenser should kick on. Did you hear it? The answer should be "yes" if your machine is functioning as it should. Allow it to freeze for 30 to 40 minutes. Leave the function on for the next test.

2. Test the Vacuum function

After at least 30 minutes have passed with the previous test, touch the OFF button underneath the word Vacuum to turn it on. The pump should turn on. Again, if you hear the sound start, it has been activated. Allow the test to run for 20 to 30 minutes.

- The pressure inside the chamber will be measured in very small units specific for high vacuum measurements called Millitorr or mTorr. We want our machine to be able to go below 500 mTorr for the best performance. Watch the interface screen for the pressure reading to decrease. Once it is below 500 mTorr, your appliance has passed these function tests successfully.

- Once this evaluation is complete, open the drain valve slowly to release the pressure. ALWAYS OPEN THE DRAIN VALVE SLOWLY. This should take about five minutes to complete. Once it is fully opened and all the pressure has been released, you can safely open the door.

If your freeze-dryer does not reduce to 500 mTorr or lower, you will need to check for air leaks. Ensure the door is closed correctly and there is a seal line all the way around the gasket. Check that the drain valve is closed tightly (perpendicular.) The vacuum pump hose needs to be tight at both ends. Things do not always go smoothly, so if you cannot successfully complete the functional testing, call the Harvest Right™ customer support hotline at 801-386-8960.

Setting Up Your Freeze-dryer Interface

The interface allows you to program your freeze-dryer. Your freeze-dryer will come with pre-programmed settings. These will work for most of the foods you'll want to freeze-dry. Most of the time, you'll only have to press the Start button. There are a few screens that you will need to learn. We already covered the "*Leaf*" Screen, which has the functional tests.

Harvest Right™ has a place for naming your newest appliance. Some fun names I've run across include Frosty, Subliminator, The Preserver, Jack Frost, Vanilla Ice, Elsa, Mr. Freeze, Olaf, Boss Lady Fuel, The Beast, Liberty, Large Marge, Munchkin, Big Bertha, Hercules, Vader, The Winter Soldier, New Hope, Space Food Oven, R2D2, Chilly Charlie, My Precious, Garfield, Coldilocks, Glacius, and Yeti. Get creative and pick a name that matches your style! Set it up by pressing *System Name* at the top of the screen. Enter your preferred name and touch *Save*. You can change the name at any time.

Become familiar with the other two interface screens - press *Harvest Right* in the middle of the screen. Look over the options here. This is where the appliance log is located. It will tell you your serial number, hours running, and the number of batches. You can change Fahrenheit to Celsius if that is your preference.

On this same screen, you can press *Set Time* to enter another area to adjust the date and time. Do this by touching the up/down arrows and pressing *Done* when finished. You can set the date mode and select "repeat" for the alarm at completion. Also on the *Harvest Right* Screen is the pump info. Press on the word 'pump,' and you can select the type of pump and reset the running hours.

The *Customize* screen is the most important to learn as you'll use it regularly. Press it and look at your options. Right now, you'll want to change the extra dry time, and I recommend changing it to 12-24 hours. After your freeze-dryer completes the standard Drying cycle, it will go into the Extra Dry phase to keep your food in limbo until you can do your dry check. Setting your Extra Dry time to 24 hours allows you plenty of extra time to get to the appliance after the drying stage completes. So, if it stops in the middle of the night, you don't have to get up to package food; it can wait until you get there.

It's always okay to give your food more drying time. You cannot overdry. If it takes you longer than 24 hours (or the hours you set), it will refreeze the chamber for safety. If that happens, add an hour of Extra Dry Time before doing the first weight check, weigh the trays, put them back in for 2 hours, and then weigh the trays. If the moisture content didn't change, the weight in grams would be the same, and your food will be dry.

Also on the *Customize* screen are the temperature and time settings for Freezing and Drying. When you need to, you can change the Dry temperature from as low as 35°F to as high as 150°F. Your temperatures may be limited by the software installed on your machine. Herbs should be processed at 90°F, and most candy needs to be at 145°F. It's easy to adjust these; just make sure you do this before hitting the start button. We recommend always pre-freezing your food before putting it in your freeze-dryer.

In the *Customize* screen, you can add Extra Freeze Time to ensure your food items are frozen before the pump turns on. Often, explosive messes are caused when the pump turns on, and the food is not yet fully frozen. Another occasion to use Extra Freeze Time is when you are processing something that will melt, such as ice cream. You'll want the chamber frozen for around 60 minutes before placing the trays on the shelves. You can also lower the Initial Freeze temperature to -20°F to ensure the foods stay completely frozen before the start of the process. You can reset the entire screen to default from here as well.

The Customize screen defaults are:
- Initial Freeze: -10°F
- Extra Freeze Time: 0:00
- Dry Mode Normal
- Dry Temp.: 125°F
- Extra Dry Time: 2:00

Learning the different screens of the freeze-dryer interface is important as this will allow you to use the machine to its full potential. To summarize:

The Interface Screens:

- Start: This button starts the freeze-drying process.
- Leaf: Functional Testing: Freeze, Vacuum, Heater, & Aux Relay
- System Name: Your Choice of Name
- Customize: Freeze & Dry Temperatures & Times
- Harvest Right: Setup Configuration: Appliance log: serial number, hours running, number of batches. Temperature °F to °C, the pump button, and the time button.
- Set Time: Date, Time, Alarm
- Pump: Select Type, Reset Hours

The Bread Run

Brand new freeze-dryers need a "one batch burn" to eliminate manufacturing odors and ensure the freeze-dryer is working correctly. During this first run, the appliance will also ask about your pump.

- Close and latch the acrylic door with two quarter-turns.
- Press Start, select your vacuum pump and touch Save.
- Press Start again. The freeze-dryer will start cooling the chamber down to 32°F, which usually takes about 15 minutes.
- Lay out slices of bread onto all of your stainless steel trays. Spritz the bread with water, so they are damp.
- When the cooling is done, you will be prompted to close the drain valve and load your food. Make sure the drain valve is perpendicular to the tubing. Open the acrylic door, slide your trays onto the shelves, and close the door completely. Ensure the seal around the gasket is present, or adjust it as needed.
- Press Continue, and your freeze-dryer will begin running automatically. It will go through the following phases: Freezing, Vacuum Freezing, Drying, and Extra Dry Time.

You don't need to do anything until the final phase of Extra Dry Time. Your bread run may take up to 24 hours to complete. Be patient and allow the freeze-dryer to do its job. Read over the next section on the phases of the freeze-dryer, and then come back when your appliance is ready. Once your freeze-dryer reaches Extra Dry Time, you can cancel the function anytime. It's fine if it continues Extra Dry Time for many hours.

- Press Cancel to stop. The Process Complete screen will pop up.
- Open the drain valve slowly to release the pressure. This should take about five minutes. Once it has released all the pressure, you can safely open the door. Make sure there is a bucket below the drain valve.
- Remove the bread from the chamber and do a few touch tests. Break it into pieces. Is it crisp? Does it crumble? Is it warm? Don't forget that the most accurate way to test your foods for doneness is to follow the two-hour check method. But this isn't necessary for the burn batch. Toss this test bread in the trash, as it may have absorbed lingering manufacturing odors.

Since your test batch is done and does not need additional time, you can now Defrost. I prefer to open the door and allow a fan to melt the ice naturally, so I select No Defrost. After 15-30 minutes, the ice rings can be removed manually by sliding them into a bucket. (Remove the gasket and the shelf unit first.)

You can clean your appliance when the ice has melted completely and the water has drained from the tube into the bucket. Cleaning the chamber and shelves is not necessary every time. Still, they should be wiped down with a clean, wet washcloth regularly. Because the bread run was the first time the freeze-dryer ran through its phases with food, this would be a good time to clean it.

Remove the gasket and slide out the shelving unit. The shelves are pretty heavy, so prepare yourself. Keep it connected and place it on the table or countertop next to the freeze-dryer. The cord should be just long enough to do this. If you do not have a counter space to place it on, disconnect the cord each time to clean it.

Wipe down the inside of the chamber with a soft cloth and warm water. Isopropyl alcohol and Everclear are also safe cleansers. Wipe down the shelves and carefully slide the heavy shelving unit back into the chamber. Wipe down the gasket and put it back in place.

Your freeze-dryer is officially ready to go! The next chapter helps you understand the process and lays out a step-by-step checklist to make the process as simple as possible.

4

USING YOUR FREEZE-DRYER TO PRESERVE FOOD

Your freeze-dryer is such a cool appliance! It takes raw or cooked food and preserves it so perfectly it can last for decades. To do its magic, the freeze-dryer must complete six phases for each batch.

The Phases of the Harvest Right™ Freeze-Dryer

Pre-cooling

The pre-cooling phase prepares the machine to drop in temperatures by getting the chamber down to 32°F within 15 minutes. This time can be extended (in *Customize*), so the chamber is even colder for fragile foods, like ice cream, which will melt. (Customize pre-cool for 60 minutes when doing ice cream.)

Freezing

The freezing phase is when the appliance drops the temperature to extremes, so the foods are frozen completely solid. Not exciting, but it is essential, and it does take time to get there.

Vacuum Freezing

This phase is both freezing and vacuuming. The chamber continues the task of freezing while the vacuum pump turns on and starts to create a vacuum.

Drying

This phase is initiated by the freezing temperatures reaching the correct point and the vacuum pump reaching adequate vacuum. The trays are gently warmed, and moisture in the food sublimates (turns from ice to vapor.) The Drying timer starts. This stage is where the bulk of the time will be. Most batches will take between 24 and 60 hours, but some will take 72 hours, and some will only take 18 hours. It will depend on what kind of environment the freeze-dryer is in and how much moisture is in the food on the trays.

Extra Dry Time

Once your freeze-dryer has reached this phase, it's time to test the food. You can start or stop the appliance at any time during this phase. Your machine will automatically flip into Extra Dry Time when the sensor can tell it is near the end. This is the time when human judgment is needed. During the first check, look at the food, touch it, weigh each tray, and take notes. (Printable batch logs are available in Appendix 3.) Put it back in the freeze-dryer for Extra Dry Time and recheck the weight after two hours. It needs more time if the weight changes. Just put it back in and add more dry time. Weigh the trays in grams, so it's easy to tell if the weight changes. Once it doesn't change, you know your food items are completely dry.

Batch #		Start Cooling		Trays In		Trays Out		Run Time		Extra Dry		Total		
			am pm		am pm		am pm		hrs		hrs		hrs	
Start Date:		Customize	Temp	Time		Check Time:			am pm		am pm		am pm	MHE
End Date:		Freeze												
		Dry				mTorr:								
Tray Contents Description:		Examples: Raw, Cooked, Thickness, Liquid, Spread		Pre-Frozen		Wet grams		Check 1 grams		Check 2 grams		Dry grams		Subtract Dry from Wet for Water Loss
1				Y / N										
2				Y / N										
3				Y / N										
4				Y / N										
5				Y / N										
6				Y / N										
Notes						Chamber Cleaned:	Y / N	Oil Changed:	Y / N	Maint. Needed:	Y / N			

You can't over-dry, so don't worry about running Extra Dry Time. Some food will ALWAYS need more dry time. Thicker areas may still be frozen. Extremely moist food may become sticky, indicating more time is required. You'll learn your machine as you keep track of your batches. I've found through experience that paying attention to the mTorr has helped to know when food is done. The lower the pressure the vacuum achieves, the dryer the food.

Remember that during this phase, you must slowly open the drain valve and allow it to vent for five minutes before opening the door. And when opening the vent, make sure the drain hose is not sitting in water from the previous batch. If the valve is opened too quickly, it can cause a burst of air to enter the chamber, blowing powdered foods everywhere. Caution: If the drain hose is sitting in water when the valve is opened (and there are no Y fittings), the hose will suck the water up into the chamber, spraying the food inside with dirty water ruining the entire batch.

Some may worry about the extra expense of allowing the machine to run Extra Dry Time. We have found it doesn't add too much additional electrical cost. To save on costs, you will simply have to watch the machine more closely because you won't know when it will switch to Extra Dry Time. We have found it much easier just to let the freeze-dryer run its course, and when we get back to it, we do a weight check and run it for another two hours. If you don't have a tight budget, it may be worth getting a FLIR thermal imaging camera to test your trays at the end of the cycle.

Defrost

The Defrost phase is a two-hour warming of the chamber to melt off the ice and allow it to drain out. Make sure you have your drain hose in a bucket to catch the water. The chamber and shelves will be slightly warm after the defrost cycle. You can give your freeze-dryer a break by not running a defrost cycle. If you aren't in a hurry, open the door, and it will melt slowly on its own. Then you have a cold chamber to start the next batch. *Tip: If you have a batch waiting, you can manually defrost your freeze-dryer in under an hour by opening the door after the batch has run and directing a fan to blow on the chamber. Have a towel handy, and after 15-30 minutes, remove the gasket and shelves. The ice rings can be slid out of the chamber, and you can wipe down the interior. However you choose to do it, defrosting is a must, so don't skip it.

Notes:

- Unless there is an error on your screen, there is no reason to cancel the process until you've reached Extra Dry Time and are ready to do the two-hour check.

- You absolutely must NOT run a second batch of food after completing a run without defrosting in between and starting over. Your pump needs to cool down and rest, and your freeze-dryer needs to be cleaned of ice. Putting a second layer of ice in the chamber will stress the freeze-dryer and could damage the pump.
- Piggybacking is when a no-moisture item, such as skittles, is placed in the freeze-dryer after a regular cycle has been completed. This allows the vacuum to work on the item and create the famous puffed look. Piggybacking is never recommended. Too many people mess it up. And for newer machines (2017+), there is a candy software update. The update is for machines running a software version of 3.6.11 or higher. This means that candy can do short runs without piggybacking. And it's awesome.

Step-by-Step Basics of Running the Freeze-dryer

Once you have set up your freeze-dryer, gotten acquainted with the interface, and completed the bread run, you're all set to start freeze-drying your first batch. Appendix 3 has a reminder step-by-step worksheet you can print off. The 20 steps for making sure everything goes well are:

1. Before freeze-drying, wash and prepare the food into chunks or slices that are no more than ¾" thick and liquid no more than ½" deep.
2. Pre-freeze the food on trays for 24 to 48 hours to improve appliance efficiency & avoid explosive messes.
3. Check the oil in the pump. It should be completely clear and between half-full and max.
4. Plug in the freeze-dryer, flip the switch to the on position, seat the gasket, close the door, check the seal (re-seating the gasket if needed,) and fully latch the handle.
5. Press Customize from the Start Screen and set any changes in temperatures or times.
6. Press Start to begin pre-cooling the chamber and wait 15-90 minutes.
7. Turn on a fan and ensure it is pointed at the left side of the freeze-dryer.

8. When pre-cooling is done, the screen will prompt you to close the drain valve. The black handle on the valve should be perpendicular to the drain hose.
9. Weight the trays. Put the food in, close the door, check the seal, and fully latch the handle with two quarter-turns.
10. Press Continue. Wait for 24 to 60+ hours while the appliance cycles through the phases of Freezing, Vacuum Freezing, & Drying. Prepare your next batch while you are waiting.
11. When the phases are completed Extra Dry Time will run up to 24 hours (if you set it as suggested.) Otherwise, the default is two hours. When the screen says Extra Dry Time, you can stop the machine at any time by pressing Cancel and then check the food to see if it needs more dry time. Some food will ALWAYS need more dry time.
12. Ensure the drain hose is in an empty bucket. Press Cancel and open the drain valve slowly to release the pressure. You may need to wait five minutes to avoid any explosive change in pressure.
13. Open the door, carefully remove the food, and check for cold or soft spots. Weigh each tray and take note on a batch log to give yourself a starting point for comparision.
14. Put the trays back in, close the valve, and press Extra Drying Time to add additional hours; at least 4 (because it's okay to dry longer), and then check on it after two hours or when you have the time. Re-weigh all the trays. If the weight changes, repeat #14. Once the weight stays the same, the food is completely dry and can be packaged.
15. Quickly remove the finished food from the trays and place it immediately into proper storage. Thick 7-mil Mylar bags are the recommended thickness for long-term storage (25+ years). Thinner 5-mil Mylar bags and vacuum-sealed canning jars work well for intermediate storage (up to 10 yrs). Canning jars are the best for short-term storage because you can see the food through the jar!
16. Add the right amount of oxygen absorbers and seal your packaging. I recommend using an Impulse sealer for Mylar bags and a FoodSaver® for your canning jars. You'll need 300cc OA for each 1-gallon Mylar bag and 100cc OA for each 1-quart canning jar or mylar bag.
17. Remove excess oxygen by pressing gently on the mylar bags before heat sealing with the impulse sealer or by using a FoodSaver® vacuum on canning jars, which removes the oxygen and seals the jar at the same time.
18. Defrost the chamber with the Defrost button or select No Defrost and open the door to let the ambient air melt the ice. Remove the shelves after 15 minutes and slide out the ice rings to speed up the defrost process.
19. Afterward, clean the freeze-dryer with a soft cloth and warm water. (Isopropyl alcohol and Everclear are also safe cleansers for the appliance.) Make sure to do a thorough cleaning occasionally, and every time there is an accidental mess.
20. Allow the chamber to dry. Aiming a fan at the chamber will speed this up. Then you are ready to start the next batch.

Mistakes to Avoid When Freeze-Drying

A freeze-drying fail is bound to happen to you at some point. It happens to all of us, especially when still gaining our footing with this skill. Many have had failures and shared their learning moments on Facebook groups. If you run into a snag, check out the Customer Support troubleshooting wizard on the Harvest Right™ website in the upper right-hand corner at this link: https://harvestright.com/support/. I hope to save you from as much of that headache as possible. Therefore, here is a quick list of mistakes that are commonly made so you can avoid making them:

Not cleaning the freeze-dryer often enough

Keep it clean! While you do not have to clean your freeze-dryer after every use, you should set up a schedule for regular cleaning that should be performed with a soft cloth and warm water. Never use abrasive cleaners, brushes, or pads to clean your freeze-dryer.

Clean the interior, carefully removing the shelving unit. If an odor lingers after you have processed a batch, use a solution of water and either isopropyl alcohol or Everclear to wipe down the interior and shelving unit. Once you're done, dry it with a soft cloth.

Also, ensure that the exterior of your machine is kept clean. Every now and then, clean out the drain hose, too. Simply closing the drain valve and pouring alcohol or soapy water down the hose and letting it set for 20 minutes will sanitize the drain line.

Not performing regular oil changes

Changing your oil regularly ensures that your pump remains in good working condition. Always check the pump's indicator window's oil level before starting each new batch. If the oil has food particles or is cloudy, it is time for an oil change. Make sure to check how often your pump needs its oil changed and keep it running smoothly.

Freeze-drying food that is too thick or too heavy

I get it. Sometimes we're in a hurry or just plain impatient to get started with the process, so we slice and dice our food into pieces that are too thick. This could hurt the quality of the finished product by shortening the food's shelf life and putting unnecessary strain on your machine. It is necessary to prep your food to the correct thickness before placing it in the freeze-dryer. You want slices that are ½" thick (absolute max of ¾" thick,) liquids up to ½" deep, and chunks up to ¾" pieces.

Not Pre-Freezing

Food that isn't completely frozen before the pump activates is one of the main reasons for explosions in the freeze-dryer. This issue is avoided entirely by always pre-freezing your food for 24 to 48 hours. By ensuring the food is totally solid, the freeze-dryer will endure less stress, extending its lifespan and reducing the time needed to process the food. Only a few foods should be put in without pre-freezing because they must have very low water content, such as herb leaves or shredded cheese.

Not performing a dry check after processing a batch

Always check that the food is completely done. While there are a variety of ways it can be tested, the absolute best way I've found is to measure weight. After the food has gone into Extra Dry Time, you can check it. Write down the weight. Put the trays back in for four hours extra dry time and check it at two. If the weight stays the same, then you know it's dry. If it did change, put it back in until the weight stops dropping.

Remember, you can add as much dry time as needed; the food cannot be over-dried. Other ways to check for doneness, such as feeling the bottom of the trays for cold areas or checking for soft parts, are unreliable. Infrared FIRA meters can also facilitate this, but they are pricey. Just make sure to check it! You don't want to open a package and find out it went bad.

Not storing the freeze-dried food with oxygen absorbers

Package the freeze-dried food quickly after the process is done so that the food does not reabsorb moisture from the air. Keep the humidity in the room low with a dehumidifier or air conditioner, if needed. After placing the food in jars or bags, line them up neatly. Open the oxygen absorbers, take out the required number, and reseal the package (dial level 5). Place the oxygen absorbers in the packaging and seal the containers. Nitrogen (the other air in the bag) is good to have in the bag, so don't worry if it doesn't suck out all the air. It's just the oxygen you need to remove; 100cc for a quart jar and 300cc for a gallon Mylar bag.

Not sticking to the recommended foods

Failure to adhere to the recommended foods for freeze-drying can result in a range of issues. Foods that should not be freeze-dried (such as those high in fat or sugar) go rancid, explode into a mess, and have decreased shelf life. To ensure that your completed product is of the finest quality and has a long shelf life, stick to the recommended ingredients for freeze-drying. Avoiding items high in fat or sugar will keep your food fresh and safe to eat for a longer amount of time.

While it is always best to stick to the recommended foods for batch freeze-drying, you are welcome to experiment with small amounts of these foods mixed into your recipes. This can add unique flavors and textures to your freeze-dried meals.

Additionally, if you are planning to use the food soon, such as for a camping trip, it may be okay to use foods that are a bit higher in fat, as they will still be consumed within a relatively short period of time. However, it is crucial to be aware of the risks associated with using these types of foods and to use them correctly and safely.

Generally Recommended Dry Times

According to the manufacturer, the freeze-dryer should typically complete a batch in 24 to 60 hours. However, you might find that your friend's sliced grapes took 48 hours to freeze-dry while your process lasted 52 hours. Why does the same item have different drying times? The short answer is variation. The difference in the food moisture content and the environment in which the freeze-dryer is located will affect your experience.

Variation in Foods

The type of food being freeze-dried significantly impacts the time range for freeze-drying. In fact, this is the factor with the heaviest contribution. Fruits and Vegetables tend to have high moisture content and will take quite a while in the freeze-dryer. Other foods like meat or herbs have far shorter freeze-drying times.

The Thickness of the Food

The thickness of the pieces of food placed in the freeze-dryer also plays a significant part in determining the length of time. Always drain off excess juices and keep pieces ½"-¾" to facilitate more efficient freeze-drying. This will allow you to use your freeze-dryer more sustainably as you save on electricity. Proper preparation benefits you in so many ways, and freeze-drying time is one of the ways you can save. Pay attention to your machine and do your weight checks to determine when it's dry.

Differences in Environment

There will be variations in the environment where the freeze-dryer is located. The location's conditions, such as the room temperature, humidity, and elevation, will significantly affect how efficiently the machine runs and, therefore, how long each batch will take.

Equipment

There are various ages of machines, varying software, and different pumps being used, which will produce a range of experiences and results. As such, understand that drying times will vary. Harvest Right™ is a brand that has proven machine efficiency in getting you to the final freeze-dried product in as little time as possible.

Outliers

Some things refuse to fit the mold and, when freeze-dried, fall outside the typical range. For example, pineapple typically takes 60-72 hours to freeze-dry (far outreaching the norm for fruits). Ours consistently takes over 65 hours. Seeds are another exception. For berries, tomatoes, and other foods with seeds, it usually takes 45-55 hours. My berries have always needed at least 6 hours of extra dry time before even starting the weight check. An example of the opposite happening is peas, which may only take 12 hours to be successfully freeze-dried. Just remember that if there is a lot of moisture in the food, such as in watermelon or squash, expect longer batch times.

In just a few days, you can change fresh food into freeze-dried! And it will last and last for years. Isn't freeze-drying amazing! And it's relatively simple once you get the hang of it. Just follow these lists, and you'll be freeze-drying like a pro in no time. Next up, we'll dive into the preparation process. We want the best possible outcome, so following a few simple rules to prepare the food properly beforehand is essential.

5

PREPARING FOOD TO FREEZE-DRY

Now we'll get into the specifics of your part of freeze-drying. In this chapter, we will focus on the critical aspects of food safety and preparation for freeze-drying. By now, you should have a good idea of how things work. Still, taking the proper safety measures is essential to ensure your food is handled and preserved correctly.

Processing foods to the correct size is also necessary to avoid prolonged batches. We'll also talk about which foods are best suited for freeze-drying. The possibilities are endless, from fresh fruits and vegetables to meats and dairy products. It's crucial to remember that not everything can be freeze-dried, so we'll also give you a list of foods to avoid. By knowing which foods can cause explosive messes, you can avoid those issues entirely. Stay with us as we continue our journey through the fascinating realm of food preservation.

Freeze-drying and Food Safety

According to FoodSafety.gov, more than 15 percent of Americans get sick from food poisoning every year, with 128,000 needing hospitalization. Some people suffer the consequences with a terrible impact on their health for years after that. The adverse effects can even last their lifetime. When freeze-drying, please remember that what you put in, you will get back out. Do not expect a freeze-dryer to destroy any pathogens. Process clean food safely and correctly.

We can do our best to avoid becoming sick by following four practical steps when handling and preparing food of any type:

1. Practice general cleanliness.

You can keep yourself clean and prevent sickness caused by foodborne bacteria and viruses.

- Keep your hands clean. Wash them with soap for at least 20-30 seconds before touching foods and after preparing foods. Also, always wash your hands before eating.
- Clean the area frequently while you handle food. While preparing food, wash your tools with soap and wipe down all surfaces you've used. Always start with clean trays and equipment.
- Separate food types. Keep the various foods separate to avoid cross-contamination. Don't allow the juices of raw meats to spread to other kinds of foods. Use different cutting boards for preparation: one for raw meats, one for fresh produce, one for bread, etc.
- Cook the various foods at the correct temperatures. Using a food thermometer will let you know if the internal temperature of a food is high enough to make it safe.
- Refrigerate food promptly (within 2 hours) when it has cooled after cooking. Set your fridge to 40°F or below and your freezer to 0°F or below. Always thaw frozen food in the refrigerator or in cold water.

2. Handle produce with care.

All produce should be cleaned before you eat or use them in dishes. Tips for ensuring they remain safe to consume include:

- Wash and rinse them just before use. Dry thoroughly with a clean paper or cloth towel.
- Wash produce under running water while rubbing to remove solid particles like dirt and pathogens.
- If you must immerse the produce in water, use a clean bowl instead of the sink, as the sink area typically houses pathogens.
- Scrub produce with firm skin, such as carrots, with a vegetable brush.
- Rinse water should be lukewarm for best results.
- Do not use bleach, detergent, or soap to wash the produce, as this will affect the taste and could make it unsafe to eat. Clean water is usually sufficient.
- Do not store fresh produce on the same shelf as raw meat, eggs, poultry, or seafood.
- Ensure you have washed and cleaned your hands before handling produce, as pathogens are easily transferred if they are on your hands. Also, ensure surfaces like cutting boards are clean.

3. Handle raw eggs safely.

Eggs are perishable, just like raw poultry, fish, and meat. As such, they must be handled safely, cooked, and stored correctly. If not, broken uncooked eggs can

cause foodborne illness due to the presence of bacteria. There are a few rules that will ensure you don't get food poisoning from handling or eating eggs:

- When buying refrigerated eggs, quickly get them home and back in the refrigerator. Those gathering eggs from backyard chickens have slightly different rules. Freshly laid, unwashed eggs don't need refrigeration and can stay on the counter for 30 days. They are good for 90 days when refrigerated.
- Don't keep eggs out of the refrigerator for more than two hours. Once eggs are stored in the fridge, they stay there until used. Use purchased eggs within 3-5 weeks. If you want to keep eggs longer, process them for storage. (Eggs can be freeze-dried, water glassed, and frozen.)
- If a recipe requires raw eggs, ensure it is cooked within two hours (or refrigerate the entire mixture and cook it within 24 hours).
- Never eat raw eggs. Those who are at high-risk for foodborne illnesses should avoid eating soft-cooked eggs.
- Always wash your hands, the utensils, and the equipment used with the eggs before and after handling eggs or foods that contain eggs.

4. Handle raw meat, poultry, and fish safely.

Bacteria tend to grow rapidly on animal-based products. It is important to handle, store, and cook these products correctly to prevent food poisoning.

- When selecting raw meats from stores, never buy items that are discolored, have a strong odor, or feel slimy or tough-textured. Also, don't buy meats that appear bruised or are wrapped in torn or leaking packaging.
- Don't mix different types of meat, poultry, or fish. Store them separately as well.
- Wash your hands with soap often when handling raw meat products. Keep your utensils and equipment clean. Avoid any other food items from coming into contact with the raw meat or the equipment that has touched it.
- Raw items can be safely stored for about three days in the refrigerator before needing to be preserved. Ensure the meats are in sealed, airtight bags. The freezer temperature needs to be 0°F (-17.8°C), while your refrigerator needs to be kept around 34°F (1.1°C).

Health and Safety

Health and safety practices that are specific to freeze-drying include:

- What goes in is what comes out. Some pathogens will be killed due to the temperatures, but not all. The purpose of freeze-drying is not to kill bacteria but to eliminate water from your food. Start with a clean product and handle it correctly.
- Keep raw with raw. Treat the raw meat as such, even after freeze-drying. It needs to be marked RAW on the outside of the Mylar bag or canning jar. Clean all items that have touched the freeze-dried product as you would typically with raw meats - in hot, soapy water.
- Process cooked meals with other cooked foods. It's always best to keep the same types of foods together. You can freeze leftovers as you make them, and when you get enough for a load, run it through the freeze-dryer.
- Liquids contain a lot of water and will take a long time, so all the trays should be liquids. Some liquids must be watered down by as much as 1:1 to avoid bubbling and blowouts due to the sugar content, including fruit juices, BBQ sauce, smoothies, etc. It seems counterintuitive, but it works.
- Fruits can sometimes bubble up. Give them adequate space on the trays. Berries have seeds and will take extra dry time. Watermelon and pineapple have high water content and will take much longer than most fruits.
- Keep likes with likes. You do not want your pineapple to taste like garlic. Some have found placing bread slices on top of garlic is a great way to eliminate odor while making flavored croutons or bread crumbs.
- It's good to have the trays holding approximately the same moisture content, but if there is one that is heavier, place it on a middle shelf. There is a sensor on one of your shelves, but because these things change, you'll have to call customer service with your serial number to find out which shelf has your sensor.
- Chewy or hard candies puff up fantastically by raising the temperature, typically between 135-150°F, depending on the candy. Solid chocolate will only melt in a freeze-dryer. Some candies will puff up ten times their size, so give them plenty of space. Candy should only be run with other types of similar sweets.

Preparation Prior to Freeze-drying

With health and safety covered, you can dive right into freeze-drying. Select the food you'd like to start with and prepare it. We started with frozen strawberries we'd picked ourselves the month before. Good foods to start with are not oily and not sugary. Choose something simple like apple slices or frozen peas. (It's a good idea to have extra foods for "simple" batches in the freezer.) Individual items like produce will need to be prepared. Keep safety in mind at all times, and wash your hands frequently.

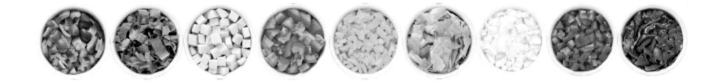

Cut Food in Small Pieces or Slices

Process the food and load up your trays. Most items do well on the stainless steel trays. Process the food into slabs ½"-¾" thick or pieces ¾" or smaller. Larger pieces will take significantly longer in the freeze-dryer. Pack your trays up to the maximum weight allowed for your size.

Liquids in the Trays

You can also make a favorite low-fat liquid recipe. Spread prepared juicy meals onto the stainless steel trays, keeping to the ¾" thickness. Liquid purees should not exceed ½" of your tray. Place your tray in the freezer, pour a pre-measured amount onto it, and allow it to freeze solid. Or pour into molds and pre-freeze and place those onto your trays.

Shelf Weight Limit

Remember to stay within your shelf weight limit, or you risk releasing too much water, which could create too much ice build-up, forcing you to remove the food and put it in the freezer, defrost the appliance, and run the food a second time. The small freeze-dryer trays hold 2.3 lbs. or 3 cups. The medium trays hold 2.5 lbs. or 4 cups. The large trays hold 3.2 lbs. or 5 cups. The X-large trays hold 5.8 lbs. or 10.5 cups.

Sugary Foods

Foods high in sugars will bubble up and exude stickiness, so they do best on silicone mats. This includes most fruits, like pineapple and peaches, and desserts. Berries and other thick-skinned produce must be punctured for freeze-drying so the juices can escape.

Candy that swells, such as taffy, does well on parchment paper with the dividers in place, so they don't stick to each other. Some foods need extra space on the trays to expand. Marshmallows and gummy worms do just that and become crunchy.

Pre-Freezing

Do you want to avoid a messy explosion? One of the biggest causes of explosions in the freeze-dryer is when the food isn't fully frozen before the pump turns on. I've found that following the rule of always pre-freezing your food for 24 to 48 hours eliminates this problem. You will avoid these horrid messes with the food completely solid before the vacuum pump turns on. This will reduce strain on the freeze-dryer and extend its life. It will also shorten the time it takes to process the food. I have two sets of trays. One set is in the freeze-dryer, and the other is in the freezer after being prepped with food.

Pre-cool Chamber

Pre-freeze the food on the tray when doing delicate items, like jello shapes or ice cream. Then set the pre-freeze on the freeze-dryer for 60 minutes so it's ice cold when you put these delicate foods in; otherwise, they will start melting on the trays.

Preparation Summary

- Select food, wash hands and prepare thickness.
- Individual food items need to be in ¾" or smaller pieces.
- Large foods need to be cut into ½" - ¾" thick slices.
- Meals should be spread onto the trays up to ½" thick.
- Liquids should be poured onto the trays, up to ½" deep, when sitting inside the freezer.
- Give plenty of space to sugary foods. Dilute sugary liquids.
- Always stay within the weight limits for your trays.
- Always, always pre-freeze your foods.
- Pre-cool the chamber for 60 minutes before doing ice cream.

Foods You Cannot Freeze-dry

As promised earlier, I am providing a more comprehensive list of foods that cannot be freeze-dried and those that can be (in the next section). Some of the foods that you should not try freeze-drying are:

- **Oily or fatty foods.** Examples include all oils, peanut butter, Nutella, nuts, butter, pure chocolate, and mayonnaise. The nature of fats and oils makes them harder to freeze-dry as they go rancid over time. It is possible to freeze-dry high-fat foods. However, they typically have a shorter shelf life, which should be kept in mind. Some may only last 6-12 months. Occasionally, rehydrating can be more difficult for fatty foods as well.
- **High-sugar syrupy foods.** Such foods do not freeze-dry well because of the structure of sugar, and they can cause an explosive mess in the chamber when the pump turns on. The list of high-sugar foods I do not recommend freeze-drying includes honey, jam, syrup, jelly, preserves, and sodas.
- **Foods that just don't work:** Oreos, Twizzlers, Swedish Fish, fruit snacks, candy canes, and licorice do not work in the freeze-dryer. They condense and get harder. Some have had success with Pop-Tarts, but they usually turn hard.
- **Alcohol.** While items with higher alcohol concentrations do not freeze-dry well, those food items with small amounts of cooking alcohol in the recipe will freeze-dry just fine. The main issue with alcohol is that it sublimates out of the foods just like water, so you can't store it freeze-dried.
- **Vinegar.** Just like alcohol, vinegar will sublimate, so it cannot be stored freeze-dried. Vinegar is an acid and shouldn't be used within the chamber for cleaning, either. Small amounts in recipes will be okay.
- **Bones.** Some people hope to be able to freeze-dry bones to make fresh bone broth, but this doesn't work. It is best to make the broth and freeze-dry that.
- **Water.** LOL! Can't freeze-dry water, I'm afraid. It reminds me of my mother-in-law's shiny can on her fridge that says "Dehydrated Water." Of course, it is an empty can with directions that say, "Just Add Water!" Haha!

Great Picks!

Good Foods to Freeze-dry

So many foods are fantastic for freeze-drying. Almost everything! See a complete list of the best foods to freeze-dry in Appendix 2. Let's start with the freshest of foods: Produce.

Vegetables

All home garden and store-bought produce can be freeze-dried successfully as long as it's been properly prepped. Did you catch that? All those delightful foods you can grow in your garden can be preserved with a freeze-dryer. Vegetables are the simplest and fastest. They have no fats, and many have lower water content, so they process quickly. Most vegetables will do fine straight on the tray.

Fruits

Fruits have a higher sugar content and can sometimes bubble up. Lay down silicone mats for easy cleanup and give them adequate space on the trays for any bubbles. Berries have seeds and will always take extra dry time. They must be punctured or sliced in half to allow the water to escape. Watermelon and pineapple have high water content and will take much longer than most fruits. Some fruits become sweeter, and some become tarter.

Meats

All lean raw, and cooked meats and their broth can be freeze-dried. It is best to use lean versions of meats, including seafood and fish, as fat content reduces shelf life. Remove excess fat from raw meats and cut them into ¾" thick slices or chunks. You can also pre-cook your meat to remove fat. Don't cook in oil, as the oil will reduce the freeze-dried shelf life. Rinse meats in hot water to remove residual fats.

Poultry

Almost all variations of poultry, including pre-cooked pieces, deli slices, and ground poultry, freeze-dry wonderfully. Poultry can be stored for up to 25 years, and cooked chicken that has been shredded is excellent. You can make your own or pick up bags of chicken pieces from a retailer. Place them on a tray after ensuring none are too thick and freeze-dry using the process outlined in the previous chapter. Breaded items, such as chicken patties and

nuggets, can be freeze-dried as-is, and all you have to do to rehydrate them is wrap them in a damp paper towel. Remember that items with high fat need to be consumed in 1-5 years.

Red Meat

Lean red meats can be freeze-dried successfully. When done correctly, they can last ten or more years. Versions of cooked or raw beef that can be freeze-dried include ground beef, roast beef, and steak. Be mindful of the items that tend to contain a high amount of fat, and purchase the leanest versions possible. Low-fat meats like goat or rabbit can go into the freeze-dryer as is, whereas fatty meats, such as ground beef or sausage, need to be washed. After you have cooked the meat, drain off any excess fat. Rinse the meat in a colander or strainer with hot water, and drain off the water. This helps with the removal of excess fat. These meat items will still have a shorter shelf life (between 5 and 10 years) compared to other freeze-dried foods. Please consume high-fat meats within 1-5 years.

With pork, just like beef, you have to be mindful of the fat content shortening the shelf life of cooked pork, including pulled pork and pork sausage. Bacon is delicious and my absolute favorite, but it is quite fatty, so it will typically only last 6-12 months. Luckily, rinsing to remove excess fat is unnecessary for some pork items, such as ham. I like to process cubed or chopped ham for freeze-drying. Sausage is usually fatty and has a short shelf life, generally less than a year. But freeze-dried chopped or cubed ham is excellent to have on hand for breakfast, especially when I'm making omelets. Game meat (and even jerky) can be freeze-dried. Goat and rabbit are some of the leanest meats available.

Seafood

All kinds of seafood can be freeze-dried: raw or cooked seafood, freshwater fish, saltwater fish, and shellfish can all be processed as long as they are flaked, shredded, or chopped small enough. This includes lobster, crab, clams, mussels, scallops, and shrimp. Seafood that is best to freeze-dry raw: "fatty" fish (salmon, tuna, mackerel, swordfish); filets that are in large sections (cod, halibut, pollock, haddock, monkfish); and shellfish (lobster, clams, scallops, or squid.) The seafood that is best to freeze-dry pre-cooked is out-of-its-shell crab, lobster, and fish that has been smoked.

Eggs

Raw eggs, cooked eggs, scrambled eggs, and eggnog process well. All these eggs and egg-containing items can be successfully freeze-dried. Storing raw eggs allows you to have fresh scrambled eggs as well as an ingredient for baking. Beat the eggs prior to pre-freezing on trays. We have found pouring the beaten eggs onto the trays much easier when they are already in the freezer. Reconstitute 2 T. egg powder to 2 T. water for one large egg.

Dairy

Remember that when it comes to dairy, lower-fat items will always have better outcomes in the freeze-dryer. If you want to do a higher-fat dairy item, such as heavy cream, dilute it 1:1 with water. Please note that butter cannot be freeze-dried because of its high-fat content. Let's break down some popular dairy a bit further. Freeze-dried milk tastes better compared to dehydrated milk. (Side Note: Non-dairy milk, such as oat or rice, will freeze-dry well also.) Cheese curds, shredded cheese, and sliced cheese can be loaded into your freeze-dryer and turned into beautiful, yummy creations. Place a paper towel below the cheese to absorb the oil. Ensure that ice cream is super cold to start so that it does not melt. Pre-freeze your machine for an hour to get the chamber extra cold before putting in the ice cream. Most people prefer to eat freeze-dried ice cream dry. All you have to do to freeze-dry sour cream is spread it out on a tray and run the batch. It becomes crumbly after being freeze-dried. Ensure that cream cheese is really cold and cut into ⅛" slices before placing it on the trays for freeze-drying. There is something wonderfully delicious about yogurt drops. (Greek yogurt does not do drops very well.) All you have to do to make them is place yogurt in an icing bag (or Ziplock bag with one corner cut off) and squeeze the drops onto the freeze-drying tray. *Turn the tray temperature down to 90°F. Other dairy items that can be freeze-dried include buttermilk, whipped cream, cottage cheese, heavy cream, kefir, and eggnog.

Legumes

Legumes don't necessarily need to be freeze-dried because they store very well in their uncooked form (as long as they are stored correctly.) Storing in airtight containers, keeping them in the dark, and placed in a location with a cool temperature are usually more than enough to get ten or more years of shelf-life. I generally only freeze-dry legumes if I use them in a specific recipe. Hummus can be freeze-dried when used within 6-12 months.

Grains

Like legumes, grains don't need to be freeze-dried. Grains store perfectly fine in their uncooked form when stored correctly. They should be stored in a cool, dark location using airtight containers, and then you can expect to get ten years of shelf-life easily. A few cooked grains work quite well in the freeze-dryer, including Oats, Rice, and Quinoa.

Herbs

Freeze-drying herbs means you have ingredients to flavor your favorite dishes for years. Lower your dry temp to 90°F. They can be reduced to powders, which makes them all the easier to use. The scent of herbs and spices is quite strong, so do not freeze-dry with other food unless you don't mind if they pick up that smell. One thing to remember is that freeze-dried herbs have more flavor and nutrients, so when adding to recipes, use 1/3 to 1/2 of the amount.

Meals

Most of the meals you have on a regular basis can be freeze-dried. Low-fat meal options have the longest shelf life. Typically these foods should be consumed in 1-5 years, depending on the fat content. You can enjoy many different types of meals. Your leftovers and sides can also be freeze-dried as long as the fat content is not too high.

Snacks

Freeze-drying lets you turn your favorite guilty pleasures into a delightful crunchy burst of flavor! You can freeze-dry salsa, guacamole, and nacho cheese. And when you add some freeze-dried sour cream, refried beans, and jalapeños, you've got yourself a nacho bar!

Desserts

Be careful when freeze-drying sugary dessert items, as the process may be more complex than other freeze-dried foods. Keep the pieces small and give them plenty of space. Read through the various tips sections, so you are ready to handle whichever food you choose.

Candy

Not all candies will freeze-dry. Some will turn hard like rocks, some will expand into an explosive mess, and some will melt into a puddle. Allowing enough space for the candy to expand is critical to freeze-dried candy making. Successfully processed candies will turn either crunchy or expand into an air puff. We use dividers to keep them from touching each other. Many candies should be cut into pieces because they puff up so much. Learn more about this in Freeze-Dried Candy Making for Selling & Fun, coming soon to Amazon.

Drinks

Freeze-drying is a great practice when dealing with excess drinks when you want to save leftovers. Smoothies, shakes, broths, milks, and other beverages are easily freeze-dried. High-sugar drinks must dilute at least 1:1, including fruit juices and smoothies. Pre-freeze all drinks completely solid in a freezer before putting them into the freeze-dryer.

Edible Flowers

These can be used with cakes, cupcakes, cookies, salads, or cocktails. Their presence adds a touch of something magnificent to the final process. Make sure you know where your flowers came from. Pesticides and herbicides should not be consumed. If you have a flower garden, like me, you can control what goes into your edible flower beds. Popular edible flowers that can be freeze-dried include: Roses, Calendula, Pansies, Violas, Begonia, Lavender, Snapdragons, Dianthus, Cornflowers, and Nasturtium.

The conditions and packaging of your freeze-dried foods determine how long they last in your pantry. The next chapter dives into food storage packaging specifics to ensure your freeze-dried goodies do not spoil prematurely.

UNLOCK THE POWER OF FREEZE-DRYING

-Freeze-drying brings people together by preserving the community's knowledge and tradition in every bite.-

As you delve deeper into the world of freeze-drying, you may want to keep your newfound knowledge to yourself. But did you know that sharing your experience can be beneficial for the freeze-drying community as a whole?

By sharing your experience, you can help others interested in learning about freeze-drying and its many benefits. You can help guide them on their freeze-drying journey and improve their overall understanding of the technique. I encourage you to share your experience with others.

By leaving a review of this book, 'The Only Beginner's Freeze Drying Book You'll Ever Need' on Amazon, you'll help other potential freeze-drying enthusiasts find the information they need to get started. Your support and feedback will be invaluable in spreading the knowledge of freeze-drying technique and its benefits.

Thank you for your support and for being a part of the growing freeze-drying community.

To leave a review scan the QR code or visit: BFDR.2MHE.COM

6

PACKAGING FREEZE-DRIED FOOD SAFELY

The process of making freeze-dried food is fantastic; no doubt about that. But as exciting as the process is, it will do you no good if your food ends up spoiling due to a packaging mistake. That begs the question: how do you ensure that your freeze-dried foods last as long as possible? The simple answer to this: invest in good storage practices.

Most people have heard that your storage area should be cool, dark, and dry. As such, basements and root cellars are excellent food storage areas. Garages are not a good option because they are usually not climate-controlled like inside a house. They often retain moisture and fluctuate widely in temperature, both conditions that lead to food spoilage.

If you do not have a basement or a root cellar, find an area in your house that remains cool or can be temperature-controlled all year round, such as under the stairs, under a bed, or in a closet. If you don't have the perfect location, know that any food storage is better than none.

Long shelf life can only be achieved through the proper storage of freeze-dried food. The freeze-drying process removes almost all the moisture in food, which is why it can sustain such a long shelf life. However, you will need to store the preserved food in the right conditions to allow it to maintain this state. Let's talk about the significant contributors to food breakdown and spoilage.

KNOW YOUR ENEMIES

The 7 Enemies of Food Storage

Food has seven foes that will destroy all that is good and wonderful about your food storage if precautions are not taken to eliminate them. These enemies are:

- **Moisture** (including the humidity in the air) - Encourages microorganism growth and causes mold
- **Light** - Deteriorates the flavor, color, and vitamins in food
- **Temperature** - Specifically, heat above 70°F causes a loss of nutrition, flavor, texture, and appearance
- **Oxygen** - Changes the texture and flavor of foods and makes fats rancid/Encourages the growth of microorganisms, leading to yeast and mold growth
- **Pests** (such as rodents and insects) - Expose food to the elements and spread pathogens
- **Time** - Even with a shelf life of 20-30 years, everything eventually degrades over time
- **Kids** - The little sneaks can empty out a pantry favorite in record time

Food Storage Done Right

Luckily, you can fight back against these food storage adversaries by implementing the tips outlined next:

Store the food in a dry place to protect against moisture

The humidity level of your food storage area needs to be controlled. The food will rehydrate quickly if exposed to moisture, which becomes a prime situation for bacteria to proliferate. The humidity level should be kept at no more than 15 percent. Consider a dehumidifier or air conditioner to ensure this condition is met. We have our freeze-drying in the basement and have a dehumidifier, draining into a sump pump, running at all times. This helps lower the humidity levels, but we still move quickly when the food comes out of the freeze-dryer to get it packaged rapidly.

Store the food in a dark place to avoid light

You must keep your food from receiving direct sunlight. Direct sunlight exposure encourages oxidation and, therefore, causes the food to lose much of its good quality and nutritional value. Some nutrients are particularly susceptible to light degradation. Examples include fat-soluble vitamins such as A, D, E, and K. Block out the sunlight by using heavy curtains or shades on windows and skylights. Rely on artificial lighting in your storage area and keep the room dark, with the lights off, when not in use. Mylar bags completely block out the light, and amber canning jars help block the light.

Store the food in a cool place to protect from temperature

The cooler your storage area, the better. In fact, the recommended temperature range of a food storage area is between 50°F and 70°F. Every increase of 18°F shortens the shelf life of most stored foods by half. Cooler temperatures reduce respiratory activities that can cause moisture to develop in the air. In addition, it slows the production of agents that causes ripening in foods like fruits and vegetables. Ripening paves the way to rotting. Always remember that no matter how well food is preserved or what method is used for preservation, food will rapidly go bad if it is stored in a hot location.

Store the food air-tight with an Oxygen Absorber (OA) to eliminate oxygen

An oxygen absorber and a strong seal are the best methods to store food long-term. The oxygen absorbers remove the oxygen, which makes up 21 percent of the atmosphere. The oxygen absorber will remove all the oxygen in the bag in a few days. Nothing will be left behind except nitrogen. Nitrogen safeguards food as it is an inert gas. This is a highly advantageous way of doing things, as nitrogen protects your food. The nitrogen will also shield your food and prevent it from pulling too tightly on Mylar bags. This stops the food from ripping holes through the bags or crumbling from the pressure.

Store the food in sealed containers that is rodent-proof to protect against pests

The container you store your food in should have an air-tight seal. Such storage devices keep moisture, insects, and oxygen from reaching the food. Keep in mind that some pests (such as rodents) can chew through Mylar bags (and even a plastic bucket, if given enough undisturbed time). It is crucial to put Mylar bags inside a container (such as a plastic bucket or tote) to avoid this problem. Another important practice is to store your freeze-dried food at least six inches off the floor which makes your freeze-dried food less accessible to pests and rodents. These creatures have a nasty habit of contaminating food they are near or touching. Storing your food off the floor also ensures that it is more likely to avoid moisture, dust, and debris. Using poison-free traps is a fool-proof way to keep rodents at bay.

Store the food in a manner that makes it easy to rotate to combat time

Rotating your food storage is essential to keeping your foods safe to eat. Foods degrade over time, slowly losing their nutritional value and changing in taste and appearance. By rotating your food storage, you can ensure that you use the oldest items first. When packaged correctly, many freeze-dried items will last for decades, which helps with shelf life. Check on your stored foods regularly and make sure you are using up anything that will expire or start losing its nutritional value.

Store the food out of sight to avoid snitching kids

Kiddos can disrupt your food storage goals if they are sneaking their favorite treats. A jar of freeze-dried peaches or a box of granola bars can disappear in minutes! If possible, keep your kitchen pantry food separate from the area where you have your food storage. Make sure your kids know which items are allowable snacks, and safeguard the rest! It can also help when you get the kids involved in building your food storage. Then your goals become their goals too, and they are more likely to leave the food alone.

The BEST Food Storage Containers

Some of the best storage containers for freeze-dried food include:

Mylar Bags

These are the most commonly used storage containers for freeze-dried foods. Mylar bags are the absolute best choice. You will recognize them by their shiny silver color. They hold an airtight seal from an impulse sealer. The right type, 7-mil, is rather thick and completely protects against light, moisture, and oxygen. They are easy to label and pack away neatly. They will need to be placed inside a rodent-proof container for perfect protection.

Glass Canning Jars

Another standard storage container that works well for freeze-dried foods is the canning jar. Created to hold up to intense pressure, these canning jars (aka Mason Jar, Kerr Jar) are a great choice to keep your food safe from oxygen, moisture, and pests. They are easy to seal using a FoodSaver® (with attachment) and stack nicely in their original box. Choose amber-colored jars if possible because light will be a constant enemy, and you'll want to store them in a dark place. Be mindful that they are breakable as well.

Metal Cans

Tin and aluminum cans make a great option because they are airtight, do not allow light in, are rodent-proof, and stack easily in their box. Metal cans protect against light, moisture, oxygen, and pests. However, they are less feasible for a home preserver, as the equipment to seal the cans may be cost-prohibitive. You will also need to invest in some heavy-duty can openers.

Other containers you may want to use include:

Plastic Buckets, Totes, Tubs

To protect Mylar or vacuum seal bags from rodents, they can be placed inside plastic buckets, totes, or tubs. Some mylar bags are large enough to fit snugly in a 5-gallon bucket. Plastic containers add an extra layer of protection, which can lengthen the foods' shelf life. Just remember that rodents can chew through plastic, if given enough time, so be sure to have other methods in place to keep rodents out of your food storage.

Vacuum Seal Bags

This type of plastic bag helps preserve your freeze-dried foods by removing the air from the package. FoodSaver® makes some great sealers and bags. They are clear and will not keep out light or prevent the oxidation process. They are meant to be immediate storage (under a year). Be careful what you store in these bags as it is easy to puncture the plastic. Ensure that foods kept in these bags are stored in a cool, dark room and inside a bucket. Remember that any delicate freeze-dried food will be crushed in the sealing process.

Plastic Ziplock Bags

These should only be used if you want to hold a small amount for a short time. The bulk of your freeze-dried food needs to be stored securely. But Ziplock bags work great for keeping aside a bit for a tasty snack. They will not stop light, oxygen, moisture, or pests. But they are perfect for kids' snacks!

The 3 Categories for Packaging

Packaging should be done right. Always. Skimping on the packaging means you will end up with sorrow and spoiled food. A good guide for doing this right is to think of food packaging in three categories:

1. Immediate use (up to 12 months)
2. Short-term (1-4 years)
3. Long-term (5-25 years)

Let's tackle the best practices for each of these categories individually:

Immediate use

You may want to set aside some of the freeze-dried food you process to nibble on over the next few months. While you can store all your freeze-dried foods in heavy-duty long-term packaging, it isn't always necessary. Plastic vacuum bags are one of the best options for immediate-use packaging. They last a few months to a year, and I have found they also work wonders with fresh foods in the fridge. Zip Mylar bags with clear windows or a clear side will last a few weeks but eventually give in to oxygen, moisture, and light. Ziplock bags can be used for a few days. Remember that these options are temporary and are only good for keeping food fresh if used within the appropriate time frame. If you will be using the food soon (such as in the weekend meal), you can leave out the oxygen absorber and just store it in a canning jar.

Best Packaging for IMMEDIATE use:
• Vacuum seal bags with an OA (good for a few weeks to a year)
• Zip Mylar bags with clear windows (good for a few weeks)

The steps to package food in a vacuum seal bag for immediate use:
1. Place the freeze-dried food inside the vacuum seal bag.
2. Add an appropriately-sized oxygen absorber (1-quart bag = 100cc).
3. Make sure the area to be sealed is flat and free of debris.
4. Vacuum and seal the bag with a vacuum sealer (such as the FoodSaver®).
5. Inspect the seal for folds or missed areas and reseal as needed.
6. Label the vacuum seal bag with the date and an item description.
7. Store in a plastic container and use it within a year.

Short-term use

Freeze-dried meals and ingredients containing fats will store for 1-4 years but will need to be consumed. Keep this in mind for your rotation. There are two excellent options: glass canning jars and Mylar bags. We prefer to keep our 7-mil heavy-duty Mylar bags for long-term storage, but 5-mil Mylar bags work great for the short-term! They are cheaper than thicker bags, so that's a plus. But they will be more susceptible to puncture, so select what is stored carefully. The best option for storing food between one and four years is vacuum-sealed canning jars with oxygen absorbers. (*Quick Tip: The FoodSaver® regular mouth attachment will get a much stronger seal if two lids are used during the sealing process. Don't worry; only one lid will stay attached to the jar.) For best results, keep the jars in a dim area. Food left in locations with lots of light loses its color and nutrients over time.

Best Packaging for SHORT-TERM use (1-4 yrs):
• Canning jars with an OA stored in darkness (good for 5+ years)
• 5-mil Mylar bags with an OA stored in a tote (good for 5+ years)

The steps to package food in a canning jar with a FoodSaver® for short-term storage::
1. Place the freeze-dried food inside a glass canning jar.
2. Add an appropriately sized oxygen absorber (quart jar = 100cc).
3. Place a lid on the canning jar. (Use two lids for the regular mouth jars.)
4. Attach the vacuum fitting and remove the air out of the jar.
5. Test the seal with your fingers.
6. Place a ring on the jar for added security.
7. Label the jar with the date and an item description.
8. Store the canning jar on a shelf using the strategies outlined in this chapter.

Long-term use

The most dependable solution: Mylar bags for the win! 7-mil Mylar bags are the standard needed for long-term storage. Add an oxygen absorber and store it in a plastic tub for the highest quality product. The 5-mil Mylar bag can also be used for long-term storage, but only for foods like powders with no jagged edges. The sharp edges of many freeze-dried foods can puncture the less expensive, thinner bags.

Best Packaging for LONG-TERM use:
• 7-mil Mylar bags with an OA stored in a tote (good for 30 years)

The steps to package food in a Mylar bag for long-term storage:

1. Place the freeze-dried food inside the Mylar bag.
2. Add an appropriately sized oxygen absorber (1-gallon bag = 300cc).
3. Gently press to remove any excess air.
4. Make sure the area to be sealed is flat and clean. (Wipe with a microfiber cloth.)
5. Seal the open end with the impulse sealer.
6. Inspect the seal for folds or missed areas and reseal as needed.
7. Label the bag with the date and an item description.
8. Store in a plastic container.

Using Mylar Bags & Impulse Sealers

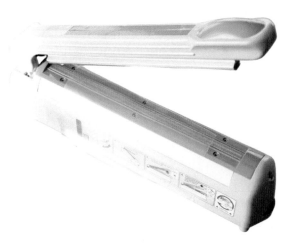

Mylar bags should be one of your go-to storage solutions for freeze-dried foods. Therefore, it is only fitting that we spend more time on the particulars of this storage option. Never vacuum seal Mylar bags. The fragile cellular structure of freeze-dried food is easily broken down during vacuum sealing. Even the highest quality Mylar bags can develop puncture holes during this process. Not only can vacuum sealing cause holes and crushed food, but it's also not even helpful to remove the air. The oxygen absorber removes all the damaging oxygen, leaving you with a cushion of nitrogen, which helps protect the food.

An impulse sealer is used to seal Mylar bags to ensure the highest probability of keeping food safe and sound from elements that would otherwise remove its freshness. It is easy to use.

To Use a mylar bag with the impulse sealer:

1. Place the food and oxygen absorber in the bag and make sure the seal area is clean.
2. Plug in the impulse sealer and set it to the right setting.
3. Place the bag against the strip, ensuring it lays flat.
4. Press down the lever and hold as the light turns on. This should take about five seconds.
5. Continue to hold after the light turns off for about five more seconds.
6. Move the Mylar bag down a little and repeat the process for a double seal.

The impulse sealer works better when the bar is pressed down firmly during the process. Let the seal cool before checking it. A quality check means ensuring there are no folds or creases and that the seal holds well. If the Mylar bags were sealed with a wrinkly look, then the heat was too high. 400°F is hot enough to seal Mylar bags. As such, you can also use a hair straightener or a clothes iron (on the wool setting) as a substitute in an emergency.

Typical settings for sealing bags with the impulse sealer:

- Setting 7 for 7-mil Mylar bags (May need to adjust to 8 if the seal does not hold well.)
- Setting 6 for 5-mil Mylar bags
- Setting 5 or 6 for zip Mylar bags with windows or a clear side
- Setting 5 for vacuum bags and also the plastic bags that hold oxygen absorbers
- *Quick Tip: Setting 4 or 5 also works for resealing chip bags.

Depending on your situation, you may have to adjust your setting up or down. The impulse sealer will also need to be turned down slightly if you are doing a lot of bags at once (such as prepping bags of freeze-dried candy for sale).

Mylar bags are still susceptible to attacks from rodents and some pests. Therefore, it is best to store these bags in a plastic tote or some other container that serves as a barrier between your food and these nuisances.

The Magic of Oxygen Absorbers

Humans need oxygen to live, and so do the microorganisms that cause yeast growth and mold on food. Additionally, oxygen can cause oxidation, which deteriorates your food's quality and nutritional value. Ensure that oxygen absorbers are always placed inside the container to be sealed with your food. Oxygen absorbers add a layer of safety when storing your food in sealed bags and containers by removing the oxygen that was sealed inside during packaging.

ALWAYS use Oxygen Absorbers

Oxygen absorbers must always be used for long-term food storage. Using an absorber big enough to counteract all the oxygen in the container is crucial. Going overboard and using "too much" is okay because it will simply stop absorbing. However, having too little is a significant problem. New oxygen absorber packets will feel like coarse sand because they include a granular iron component. A telltale sign that the oxygen absorber has been depleted is when the packet is stiff and crunchy - a consequence of the iron inside the packet rusting from exposure to oxygen for an extended period.

Oxygen absorbers need "headspace" to function well. This room allows the extraction of oxygen from the atmosphere around the food. The oxygen is subsequently drawn from the food and captured by the oxygen absorber. Move quickly when using oxygen absorbers. They start absorbing oxygen immediately when removed from their sealed packaging. When everything is ready, remove what you need, and reseal the container immediately. Place the absorbers in your storage container, push out any extra air, and seal them quickly to maintain the efficiency of the oxygen absorbers. Remember that oxygen absorbers do not remove nitrogen or other gasses from the air, so the bag should not have a tight vacuumed look after it's sealed.

Tip If you plan to use your freeze-dried food within a short amount of time (such as in your kids lunch this week) you can skip the oxygen absorber and just keep it in a canning jar until use.

Always Use the Right Size

Another consideration in the proper use of oxygen absorbers is sizing. Oxygen absorbers come in various sizes from 50cc (for a pint) up to 2500cc (for 5 gallons.) Ensure the oxygen absorbers' size matches the packaging you are using.

- **100cc for a quart** canning jar or 8" x 8" Mylar bag.
  Loosely packed food with air pockets will need 200cc.

- **300cc for a gallon** 10"x 14" Mylar Bag.
  Loosely packed food with air pockets will need 500cc.

- **2000cc for a 5-gallon** 20" x 30" Mylar Bag.
  Loosely packed food with air pockets will need 2500cc.

Oxygen Absorbers vs. Desiccants

A desiccant is an item used to control the moisture content of a product. In essence, it is a moisture absorber. There are several types of desiccants, though the most common and only FDA-approved is silica gel. These are NOT to be used with your freeze-dried food. Desiccants are great for keeping items such as medication tablets safe and dry.

Never place desiccants and oxygen absorbers in the same food storage container. Some assume that using both together would be an even better strategy, but that is untrue. Desiccants remove humidity from food, and as great as this benefit is, they cannot be used simultaneously with oxygen absorbers. When moisture is removed from the food by desiccants, the consequence is that the oxygen absorber becomes ineffective. Oxygen absorbers require that there be some level of moisture to absorb oxygen. This makes the 2-3% moisture left in freeze-dried food perfect for an oxygen absorber.

The general rule of thumb is that freeze-dried foods should be consumed between 6 and 12 months after the sealed package has been opened. The next chapter discusses the best ways to store freeze-dried food.

7

STORING FREEZE-DRIED FOODS LONG-TERM

We live in a time when there is a grocery store or restaurant around every corner. It is easy to pick up food at any time, which has lulled us into a false sense of security that food will be available anytime on any given day. When a catastrophe strikes, there is typically little to no warning, and most people don't have a backup food supply. Add to this the fact that most grocery stores only stock enough food to supply their community for three days (and even less in some cases). You have a recipe for disaster as the food supply chain completely breaks down during an emergency.

A disaster can easily strip away this convenience of obtaining food that we have gotten used to and leave us with nothing to survive. If the Covid-19 pandemic has taught us anything, it is that life as we know it can become null and void in what seems like the blink of an eye. When such an event happens, we will need food stored in adequate amounts available to us.

A few short decades ago, it was impractical for people to go to the grocery store every week, simply due to the traveling distance, so having a pantry in your home was an absolute necessity. Our society has come to rely on the grocery store as our pantry. Back when utilities were not part of every household, food had to be stored using methods such as canning, drying, or placing in a root cellar to ensure there would be something to eat during the long winter months.

Why Food Storage is Essential

In addition to the benefit of being prepared for an emergency, food storage is an essential part of modern life for the following reasons:

Healthy Homemade Meals

Most of us live fast-paced lives, and cooking can get placed on the back burner, especially when supplies are not readily available in our homes. However, study after study shows that eating out is less healthy compared to eating in. You control what goes in your body when you make your own meals.

Having freeze-dried food (both ingredients and full meals) stocked in your pantry helps with meal planning and preparation and ensures you will have more homemade meals as the norm. Freeze-dried food hydrates rapidly, making these ingredients relatively easy to use in meals.

Save Money

A large storage area, such as a pantry, allows you to buy food in bulk. Buying in bulk will enable you to take advantage of sales and the lower price per unit of these items. Savings also come in the way of being able to stock food that you grow in your garden.

Having a well-stocked pantry can eliminate the need to go to the grocery store as frequently, which saves you on travel expenses. Fewer trips to the grocery store also lessen impulse buying, so you can keep more dollars in your wallet.

Commercially prepared freeze-dried foods are expensive. Having a home freeze-dryer producing the same—or better—types of foods can quickly pay for itself. It will be the food you choose, prepared the way you want to eat it, without all the additives and preservatives!

Food Security

Food security is having reliable and sustainable access to affordable, nutritious food. Disasters are not the only reason why a household's food supply can become short. Circumstances such as a family member becoming ill, the breadwinner losing their job, having a fluctuating income, and seasonal work can put a dent in your food supply. However, having a stocked pantry can remove this worry and help you sleep easily at night, which gives you one less thing to worry about during stressful times.

The Foods You Should Store

With the plethora of options we have when it comes to food nowadays, you might be overwhelmed as to what you should stock in your pantry. The most straightforward answer is to store what you like to eat. It makes no sense to have a pantry stocked entirely with products that will make you cringe with every bite. (I'm looking at you, MREs!)

When an emergency happens, you will be under extra stress and want familiar foods you enjoy. Eating something that does not agree with your palate (or your digestion) will only make that situation more challenging. Make your food choices with this in mind so they will comfort you during these times.

Another reason you should stock items you enjoy eating is that it makes rotating your inventory even more effortless. Rotation ensures that you use food before it expires. You will want to keep track of your food and monitor the dates so those expiring get used before others. When you like something, you don't mind using it to make a meal, and then you just replace that meal. Keep in mind that canned food that is about to expire can be opened and run through your freeze-dryer so it can be stored for an additional amount of time!

Once you have narrowed down what you should stock based on your preferences, follow these criteria for storing in your pantry:

- What you like: This includes full meals as well as ingredients. You'll want to store raw egg powder to make scrambled eggs and as an ingredient in baking!
- The shelf life of the items: It is best to stock items with the highest longevity to avoid wastage and not have to restock the space prematurely. Single ingredients that are low in fat (such as freeze-dried vegetables) store the longest.
- The nutritional value: You need to keep food that will allow you to eat a balanced diet even during an emergency. Stock food from all the food groups.
- Allergy issues: Avoid food that incites allergic reactions.

Shelf-stable foods should be the top priority when stocking food in your pantry. Shelf stability is about how long a food item can safely be used after sitting in the pantry. Aim for a minimum of one year. Most freeze-dried items last 5-25 years. It's easy to store traditional shelf-stable foods, including:

- Ready-to-eat canned items, including meats and soups
- High-energy foods like peanut butter, jelly, honey, granola bars, and trail mix
- Staples like rice, oats, potato flakes, dried beans, and dried peas
- Baking items like flour, sugar, baking powder, and salt
- Vitamins and supplements

Freeze-drying allows you to incorporate foods not traditionally on the shelf-stable list, like fresh fruits, vegetables, dairy, and meats, into your diet. You can safely store freeze-dried raw lean meat for a decade, and dairy can safely be stored for 5-15 years. Fresh vegetables and fruits can be stored for 25 years! This means you benefit from having vitamins, minerals, protein, and fiber in your diet!

Meeting Your Food Goals

To have foods you enjoy eating available for everyday use or as an emergency supply, you must have a plan. It may seem easier to purchase ready-made food supplies, but your budget and palate will suffer. Get the delicious meals you desire by taking a systematic approach to fill those shelves. Utilize all the options you have at your disposal and fill your pantry with staples, canned goods, and freeze-dried foods. Whether you plan to freeze-dry complete meals or the ingredients to make your meals, you will need to set some goals.

Recipe-based Plan

Adopting a recipe-based approach to food storage unites the benefits of freeze-drying with meal planning. Instead of buying and storing a list of individual ingredients, you design meals and store them either complete, as Just-Add-Water meals, or as ingredients. I consider this a superior approach compared to straight food-type storage because:

- You will be 100% certain of the items and quantities to store.
- You can ensure every component you will need is on hand.
- Your family will want to consume the food you've planned.
- You can get offers and discounts on the things you'll buy.

Committing to this kind of plan is super simple! You just pick your favorite recipes and go for it. You can do a trial run first, starting with preparing two weeks' worth of freeze-dried meals. Test them out and determine how you want to proceed. Once you have gotten the hang of this and decided it is the right path for your food storage needs, you can process more food. A foolproof way of going about this includes the following steps:

1. Decide how long you want to provide meals.
2. Decide your breakfast, lunch, dinner, and snack recipes.
3. Determine how many meals you need by the number of people in your household.

With that foundation set, you can create a shopping list and gather ingredients you already have stocked, saving time and money.

Store what you Eat, Eat what you Store

I recommend combining these methodologies to have a well-rounded experience with freeze-drying and all it offers you and your household. Do not freeze-dry things you will not eat to ensure that happens. It does no good to store foods just because you think you should. Don't bother storing foods your family will not enjoy because they will remain in your pantry and go to waste. Forcing "gross" food on your family will be a painful process. If your household doesn't eat it fresh, they won't eat it preserved, regardless of how nutritious it is. If it won't get consumed, then it's a waste of your time and money to store it.

The only exception would be when you want to sneak in added nutrition. Take that spinach your kiddos typically turn their noses up at and turn it into a powder. You can even trick yourself into eating a more well-balanced diet. In such cases, freeze-drying can become your best friend. Many foods can be powdered and added to your recipes for a nutrient boost without anyone noticing! The flavor and appearance will likely be unaffected depending on the additions to particular meals. Just think about how many casseroles could use a "green shot" of veggies. Add powdered kale, carrots, cauliflower, or any other vegetable or fruit to smoothies. Pancakes and waffles can be infused with powdered pumpkin or squash. Powdered broccoli can be added to scrambled eggs for a tasty twist to green eggs and ham. You can get creative with adding nutrition to your family's meals.

Not sure how a freeze-dried item will go over with your family? Try it first and find ways your family will use it before committing to freeze-drying a large batch. Such ways include:

- Place a magnetic notepad on your refrigerator. Freeze-dry small amounts of the items you think your family enjoys. Every time a particular freeze-dried item is consumed, take a note to represent the items your family most enjoys.
- Using the list created, divide the foods into sub-categories such as fruits, vegetables, proteins, dairy, etc. Obtain more ingredients and modify them to suit your family's taste buds. Tweak and adjust amounts over time and note which foods are consumed the fastest and in what quantities.

- Study your grocery list and note the items you buy most frequently. Can some of the not-so-healthy options be replaced with more health-conscious items? Can any of these items be freeze-dried? If they can, make snacks yourself using your freeze-dryer.
- Create weekly and monthly menus for your home, not only to save time and money at the grocery store but also to create Just-Add-Water meals and to make use of leftovers.

Start small so that you don't overwhelm yourself. New habits will take time to get used to, and there is no need to rush. Take it one step at a time, and be mindful as you learn how to add freeze-drying to your food storage.

Rotating Freeze-dried Foods

Rotating your food ensures two things: nothing goes to waste, and you keep your food the freshest possible. Food rotation means consuming the foods in your pantry (and other food storage areas) with the closest expiration dates first. Rotation will be easy if you eat what you store because you store foods you like to eat. All you need is some organization, and you'll nail it.

First-In-First-Out (FIFO) System of Rotation

This system organizes and uses inventory before it goes bad in many sectors, including the restaurant industry. The last thing you want is to forget about the food you put your time, money, and efforts into preserving. FIFO works because you are eating food before it gets trapped by the biggest enemy of food storage: time. Make putting away your groceries and preserved foods a mindful activity. You might be tempted to put the new items up front, but instead, put them in the back and bring forward the foods closer to expiration.

Food rotation can seem complicated. But once you implement a few basic strategies, it becomes a cinch. The following build on FIFO.

Date all packages with a black Sharpie

I have found it beneficial to have the package date and the assumed expiration date on each package. High fat will cause your dates to remain lower (five years), and no-fat items, like vegetables, will have 20 years of shelf-life. Mark your dates on the storage packaging with a dark permanent marker. Print this big, bold, and legibly so that this date is obvious as you rotate the food. Don't leave guesswork for your future self. For shorter-term storage, I often write the information on a piece of masking tape I put on the mylar bag. This way, I can reuse the mylar bag for another short-term item.

Sort into bins according to the food type or by date

Organizing your freeze-dried items by food type gives you an aerial view of the items you have and in what quantity. It is visually appealing, and, more importantly, it ensures cross-contamination does not occur if your food becomes unsealed. When you want to add items to these tubs, bring those already stored forward and put the new packages in the back. You can also sort your food storage by date, keeping all the foods that need to be consumed in order of how long they will last. This method works well when all the necessary items to make complete meals are included in the same bin.

Keep an inventory and update it

Even better than an aerial view, keeping an inventory allows you to note the exact quantities of the foods you have and even those you do not have. This is an easy way to keep track of your food. It also helps save time, money, and space and prevents wastage. You can use a physical pen and notebook, an electronic spreadsheet, or even step into the digital age and use an app. Using QR codes with the Argosy app is fantastic. You can even search for an item!

The heaviest containers should be placed on the bottom of your food storage

Naturally, keeping heavy items off a top shelf is best to avoid being harmed when pulled down. The entire shelf could topple if it becomes top-heavy. Placing your heaviest food storage items on the bottom is wise. Freeze-dried food is not heavy at all. Without all the water weight, the food becomes light and fluffy, so that the significant weight will come from your choice of packaging. Boxes of glass canning jars will weigh a lot more than totes of mylar bags. If you, like me and many others, store food preserved with a variety of methods, then you may have buckets of grains, boxes of #10 cans, or tubs of rice in mylar bags. These heavy items are perfect for the bottom shelves, and the freeze-dried foods are wonderful for the higher shelves. These items should also be incorporated into your rotation, so they aren't forgotten.

Use your stored food

Try it! Actually eat the food. This is the absolute best way to rotate and know what you like and what you still need. Incorporating your food storage into your everyday family meals ensures that you eat what you store and store what you eat.

Now that you've correctly stored your freeze-dried items, let's move on to the many ways you can enjoy these uniquely preserved foods.

What Went Wrong?

Troubleshooting Why Food Went Bad

"Oh no!! It's moldy!" is something you never want to hear. You do not want to take all the time and resources to freeze-dry food only to discover later that it went bad. I mean, can you imagine being excited to enjoy your favorite freeze-dried pumpkin bites only to gasp in horror as you find mold growing on the once vibrantly-colored and crunchy snacks? Let's try as much as possible to limit this to our imagination so it will not come true.

Understanding why stored food goes spoils goes a long way in helping you take preventative measures. There are several reasons why food may go bad inside your packaging, but some of the most common are:

The food may not have been completely dry

Before even placing your freeze-dried food in packaging, you must ensure it is totally dry. Testing to see if your food is dry is simple. Weigh the tray holding the freeze-dried food when you think it is done, and give it two hours of extra dry time. When the time is up, weigh the tray again. If the weight has not changed, then the food is completely freeze-dried. You can do a happy dance. If the weight changes, you must return the food to the freeze-dryer for another two hours. Repeat this process until there is no change in weight.

The packaging may not have gotten completely sealed

An error in packaging is the most common reason why food spoils. Always ensure your packages are completely sealed. If using canning jars, check the lid's seal with your fingers. If it pops off easily, it was not sealed correctly. Always add a ring to the jar for added protection. If using Mylar bags, look at the seal to ensure it is smooth and even. We generally do two seals to make sure the seal is adequate. You want to make sure there is no possible way for oxygen to get in and destroy the food.

The food you stored may have had too much fat

The fat in foods can cause them to go rancid, regardless of how well-packaged. Remember that full meals and ingredients containing a lot of fat can only be stored for immediate or short-term use. At maximum, they need to be eaten within five to ten years. Use low-fat recipes to help avoid this issue.

Now that we've covered the proper ways to store your freeze-dried foods, they'll be ready when you want to use them! The next chapter will discuss the three ways to enjoy freeze-dried foods.

8

ENJOYING YOUR FREEZE-DRIED FOODS IN 3 WAYS

ow that food storage seems less daunting, it's time to enjoy your freeze-dried foods. The meals, treats, and foods you've prepared and stored well can now be used for your meal chart. The three common ways of consuming freeze-dried food are:

1. Eating it dry and crunchy as a snack or treat.
2. Adding ingredients dry or rehydrated to recipes.
3. Rehydrating complete meals.

Let's look at each of these ways individually.

Best ways to Consume Freeze-dried Foods

Snacks & Treats

Snacking doesn't have to be the evil it is made to be. Snacking can be a part of a healthy diet, such as when your snacks are freeze-dried fruits and veggies. This needs to be a mindful task, whether an adult or a kid does it. Freeze-dried foods allow you to have healthy bites available in between large meals rather than the fat-saturated and sugar-laden options that are typically readily available.

Freeze-dried foods also rake in points in the snack department because they do not need to be refrigerated or have added preservatives (which allows you to avoid common allergens.) They are safe in hot environments (such as a locker) throughout the day. That's a lot of benefits—and it's not even counting how tasty freeze-dried treats are.

Before we move on, here is a quick word of caution. Fresh fruits and veggies have lots of water that helps with digestion. Freeze-dried foods have almost all the water eliminated from their structure. This means that water is not readily available to aid the food's movement through the digestive system. To avoid a stomach ache, remember to drink lots of water when you eat a large amount of freeze-dried foods in their dry form.

There are quite a few options for snacking on freeze-dried foods. You can snack on veggies, fruits, pieces of cheese, or other food straight out of the containers. You can also prepare snacks by adding seasonings to these plain veggies and fruits before freeze-drying.

Veggie chips are an all-time favorite! The vegetable slices can be infused with a bold flavor by adding seasoning. To get the seasoning to stick, lightly spritz the slices with water or olive oil. For a savory taste, dash with salt and pepper, lemon pepper, Italian seasoning, or any other combination that makes your taste buds happy. You can make chips out of zucchini. After you have customized freeze-dried potato chips to suit your taste, you may never want to touch the store-bought stuff again.

Freeze-dried fruit all by itself is a popular option as well. It already tastes like candy! Pineapple pieces, strawberries, and peaches are a big hit in our house. Flavorings can also be added to your favorite fruits. For a sweeter flavor, sprinkle with brown sugar or ground cinnamon. Slice your favorite fruits and season them before arranging them on the freeze-dryer trays.

A really popular snack is yogurt bites. You can mix fruit in or leave it plain. Pour the yogurt into an icing bag (or Ziplock bag with the corner snipped.) Make coin-sized yogurt drops on the freeze-dryer tray by gently squeezing the yummy goodness from the bag. Set your tray temp down to 90°F and use silicone mats to help them pop off easily. Plain Greek Yogurt doesn't hold together, as well as yogurt with fruit or sugar added.

Another delicious snacking option is oatmeal bites mixed with your favorite fruit. Cook oatmeal with your fruit (such as apples) diced or sliced thinly. Allow the combination to cool, and place small dollops onto the freeze-dryer trays. Process and, soon, you will have treats that look like mini oatmeal cookies but are far healthier.

You can also include some (unhealthy, but fun) sugary treats, such as ice cream sandwich bites. We love eating the Neapolitan-flavored bites. Tiny scoops of ice cream can also be processed into a sweet treat. Certain candies can also be freeze-dried into a crunchy sweet treat. Some favorites are Skittles, Caramel M&M's, and taffy. Yum!

In summary, great freeze-dried **SNACKS & TREATS** are:
- Plain Veggies and Fruits
- Seasoned Veggie Chips
- Yogurt Bites, Oatmeal Bites
- Ice Cream, Candies

Individual Food Items

Any food you have processed through the freeze-dryer can either be consumed freeze-dried or can be rehydrated before use. The only exceptions are raw meats and eggs, which should always be handled as raw. You can open a bag of strawberries and eat them as-is or make them into something. Add water and a little sugar to make Strawberry Shortcake Sauce (See the recipe in Appendix 2). Those same berries could also be turned into a powder and added to your ice cream. That makes my mouth water just thinking about it!

This versatility is why storing individual ingredients can be so beneficial. Now you won't have to worry about running out of the cream cheese you need for your Alfredo sauce. Just grab the powder and add it to your sauce; you don't need to rehydrate it first.

Freeze-dried foods are moisture-sensitive, as we have established. Even a few seconds of exposure to dampness can quickly cause deterioration. However, there is an advantage to this sensitivity. You can quickly rehydrate these foods by adding a small amount of cold or hot water. Then you can easily add a little pizazz to meals or even when you want a complete meal at your fingertips. Best yet? This all happens in a matter of minutes.

Rehydrated foods can be directly consumed, but they can also be incorporated into meals either in a powdered form or whole. To create a powder from freeze-dried food, all you have to do is put the freeze-dried product in a blender or food processor and process it to achieve the desired texture. You can get the equivalent of 7-8 tablespoons of fruit in just one tablespoon of powdered freeze-dried fruit. This makes the perfect replacement for whole fruits in desserts, baked items, and breakfast.

Speaking of breakfast, Get your vitamins and minerals by adding freeze-dried fruits to your pancake or muffin mix. You can use the powdered version to infuse breakfast staples with tons of flavor and nutrition, or you can use whole foods. Just rehydrate with a small amount of water first. Freeze-dried fruits can also be added to oatmeal, cereals, and smoothies. The same can be done with cakes, cookies, and other pastries.

I have always been conscious about making sure that my family eats nutritious and well-balanced meals. One of the ways I do this is by incorporating spinach powder and other healthy vegetables into our cooking. I've become skilled at blending these ingredients seamlessly into dishes, so much so that my kids don't notice.

When they do notice the color, they are fine with it. They love "monster" tuna melts and green pancakes. And it's easy to toss a few tablespoons of spinach powder into the mix. My 5-year-old happily declares she loves spinach pancakes, which shows that my efforts are paying off. Overall, it's a win-win situation for me, as I can ensure my family eats healthy while making it fun for them. Adding veggie powders to spaghetti sauce, soups, or chili is quite easy.

You can infuse water with fruit flavors and create juices and other healthy beverages. You can freeze-dry coffee, juices, and smoothies to have the powder available to whip up a drink whenever you want.

You do not even have to rehydrate items added to soups and stews. When you add water, stock, or broth during the cooking process, you can have a bowl of deliciousness in your hands in minutes. The sky's the limit. So, I encourage you to experiment.

In summary, freeze-dried **ingredients** can be used to:
- Replace fresh ingredients in your recipes
- Add flavor and nutrition to meals
- Enhance your breakfast and desserts
- Improve and flavor beverages
- Beef up your soups and stews

Complete Meals

Having complete meals on hand when needed is a fantastic benefit of owning a freeze-dryer. You can make up a double batch of chili, chicken-and-rice casserole, or another favorite and process it through the freeze-dryer to be eaten at another time. This makes it possible to have Just-Add-Water meals available anytime! It really is as simple as adding hot water and giving it a few minutes. Imagine how easy it will be to have a home-cooked meal on a night when you have no time for cooking!

One of the best things about these ready-to-eat meals is that you can customize them to your preferences. If you're vegan or vegetarian, you can freeze-dry those meals. The same applies if you are on a gluten-free diet, a paleo diet, a ketogenic diet, and any other specialized diet. You can provide meals with your favorite recipes and entirely avoid food allergens. You get to choose what your family will eat. Just-Add-Water meals are awesome for work lunches and car travel, too.

Freeze-dried meals are fast! Add boiling water, stir, and in 10 minutes, your meal is ready! That is way faster than ordering in or even picking up fast food. Just-Add-Water meals can also save you the money you would have spent on an unhealthy, fast-food meal. And these meals are loaded with nutrients and taste amazing!

Some may compare their Just-Add-Water meals with MRE meals. MRE stands for Meal Ready to Eat. Most popularly, they have been used as self-contained, individual rations consumed by soldiers in the field. However, their popularity is growing in less dangerous arenas as well. They are now seen as sustenance for potential emergencies and as easy-to-carry meals while backpacking, hiking, and doing other adventures. MREs are not freeze-dried, though, and have a maximum short-term shelf life of five years.

Freeze-drying allows you to easily create your own "dry MREs" and make them highly nutritious and calorie dense. They can be eaten straight from the bag or rehydrated with cold or hot water. You will have much less weight to carry, as all the water weight has been removed from Just-Add-Water meals. Freeze-drying elevates the ordinarily dull and lackluster appearance and taste of traditional MREs. Your freeze-dried meals will serve the same purpose but last longer and can be made to suit your taste, preferences, and needs. Check out Micro-Homesteading Education's Backpacking with Freeze-Dried Meals to learn more about this.

As we've discussed, you can freeze-dry complete meals for your Just-Add-Water meals, but you can also assemble a meal by combining freeze-dried ingredients. A good example would be soups. Package your Just-Add-Water meals the same way you would your other freeze-dried foods. Remember to keep track of your meals' fat content for storage reasons. Use an oxygen absorber and seal up the mylar bag. Label and date the bag, and you're all set. Mylar bags come in various sizes, and they make one that is the perfect size for individual meals (6.5" x 8.5".)

When cooking around a campfire, you can have an easy meal and even avoid dishes! Just-Add-Water meals are super simple because you literally just add water directly to the mylar bag. It is fantastic to have an entire delicious meal ready in minutes simply by adding water. Leftovers can also be freeze-dried, so you do not have to make complete meals. You can freeze containers of leftovers and then put them on your trays when you have enough for a batch. Fatty leftover meals should be consumed within five years. The lower the fat and oil content, the longer the shelf life will be.

In summary, freeze-dried **meals** can be used to:
- Provide quick everyday meal options
- Completely avoid food allergens
- Have easy lunches & travel meals
- Keep fast and nutritious favorites on hand
- Easily prepare food in an emergency
- Go backpacking, hiking, or camping

Cooking with Freeze-dried Foods

Cooking with freeze-dried ingredients has many additional benefits that make the activity even more enjoyable. For one, using freeze-dried foods means your produce is already clean and ready, saving you time and effort in the kitchen. This also eliminates the need for dicing, slicing, and chopping, which can be tedious and time-consuming.

The combination of Freeze dried foods can create delicious and satisfying meals. Many recipes are simple, easy to prepare, and require minimal effort. Mix freeze-dried ingredients with water in a large saucepan, bring to a boil, reduce heat, and simmer for 20 minutes or until all water has been absorbed.

Using freeze-dried foods is a great way to make quick and easy meals full of flavor and nutrition. They make fast meals as they are easy to store, lightweight, and require no refrigeration.

Another great benefit of using freeze-dried foods is that they retain much of their nutritional value, which is vital for maintaining a healthy diet. Freeze-drying removes almost all (97 percent) of the moisture from food, leaving you with a concentrated, rich flavor that makes your taste buds sing in harmony.

Using freeze-dried foods or powders also means no excess liquid to water down your sauces, stews, broths, and soups, which can be problematic when using fresh or canned ingredients.

Another advantage of using freeze-dried foods is that they are made with natural ingredients, which means they do not contain additives, dyes, preservatives, sulfites, or other chemicals often found in store-bought products. This lets you know exactly what goes into your meal and ensures that you consume natural nutrition.

Finally, using freeze-dried ingredients allows you to have various fruits, vegetables, and meats on hand, which can be a great way to add variety to your meals. You can also mix and match ingredients to create new recipes, which is an enjoyable and creative process.

In summary, **cooking** with freeze-dried ingredients means:
- No prep is necessary; it's already done.
- Concentrated flavor with no excess moisture.
- All-natural, nutrient-dense ingredients.
- Fast, delicious, and easy meals.

Incorporating Freeze-dried Foods into your diet

So how do you add freeze-dried ingredients to your meals? As daunting as it may seem, the good news is there are lots of options, and they are all tasty. They include:

- Crumbling freeze-dried ingredients on top of food for decoration or flavor.
- Adding freeze-dried powders as an ingredient, flavoring, or nutrient boost.
- Adding freeze-dried ingredients directly to soups.
- Adding freeze-dried fruits and vegetables to blender drinks
- Sauteeing freeze-dried ingredients before use
- Rehydrating or reconstituting ingredients

Crumbling freeze-dried ingredients on top of food for decoration or flavor.

Freeze-dried ingredients can be crumbled so that they not only add flavor and nutrition to dishes but can also be decorative. I love strawberry crumbles on a cheesecake! In addition to their nutrition and flavor, you can use veggies (beet powder, carrot powder, or spinach powder) and fruits (blueberry powder, raspberry powder, or pineapple powder) for their delightful colors. Another favorite treat is to freeze-dry candy and crumble that over yogurt or ice cream.

Adding freeze-dried powders as an ingredient, flavoring, or nutrient boost.

Adding powdered fruits and vegetables into smoothies is one of many ways to incorporate powdered freeze-dried ingredients. You can add them to your meals to get that added oomph of nutrition and flavor. The many uses of powdered freeze-dried ingredients are unlimited! They can embellish other dishes such as muffins, pancakes, cupcakes, burgers, lasagna, and dips. Many bakers prefer powdered freeze-dried ingredients as they do not add any unnecessary moisture to batters and doughs. You can add freeze-dried ingredients to your recipes in powdered form. To make a smoothie, toss all the ingredients into your blender together and process to a smooth consistency. You can add freeze-dried powders to soups and make delicious, smooth sauces. Generally, you will need a little less water to reconstitute a powder than was taken out during the freeze-drying process.

Adding freeze-dried ingredients directly to watery soups.

You can toss freeze-dried ingredients directly into the pot when using them in your soups and other liquid recipes. There is plenty of water to hydrate them back to perfection. When making a watery sauce (such as spaghetti sauce), add 1-2 tablespoons of water for every half cup of freeze-dried ingredients. These ingredients can be incorporated just as you would the fresh counterparts. If making a thick sauce (such as creamy white sauce), it's usually best to rehydrate or reconstitute before adding it to the sauce.

Adding freeze-dried fruits and vegetables to blender drinks

Smoothies and shakes are a great way to integrate fresh fruits and veggies into your diet. You do not have to rehydrate freeze-dried fruits or veggies when creating smoothies. Combine the ingredients in a blender with water, juice, almond milk, or another liquid. Add what you have around the house, such as a banana or yogurt, to make a delicious and nutritious health drink.

Sautéing freeze-dried ingredients prior to use

Depending on the type of dish you are creating, freeze-dried ingredients may not require rehydration before you start cooking. Examples include recipes that call for sautéing ingredients like peppers, onions, and even meat. These ingredients do not need to be rehydrated beforehand. Heat some oil in your pan and add the dry freeze-dried ingredients. Not only do you save time by not having to rehydrate first, but sautéing time is also significantly reduced. Only add water if the recipe includes it or to avoid overcooking.

Adding Moisture to Freeze-dried Foods

When you are ready to add moisture back into the freeze-dried foods, there are a few tricks to help you get it done just right.

Rehydrating or Reconstituting prior to using as an ingredient

Rehydration of food is easy. Reconstitution is a little more tricky. First, let's cover the difference between these two. To rehydrate is to restore water. An example of this would be soaking freeze-dried raw steaks in a bowl of water overnight. The meat is rehydrated by morning and will behave like typical raw meat. To reconstitute is to add liquid to a concentrate to return it to its original consistency. An example would be adding 2 Tablespoons of water to 2 Tablespoons of Egg Powder to get the equivalent of 1 egg.

Rehydrate: Restore water
Reconstitute: Add liquid to a concentrate

Freeze-dried foods are extremely moisture sensitive, so even brief exposure to damp air can cause them to lose their vibrancy and become limp and chewy quickly. This affinity for water is a benefit in the context of rehydration. The sensitivity of freeze-dried foods enables them to rehydrate rapidly with a small amount of cold, warm, or hot water. Rehydrating dehydrated foods take longer (up to 90 minutes) and require more water (often hot).

Because freeze-dried foods are almost void of moisture, they quickly soak up the moisture in the environment around them. Too much moisture is a bad thing for freeze-dried ingredients, though. Always keep them in air-tight containers. It is also possible to over-hydrate your freeze-dried foods. Remember, all freeze-dried items will behave like thawed frozen foods. This is because they freeze before they dry. So, fresh strawberries will freeze and dry in the machine, and when rehydrated, they will be like thawed frozen strawberries but be beautiful and loaded with nutrients.

There can be blunders with rehydration and reconstitution. Imagine having grand plans for lettuce you freeze-dried only to end up with a soggy pile of green mush. Lettuce would be better used as "chips" with dip or as a nutrient powder in smoothies. With greens, it is quite often better to use them powdered. Some freeze-dried foods are best used without rehydrating at all.

When rehydrating, try to use the least amount of water necessary. Some things only need a light spritz of water to be the consistency you want. Draining off excess liquid means you are throwing away some of the valuable nutrition in the form of water-soluble vitamins. Overhydration happens to the best of us, but you can avoid this pitfall with this knowledge.

Hydration must be done mindfully. The general rule of thumb is to add ½ to 1 cup of water to 1 cup of freeze-dried food. Add the freeze-dried ingredients to a clear bowl so that you have a great visual of what is happening. Add just enough water to pool at the bottom of the food. Stir the food occasionally during hydration to ensure every piece has been exposed to the water. Most foods will not require additional water as they reconstitute closely to the fresh ingredient. Typically, cooked meats require slightly more time than vegetables to rehydrate. Just continue to add a little water at a time until the item is fully rehydrated. (Raw meats cannot be overhydrated and do best when soaked.)

Foods to rehydrate prior to cooking:
1. Ingredients that will not be in any liquid during the cooking process.
2. Ingredients that will be cooked in a thick sauce.

If the food falls into either of these two groups, rehydrate before cooking and incorporate them into your recipes like fresh ingredients.

If you want to be exact, you can calculate the water loss during the freeze-drying, and then you'll know how much to add. The determined amount of water loss should be the maximum amount you want to stay within rather than an exact amount used for reconstitution or rehydration. Once you've measured the maximum, you can gradually add liquid until the ideal consistency is achieved. If you don't have this measurement, it's just as easy to add little by little until you reach the consistency you want.

Suggestions for Rehydration and Reconstitution

Specific freeze-dried foods and ingredients require different conditions for proper rehydration or reconstitution. Please note these specifics below.

Fruits

Rehydrated fruits are a great addition to cobblers and pies, on top of warm oatmeal, in or on top of yogurt, or in smoothies and shakes. To rehydrate fruit, add it to a bowl with water and let it soak until it rehydrates to the desired consistency. Hot, warm, or cold water can be used. Otherwise, you can spritz it with water, adding a little at a time. At times, freeze-dried fruit can be incorporated directly into recipes as rehydration will occur as it soaks up moisture from the other ingredients. You can powder your fruits as well. Each tablespoon of freeze-dried fruit powders equals eight tablespoons of fresh fruit.

Vegetables

The rehydration of vegetables depends on how they are used. Rehydration is not required if your veggies will be used in soups. Freeze-dried green leafy vegetables should be powdered or, if you dare, spritzed with water or placed in a large Ziplock bag along with a moist paper towel. Adding too much moisture will cause them to become soggy, so be mindful of how much water you add. Freeze-dried greens can also be powdered and added to smoothies and sauces. Other types of veggies can be rehydrated by placing them in a bowl with hot water for 5-15 minutes. They can also be cooked on the stovetop, such as in sautéed recipes.

Dairy

Freeze-dried yogurt drops, sliced cheese, and ice cream sandwiches are dairy products that can be eaten crunchy as snacks. There is no need to rehydrate them. Dairy products are versatile items for cooking as well. They allow for the creation of many rich and flavorful dishes. Reconstitute powdered sour cream to add to a meal. Powdered dairy can be added to recipes.

Dairy items like yogurt and sour cream can be freeze-dried in a thick, even ½" layer on the freeze-dryer trays. After their batch, they can then be processed into powders. Even freeze-dried ice cream sandwiches can be powdered and incorporated into other recipes to deliver a robust and delicious flavor. The same can be done with freeze-dried milk. The powdered ingredients can be reconstituted by spritzing with a bit of water or gradually incorporating water into the ingredient and stirring until it returns to its original state.

Freeze-dried grated cheese can be hydrated on the top of dishes, such as a casserole while being baked. Covering them with foil allows them to quickly rehydrate from the moisture released from the food. Alternatively, they can be rehydrated by spritzing with water. Freeze-dried sliced cheese can be placed in a Ziplock bag along with a moist paper towel until the original consistency is regained.

Eggs

Eggs can be freeze-dried, either raw or cooked. Reconstituted raw eggs create a better texture than cooked and rehydrated scrambled eggs. However, cooked breakfast skillets with eggs, veggies, cheese, and meats are fantastic. To freeze-dry raw eggs, whisk them before putting them onto the freeze-dryer tray. Your freeze-dryer can hold a lot of eggs: an X-Large holds 40 eggs per tray, a Large holds 24 eggs per tray, a Medium holds 18 eggs per tray, and a Small holds 8 eggs per tray.

Do not line the trays with parchment paper or silicone mats because the liquid seeps underneath the mat. For the easiest cleanup, it's best to stick with the stainless steel trays. Pre-freeze the trays for 24-48 hours and run them through the freeze-dryer. (Always pre-freeze eggs. Always.) Break up the freeze-dried eggs with a spoon and place the pieces into a blender or food processor to process into a powder.

Raw freeze-dried eggs can be used in pancakes, baked treats, scrambled eggs, and more. For scrambled eggs, you'll need to reconstitute them so you can cook them like regular raw eggs. For adding to recipes, reconstitute the number of eggs needed and allow to sit for 5 minutes before adding to the recipe.

To reconstitute raw eggs, mix two Tablespoons of powder with two Tablespoons of water and allow it to sit for a few minutes before mixing well again. More water might be necessary if the eggs were very finely processed.

For scrambled eggs, after they have been cooked, divide them into evenly sized pieces and place them on the freeze-dryer trays. For hard-boiled eggs, remove the shells and slice them into ½" thick pieces or chop them into bits. These can be slices for salad toppers or chopped pieces added to a tuna salad recipe, which allows the mayonnaise to rehydrate the egg pieces. Before freeze-drying, you can separate the whites and yolks for special uses, whether raw or cooked. It is not necessary to powder cooked eggs, especially if you want to retain the original texture when it is time to consume. To rehydrate cooked eggs, mix ½ cup with ⅓ cup of water and allow to sit for a few minutes before stirring.

Meats and poultry

Rehydrated freeze-dried cooked meats and poultry have the same original flavor and consistency you enjoy as a meat lover. Raw meat rehydrates well when soaked in cold water overnight in the fridge. Cooked meat rehydrates by soaking in a bowl of warm or hot water. Luckily, meat is an item that cannot be overhydrated. It never becomes soggy and only reabsorbs the amount of water it needs. Be careful, though, when rehydrating seasoned meats; adding too much water may wash away the flavoring.

After rehydration, pat the meat or poultry with a paper towel to remove the excess liquid. Cooked meat or poultry products can be eaten as-is or used in recipes. Raw meat or poultry products need to be cooked before they are consumed. Rehydrated raw steaks will have the same characteristics as fresh raw steaks when you toss them on the grill. Season and enjoy as you normally would.

Baked items

Freeze-drying does not exclude baked dishes like cakes, brownies, and breads. They just aren't as common because rehydration is a little tricky. Slice the items, place them on the freeze-dryer tray, and let your freeze-dryer do the rest.

For a rehydrated slice that tastes like freshly toasted bread, briefly dunk the bread into water and pan-fry it for a few minutes. Be careful; it will be delicate. You can also fold a moist paper towel around an item and place it in a Ziplock bag, allowing the water to be slowly reabsorbed into the item. This can take a few hours but you will end up with a moist, soft product. Thicker breads, such as banana bread, zucchini bread, or pumpkin bread seem to do much better rehydrating than more delicate breads like white bread.

Full Meals

Freeze-dried meals (prepared fresh or leftovers) can be hydrated easily by adding warm water until the original consistency returns. Add the meal to a pot with water and fully heat it on the stovetop. Pasta dishes like spaghetti can be steamed back to life by adding hot water and covering the container so that the steam works its magic. Rehydrate casseroles, like lasagna, by adding enough warm water to reach about 1/3 of the height of the dish, cover the casserole dish with foil, and bake for 30-45 minutes at 350°F.

The quality of the freeze-dried products produced in your freeze-dryer is a consequence of its superior build. Maintenance must be done regularly and thoroughly to continue getting such high-quality items from the freeze-dryer. The next chapter gives you the insight to ensure the machine serves you well for as long as possible.

9

MAINTAINING YOUR FREEZE-DRYER EFFICIENTLY

Your freeze-dryer is similar to a clothes washing machine in its ease of use. On the other hand, a freeze-dryer can also be compared to a vehicle in the maintenance department. A new vehicle runs smoothly at first, but as time passes, normal wear and tear can cause things to no longer work right under the hood. Before your vehicle breaks down on you, the smart thing to do is to maintain it regularly. You can nip any issues in the bud before they become major. The same applies to the Harvest Right™ freeze-dryer. Keep it clean, do regular oil changes, update with new software, and occasionally replace parts. The printable Maintenance Log in Appendix 3 provides more details. The subcategories below provide the basics of ensuring your freeze-dryer serves you well for years and years.

Cleaning the Harvest Right™ Freeze-dryer

Keeping your freeze-dryer in good condition is not only about keeping the freeze-dryer itself spotlessly clean. Its surrounding area needs to be kept clean, too. No matter how much effort you put into maintaining the machine, if dust, debris, and moisture are present in your location, then it will constantly attract these enemies, and they will start doing damage. This means more wear and tear on the freeze-dryer, potentially shortening its lifespan.

Keeping a Clean Environment

Keep up with regular maintenance around the room and keep it clean by taking out any trash regularly, using a dehumidifier, and keeping it uncluttered to encourage good airflow. Wipe down surfaces often, including the fans around the freeze-dryer and other items that might trap and hold dust. Your countertops should be wiped down regularly to keep your working area clean. Use warm water with mild dish soap. It's safe to sanitize with isopropyl alcohol or Everclear.

Empty the Bucket

Yes, regularly emptying the bucket is important. Getting the "Y" tubing fittings will save you heartache from ruining a batch with siphoned dirty water. If not, this is especially critical. Stagnant water is gross and unsanitary, so keep your bucket empty.

Cleaning the Exterior

Use warm water and dish soap to clean the outer door, handle, screen, and the other exterior surfaces of the freeze-dryer cabinet. Use a soft cloth to wipe it dry. That is all you have to do to upkeep the outside of the freeze-dryer as long as you care for the surrounding space.

Cleaning the Interior

Cleaning the inside of your freeze-dryer requires some special considerations as there are many parts to clean. Let's break down the cleaning process step by step.

1. Turn the freeze-dryer off and unplug it from the wall. This is an electrical device, and you will use water to clean it. Electricity and water do not mix. Ensure your safety, and do not skip this first step.
2. Open the door, remove the black rubber gasket, and remove the shelves. Disconnect the cable by unlocking the tab, pressing the tab down, and pulling the two pieces apart. The shelving unit is heavy, so be careful when moving it around.
3. Clean the chamber and shelves with warm water and dish soap, isopropyl alcohol, or Everclear. Occasionally you'll want to clean out the drain hose. Pour alcohol or soapy water down the drain hose while the shelves are out, and use a tube scrubber as needed. Dry the shelves and chamber with a soft, dry towel.
4. Reconnect the cables and put the shelves back in place. Ensure the shelves are completely dry when putting them back into the chamber.
5. Put the rubber gasket on and close the door. You may need to reseat the gasket if the seal isn't present when the door is closed.
6. Plug your freeze-dryer back in and flip the switch to "on."

Protect Your Freeze-Dryer While Cleaning

The steps above list what you should do to clean your freeze-dryer. And now here are some things you don't want to do:

- Under no circumstances should you use a dishwasher to wash the shelving unit. The heat will cause the heating pads to peel and eventually come off.
- Do not use abrasive tools to clean the freeze-dryer (interior or exterior), as these will scratch and dull the surface.
- Do not use Clorox (bleach,) benzene, or thinner for cleaning, as they will damage the freeze-dryer.
- Do not use acid, vinegar, or lemon juice, as they will damage the stainless steel chamber.

If the freeze-dryer will not be used for an extended period, turn it off and unplug it from the wall. This protects the appliance from unexpected power surges and extends the freeze-dryer's life. Ensure it is completely clean and dry inside and out during this time of disuse. Prop the door open to keep the freeze-dryer from developing odors or mold. The pump should be emptied and then filled with fresh oil to sit. Dirty oil will cause corrosion to the internal parts of the pump.

The Vacuum Pumps

Standard and Premium Pumps

If the oil in the pump ever looks cloudy, dirty, or a different color, it needs to be cleaned. The **oil change** is not complicated and can be accomplished in five steps.

1. Open the oil drain valve on your oil pump and let all the oil drain into a container. (Old yogurt containers work well.)
2. Tip the pump if needed to remove as much oil as possible. Do not tip so far that oil goes into the demister.
3. Close the drain valve.
4. Open the fill port and fill it with clean oil. Please use high-quality new or well-filtered vacuum pump oil. Do this slowly, as the oil takes a little time to settle and show up on the meter. Pour until the oil reaches the mid-line, seen through the glass at the front of the pump. Do not overfill.
5. Close the fill port.

Always follow the rules for your pump when doing oil changes. They are listed in the manual that comes with the pump. Filtered, clear oil can be reused according to the Harvest Right™ manual. Just make sure it's clean.

The **filtration process** is also not complicated:

1. Place the used oil in the freezer for at least a few hours before filtering. Overnight is even better. This is necessary since water is in the used oil, and freezing will separate the two liquids.
2. Pour the oil into the filter that came with your freeze-dryer. It should look and work like a Brita water filter. Discard any ice or sediment at the bottom of the container instead of putting it in the filter. The container needs to be wiped clean to prepare for the next use.
3. Allow time to pass as the oil slowly goes through the filter.
4. Pour the filtered oil into the original freeze-dryer quart container. The amount needed to fill most pumps is 600ml.

Oil-Free Pump

"Oil-free pumps are quiet, fast, and easy to use." This is a quote straight from the Harvest Right™ website. Some people love their oil-free pumps because they don't have to do regular oil changes. (Premier needs an oil change after every 20-30 batches and a standard pump needs an oil change after every 4-5 batches.) The oil-free pumps are louder and hotter than the premium pump but quieter than the standard pump. The oil-free pumps are more expensive and may require maintenance and sometimes rebuilds on an annual basis. If you have an older model freeze-dryer, you will need an adapter for the oil-free pump. Harvest Right™ will give you this device free of charge.

Extended periods of non-use

The pump should be emptied and then filled with fresh oil, even when it will be out of use for a long time. Remember: dirty oil will cause corrosion to the pump's internal parts.

The Software

Your freeze-dryer produces magnificent results because of its excellent build. But the hardware would only be useful with the software that supports it.

Updating

You need to update this software to ensure the continued good performance of the machine. The company will email you software updates, but you can also see the latest updates on the website: https://harvestright.com/software-update/. If you're unsure if it is time for your machine to have a software update, email customer support with your software numbers (at the top right of your freeze-dryer screen) and ask for the latest update. You will need a USB drive to install the update. A smaller size, such as 16GB, works well. To upgrade, follow these steps:

1. Download the new software for your version from the website or add the firmware from the email.
2. Once saved to your computer, open the folder by double-clicking on it. Copy all the files (with extension .hff, .hfw, or .hfr) and put them onto the root of the USB thumb drive (not in a folder).
3. Flip the freeze-dryer power switch off.
4. Plug the USB device with the file(s) into the USB port to the right of the interface screen on the side of the cabinet while it is still turned off.
5. Flip the switch back on and let the freeze-dryer boot up.
6. Once you see the home screen, it's done, and you can remove the USB device. The installation is complete, and your freeze-dryer is ready to use the new software.

The machine will read the installer and initiate the process all on its own. This will take a few minutes, and the freeze-dryer will start when the update is complete. The new version number of the software will be shown in the top right corner of the screen. You may have to reset some options in the Customize area, so go through these carefully.

Downgrading

It is possible to downgrade the software to a previous version. Just follow the same process. The only difference is that you need to place an additional file on the USB drive called ForcedUp. Keep in mind that Harvest Right™ does not provide support for reverting to a previous version. It is generally not recommended.

If you have any trouble updating, here are a few tips for updating or downgrading the software:

- Use smaller USB drives such as 16GB.
- The USB drive should be formatted, and only the installer files should be copied.
- Make sure the file names are correct. If you download the file more than once on your computer, the system will automatically rename them. This will cause conflicts when installing on the Harvest Right™ machine.
- If you encounter any issues, first try a different USB drive and then ensure the correct files are placed on the USB drive.

If the problem persists, contact Harvest Right™ customer support. However, you can be assured that the process is typically done without complications.

NEED HELP?

Where to Get Assistance

There are several avenues to get help with any issues that may arise when using your freeze-dryer.

Harvest Right™ Customer Service

The number is 1-801-386-8960.

They have fantastic customer service. They will work with you to make sure your freeze-dryer is working correctly. If your machine is out of warranty, they will help you get the info and parts you need so you can fix it.

The Freeze-dryer Problem Diagnosis Guide on the Harvest Right™ Website

This is the first step to getting help with your freeze-dryer when something is amiss. Here's a shortcut to the HarvestRight's website: FDHR.2MHE.COM or scan the QR Code.

On the website, go to the top right corner and click on Customer Support. Scroll down and pick a category from these options:

- Set Up & Basics
- Vacuum Error

- Refrigeration Issues
- Drying Issues
- Touchscreen Issues
- Power Issues
- Software Versions

From here, the Diagnosis Guide will walk you through troubleshooting your particular problem. A lot of great help is available for all kinds of issues, and you can also search the customer support articles. If you don't get it worked out with the guide, submit a ticket for personal help. You can do that on the same page.

Facebook Groups

Many have found the social media app Facebook is for more than just connecting with friends and family. Join a few freeze-drying Facebook groups to connect with people like you, check out recipe ideas and tips, and get help troubleshooting your machine if needed. Many members have the information you may need, and the compiled group knowledge is invaluable for getting helpful ideas quickly.

Micro-Homesteading Education's Freeze-Drying Facebook group is "Food Preservation with Freeze Drying." Connect with us!Scan the QR code below or visit the shortcut to FB Group: FDFB.2MHE.COM

You now know how to always keep your freeze-dryer in excellent working order and where to find help when needed. The next chapter gives experts tips and tricks to save time, money, and effort while getting the best freeze-dried products.

KNOWLEDGE IS POWER... LET'S SHARE IT!

Now that you have a solid understanding of freeze-drying and its many benefits, you're in the perfect position to help others discover the same.

Leaving your honest opinion of this book, "The Only Beginner's Freeze Drying Book You'll Ever Need," on Amazon will provide valuable insight for others interested in learning about freeze-drying. Your feedback will help guide them on their freeze-drying journey and improve the book for future readers.

We appreciate your support and for being a part of the growing freeze-drying community. Remember, the more individuals discover the benefits of freeze-drying, the more it will benefit the entire industry.

Thank you for choosing this book and being part of the growing freeze-drying community. Your support is greatly appreciated.

To leave a review scan the QR code or visit: BFDR.2MHE.COM

10

FREEZE-DRYING TIPS & TRICKS

e have reached the final chapter of this book, and it is only fitting that we end with extra information that makes freeze-drying a little easier and enjoyable activity that can save you time and money.

Keep the Freeze-dryer Running

Make your freeze-dryer do the best work it was designed to do right there in the convenience of your home. As long as you maintain the machine, it will serve you well. Certain practices ensure the best freeze-drying of your food. So, I implore you to:

Always do pre-freezing!

Pre-freezing saves time and ensures the freeze-dryer doesn't have to work so hard, which means a more extended life for the machine. The pre-freezing process ensures the ingredient or meal is completely frozen and can undergo sublimation. If your food is not completely solid, evaporation occurs. The food will not achieve the same quality of preservation that would have happened if sublimation were to occur. After your food has been pre-frozen, keep it in the freezer until it is time to freeze-dry. This ensures your food does not warm up while waiting for the freeze-dryer.

Set extra dry time to 12-24 hours.

Extra drying time ensures you have plenty of time to get back to your food after it has finished running a batch. You cannot over-dry, so don't worry about having too much extra dry time. Once you check on the food, you can take it out, weigh it, and put it back in for two hours before doing a second weight check. If you do not change this setting, your food will have the default two hours of extra dry time before re-freezing the food. Changing this to 24 hours allows you flexibility, so the machine works for you instead of you being stuck checking on it regularly.

Have frozen food on hand to keep the freeze-dryer going.

I like to keep bags of frozen veggies or fruits on hand to plop them right on the freeze-dryer trays and put them in the machine. The great thing about this is you can avoid prep time by buying these pre-chopped and cut fruits and veggies and storing them in your freezer until it's time to freeze-dry.

Freeze-drying on a Budget

A big part of the appeal for many who invest in a freeze-dryer is ultimately saving money on food. This section provides tips to help you get your money's worth.

Budget-Friendly Ideas that Make Your Money Stretch Further

With food prices skyrocketing, you'd be surprised at the many ways you can avoid overspending while keeping your family well-fed and nourished. I am talking about healthy foods and not processed stuff. A misconception is that eating healthy is more expensive than just settling for processed foods. But that is not true, as long as you know how and where to look. A few ideas you could try are:

- Use a shopping app to save money and gain cash back.
- Buy generic brands. Even if they taste different, that doesn't mean they are of lesser quality than premium brands. It is possible to save more than 300 percent on some items by making the switch.

- Shop at discount stores like Costco, where more generic brands are sold for lower prices and in bulk.
- Check out the clearance section at your local grocery store. You would be surprised at the sheer variety of meat, fish, and other items available for sale.
- Buy cheap foods like rice, oats, pasta, dried beans, and lentils in bulk.

How To Access Cheap Food

Cheap food is not automatically synonymous with substandard food. It simply means foods that are easier to come by at lower prices. The food eaten by your family, and thus your grocery bill, amounts to a large percentage of your monthly budget if you do not tame that aspect of spending.

One way to gain control is to buy the cheapest foods in bulk. These staple foods can be dressed up or down with the addition of spices (like oregano, garlic powder, salt, black pepper, and chili powder, which are also usually cheaply bought) and other foods in smaller amounts. In addition to those mentioned above, staple foods that do not (typically) cost an arm and a leg are listed below.

Apples	Carrots	Herbs	Popcorn
Baking Soda	Celery	Honey	Potatoes
Bananas	Chickpeas	Kale	Quinoa
Beans	Cooking Oil	Lentils	Rice
Bread	Cottage Cheese	Lettuce	Spices
Cabbage	Cucumbers	Milk	Spinach
Canned Beans	Eggs	Oats	Squash
Canned Fish	Flour	Onions	Sugar
Canned Fruit	Frozen Chicken	Oranges	Tofu
Canned Meats	Frozen Fruit	Pasta	Tomatoes
Canned Soup	Frozen Veggies	Peanuts	Vinegar
Canned Sauce	Grapes	Peppers	Yeast
Canned Veggies	Ground Turkey	Plain Cereal	Yogurt

The cost of such foods depends on where you live and the exact economic conditions of that area. Shop around your area to discover the nuances of food availability and prices in your location. Then take advantage of these conditions to the best of your ability.

Grow a Garden

Even better than controlling your grocery bill, growing a garden gives you significant control over what you eat. Backyard gardens are becoming increasingly popular with people with access to land. You can select which varieties to grow and use organic methods to ensure the cleanest, most-nutritious food for your family. Even if you live in a small apartment, you can grow at least a few items in pots or vertical containers. When you're ready to begin, take a look at the variety of gardening books available from Micro-Homesteading Education.

No matter your circumstances, a few tips for growing your own food include:

- Start small so that you do not become overwhelmed and give up.
- Plant things you enjoy eating.
- Ensure you have easy access to water.
- Use clean sources of compost and soil mixes.
- Select a growing location with at least six hours of direct sunlight daily.
- Using raised garden beds helps control the nutrient and soil content.
- If you don't have much space, consider using containers or pots.
- Gain advice and tips from farmers and other gardeners in your area.
- Look for community gardens or allotments if land is unavailable to you.

Forage for Wild Edibles

Foraging is the act of gaining food from natural sources that have yet to be interfered with by human practices. Therefore, picking an apple from a tree that grows in your yard is foraging. So is picking a leaf of mint on your walk through the woods nearby. Foraging is not a new activity. Ancient civilizations gathered wild edibles like plants, seeds, nuts, and berries and hunted for fish and animals. Remember that the areas you forage need to be free of chemicals, including pesticides and herbicides. Select your locations carefully.

Typical wild edible plants include:

- Greens, including dandelion greens, purslane, lamb's quarters, chickweed, wild lettuce, mallow
- Berries, including blueberries, raspberries, blackberries, currants, cranberries, lingonberries, ground cherries
- Roots, including dandelion root, wild onions, cattail root, chicory root, and burdock roots
- Nuts and seeds, including acorns, walnuts, pine nuts, hickory nuts, pecans, and sunflower seeds
- Mushrooms (foraging mushrooms requires knowledge due to toxic varieties of mushrooms)

As mentioned before, it is not just plants that can be foraged. Shellfish like clams and mussels, fish, and other seafood in rivers, lakes, and seasides near your home can become part of your diet (and also, your freeze-drying practices), and so can wild animals, such as rabbits, wildfowl, and wild pigs. Just be sure of the legalities for your area before you begin. You're limited by the environment in which you live and what is available for foraging.

Make Money with Your Freeze-Dryer

You are not limited to sharing your freeze-dried foods with just your family. You can also sell them and make a profit from your investment in your freeze-dryer.

Customer Favorites

Lots of people love freeze-dried fruits, especially pineapples, and grapes. Many fruit and vegetable powders can be made into healthy smoothies, like kale or spinach. Freeze-dried candy is becoming extremely popular.

Many people have found that others want to avoid investing in a freeze-dryer but would love to pay for local freeze-dried food. Arrangements can be made for them to "rent" space in your machine. Have your friend purchase and prepare the food and provide the packaging. You run the batch in the freeze-dryer yourself, then split the results 50:50. Or you could charge a set fee for use, such as $25 per tray, $80 per day, or $300 per week. Ensure you are charging a premium for the premium service you provide.

On a whim, I decided to try candy and surprisingly sold $131 worth of candy during the first week I had the machine! I spent $35 on materials to get candy, labels, and packaging, and my kiddos helped by putting all the stickers on. Both kids and adults LOVE freeze-dried candy. Bite-sized ice cream sandwiches are a hit everywhere. Some people like to call them astronaut treats! To learn more about freeze-dried candy tricks, check out Micro-Homesteading Education's freeze-dried candy book "Freeze-Dried Candy Making for Selling & Fun!".

Freeze-dried flowers are also in high demand. The beauty of flowers does not diminish when they are freeze-dried. Special occasion flowers can be kept forever. Some people would happily pay for their specialty flowers to last and last.

Freeze-dried items that tend to sell quite well:

- Fruits
- Vegetables
- Powdered Foods
- Puffed Candy
- Ice Cream Treats
- Flowers

Cottage Laws

You can't simply start selling freeze-dried treats from your home, though. You need to get any licenses, registrations, or permits first. This protects not only potential buyers but also you. Cottage Food Operations (CFOs) became legal in the United States in 2013. As such, under the Homemade Food Act, people can prepare, package, and sell foods deemed safe from a home kitchen. To prevent people from becoming sick, only a limited number of foods—those that don't require refrigeration—are permitted for sale.

Cottage Food Laws have specifics that are based on state and county. You will have to look up the information about your state and your specific county. Be ready to fill out the paperwork. CFOs fall into two classes:

- Class A - direct sales of cottage foods
- Class B - the engagement of indirect sales through third-party sellers that hold valid permits

The county officials you work with will let you know what needs to be on your label (usually the address of the kitchen used). They will also inform you of any kitchen requirements or inspections and tell you which classes you need to take. With those legalities out the way, you can use your freeze-dryer to earn income.

More Tips

To end this chapter, here are a few more random tips and tricks for a safe and uneventful freeze-drying journey:

- Follow the freeze-drying rules stated in the Harvest Right™ manual and their website.
- You won't know how long a food will take to freeze-dry with certainty until you try it with YOUR machine in YOUR environment. So, get to freeze-drying!
- Always weigh your trays at the end of the run, give them extra dry time for two hours, and then re-weigh. If the weight hasn't changed, your food is completely dry and ready for packaging. This is the most reliable and quite easy way to determine if your food is done and safe for storage.
- Foods with seeds will take longer to freeze-dry. Always run these foods for at least six hours extra, and then run your two-hour weight check. Seedy foods include strawberries, blueberries, Goji berries, ground cherries, raspberries, blackberries, gooseberries, kiwi berries, pomegranates, tomatoes, tomatillos, and citrus.
- When the freeze-dryer switches to Extra Dry time, it just means that it's time for you to check on the food. The human element is critical. (This is when you weigh your trays and put them back in for two hours.)
- Place a towel underneath the front of the freeze-dryer to collect any moisture that drips. Ours dribbles constantly while it is working hard running a batch.
- For a quicker defrost, wear gloves and pull out the ice as it cracks off the chamber before it completely melts.
- Some people found that purchasing a continuous sealer was the answer when their impulse sealer had issues. Others like to buy a chamber sealer. The impulse sealer we got with our freeze-dryer has worked well enough for us.
- It's normal for the temperature of the chamber to fluctuate significantly back and forth between very cold and very warm. This is part of the process.
- Blanch raw potatoes every time. They will turn black if you do not. No matter how you prepare them, always blanch them before freeze-drying if they are uncooked.

- Keep apples, pears, bananas, and other fruit fresher and brighter in appearance by dipping them in a lemon juice wash (one tablespoon of lemon juice to each cup of water).
- Pineapple may run for 72 hours. Do not be surprised if that happens. Remember that if it is still sticky, it is not done yet.
- Blanched green beans give better freeze-dried results than cooked green beans.
- Bananas should be just ripe (a few freckles are fine). Be careful using overripe bananas. The sugar content is higher, and they may bubble up in the freeze-dryer. Give bananas a little space on the tray as well.
- Don't run the vacuum without running the freezer first. It puts moisture from the drum into your pump, and your oil turns cloudy and must be changed. For example, warming skittles and then vacuuming them does NOT work. I have done it; the skittles only puffed slightly, and the oil in the pump turned cloudy. Never again will I do this, and I hope you never do!
- Occasionally, you may notice a silicone mat curling up during freeze-drying. Don't worry; once the cycle is complete, it will settle back down and be flat again when it's done.

CONCLUSION

Freeze-drying is the fascinating process of removing moisture from foods by combining low temperatures, lowered pressure, and heat as a method of food preservation. For a long time, freeze-drying was a process limited to commercial activity. We had to hand over our hard-earned cash to enjoy the benefits of freeze-dried foods.

But now, with the invention of the home freeze-dryer, we have the power to control food quality, and we can get high-quality food preservation. Freeze-drying allows the everyday person to have nutritious food that has an extended shelf life! Foods could still be good 20-30 years from now with no refrigeration and no special attention.

The best part is that rehydration of these foods is quick and easy with just the addition of water. They taste great and maintain their nutrients. Whole meals can be created, making mealtime a simple affair. And, just as a cherry on top, leftovers can be freeze-dried to prevent wastage.

Rehydration is not even necessary for consumption. Freeze-dried foods can be eaten as they are, all dry and crunchy. This makes for healthy, convenient, fun, and crunchy snacking! One of my kids loves snacking on freeze-dried cauliflower. Another favorite is corn. It does not need to be sweet to be fun and tasty enough to munch on.

Almost 100 percent of the moisture is removed from the foods by freeze-drying. The foods become light and easy to carry so they can be enjoyed anywhere. You control what goes into your food. Say goodbye to allergic reactions to unknown ingredients in food. There really is no shortage of advantages to getting your own freeze-dryer and making tasty meals and more that can be enjoyed today, tomorrow, or twenty years from now.

I promised you two things at the beginning of this book:

1. To explain the freeze-drying process in a straightforward, easy-to-understand manner to help you get the best results possible. There are printable worksheets to enhance your experience in Appendix 3.
2. To provide you with freeze-drying recipes that allow you to use all you have learned on these pages. Instructions for Common Foods are in Appendix 1, and Easy Recipes are in Appendix 2.

I delivered on those promises. Now, it's up to you to practice what you have learned. Don't be afraid of making mistakes; it's one of the ways we learn. Luckily, this book allows you to minimize the incidences of this happening so you can go straight to enjoying the fruits (and veggies, and more!) of your freeze-drying labor.

My final words to you are these: You have the basics and all the tools you need. You're ready to build a superior food storage system stocked with high-quality items that will last years and years. Help someone else enjoy the same luxury. If you enjoyed the book, please leave a review on Amazon. It might seem like a small act, but it goes a long way in helping other like-minded people find this book.

This curiosity about food preservation has made us kindred spirits. I remember how daunting it was when I first started freeze-drying. I hope my words will remove the fear so you can jump right in and enjoy all the possibilities of freeze-drying. I wish you luck as you start this new adventure and hope to hear all about it as you get in touch.

APPENDIX ONE: 108 COMMON FOODS

So many foods work wonderfully in the freeze-dryer. This section covers the instructions for the preparation of the most ordinary foods.

Freeze-dry times and rehydration information are estimates and will depend on your ingredients, environment, and methods. Experiences will vary. Please use common sense and follow cleanliness and safety practices. The food categories are:

FOOD LIST

Fruits 110

Apples
Apricots
Avocado
Bananas
Blackberries
Blueberries
Cantaloupe
Cherries
Coconut
Cranberries
Grapefruit
Grapes
Honeydew
Kiwi, Golden
Lemons
Limes
Mandarins
Mangos
Nectarines
Oranges
Peaches
Pears
Pineapple
Plums
Pomegranate
Raspberries
Rhubarb
Strawberries
Tangerines
Watermelon

Vegetables 115

Asparagus
Beets
Bok Choy
Broccoli
Brussels Sprouts
Cabbage
Carrots
Cauliflower
Celery
Corn
Cucumber
Eggplant
Garlic
Green Beans
Kale
Leeks
Lettuce
Mushrooms
Okra
Onions
Parsnips
Peas
Peppers
Potatoes
Pumpkins
Radish
Rutabaga
Scallions
Spinach
Squash
Sweet Potatoes
Swiss Chard
Tomatoes
Turnips
Yams

Meats 122

Deli Meats

Beef 122

Ground
Filets
Meatballs
Patties
Roast
Steak
Stew Meats

Pork 123

Bacon
Ham
Roast

Poultry 124

Ground
Roasted
Turkey Bacon

Seafood 124

White Fish
Oily Fish
Shellfish

Dairy 125

Cottage Cheese
Cream Cheese
Hard Cheeses
Heavy Cream
Ice Cream
Milk
Sour Cream
Whipped Cream
Yogurt

Eggs 126

Grains 127

Breads
Cake
Pasta
Oats
Quinoa
Rice

Legumes 128

Beans
Chickpeas
Lentils
Soybeans
Sprouts

Fruits

Apples

Serving: 140 grams (1 medium)

Timing: 25-35 hours

Tip: Lemon Water: 1 Tbs Lemon Juice and 1 cup Water.

Prep: Rinse and core. Slice 1/4 inch thick. To prevent browning, drop in lemon juice water. Drain. Pat dry.

Raw: Spread on trays. Pre-freeze. Freeze-Dry.

Rehydrate: Add 1/2 cup of water to 1 cup of apple and let it sit for 5-10 minutes until tender.

Use: Great as a snack right out of the bag, or throw them in smoothies or pies.

Apricots

Serving: 105 grams (3 small)

Timing: 35-45+ hours

Tip: Use silicone or parchment as these can stick.

Prep: Rinse. Cut fruit lengthwise around the pit and gently twist to separate halves. Remove the pit and slice 1/4 inch thick.

Raw: Spread on trays. Pre-freeze. Freeze-Dry.

Rehydrate: Add 1 1/2 cup of water to 1 cup apricot and let it sit for 5-10 minutes until tender.

Use: Tasty as a snack or use them in smoothies, pies, and cakes.

Avocados

Serving: 130 grams (1/5 fruit)

Timing: 25-35 hours

Tip: Use perfectly ripe fruit or it may taste bitter.

Prep: Cut lengthwise around the seed. Gently twist to separate halves. Whack the seed with a blade and twist to remove it. Scoop out of the skin. Slice or mash.

Raw: Dip in lemon water. Spread on trays. Pre-freeze. Freeze-Dry.

Powder: I powder after freeze-drying and use it to make guacamole, avocado toast, or add to smoothies.

Rehydrate: 1 cup guacamole to 1/3 cup water. Add more or less to desired consistency.

Use: Make guacamole in an instant or toss it into a smoothie for extra nutrition.

Bananas

Serving: 140 grams (1 large)

Timing: 30-40 hours

Tip: Use overripe bananas in baking and smoothies.

Prep: Best yellow or just starting to speckle. Peel and slice. To prevent browning, mist with diluted lemon juice.

Raw: Pre-freeze individually. Then add the correct weight amount onto the tray before freeze-drying. You can get a lot more on the tray, and they separate easily because they are frozen separately.

Powder: Blend with a bit of water. Pre-freeze. Freeze-Dry.

Rehydrate: 1 c powder to 1/2 c water = 2 c mashed banana. Add to desired consistency.

Use: Easy snack or great to make desserts of all kinds.

Blackberries

Serving: 125–150 grams (1 cup)

Timing: 50-60 hours

Tip: Always use silicone or parchment for berries.

Prep: Wash and pat dry.

Raw: Pre-freeze. Freeze-Dry.

Rehydrate: Add 1 cup of water to 1 cup blackberries and let it set for 10 minutes until tender.

Use: Tasty as a dry snack and they work well in pies, cakes, and pancakes.

Blueberries

Serving: 80 grams (1/2 cup)

Timing: 35-45 hours

Tip: Make sure each berry is punctured.

Prep: Wash and pat dry.

Raw: Pierce individual berries. Pre-freeze. Freeze-Dry. I like using the Roller Berry from Frozen Right for this task. It works flawlessly.

Rehydrate: Add 1 cup of blueberries to 1/2 cup of water and let it sit for 5 minutes until tender.

Use: Tasty as a snack right out of the bag, or they work well in pies, cakes, salad, and pancakes.

Cantaloupe

Serving: 150 grams (1/4 medium)

Timing: 40-50+ hours

Tip: Use very ripe fruit.

Prep: Select entirely yellow/golden on the outside. That lets the sugars set. Rinse, halve, and scoop out the seeds.

Raw: Scoop out the flesh or peel and cut into thin slices or cubes that are about 1/2 inch thick.

Rehydrate: To use in a dessert add an equal amount of water.

Use: Best as a crunchy snack.

Cherries

Serving: 1 cup (21 cherries)

Timing: 50-60+ hours

Tip: Thaw and refreeze to drain off excess juice.

Prep: Rinse. Remove stems and pits, and cut them in half.

Raw: Place on silicone or parchment-lined trays. Pre-freeze. Freeze-Dry.

Rehydrate: Soak cherries in an equal amount of water and drain off excess.

Use: Tasty as a snack right out of the bag.

Coconut Meat

Serving: 100 grams

Timing: 30-40 hours

Tip: Turn to powder for a coconut flour.

Prep: Pierce the soft eye of the coconut and drain the liquid into a bowl. Find the equator (thin line) and crack the coconut in half. Situate your knife under the flesh. Gently pry the meat from the coconut shell, twisting your knife if necessary.

Raw: Cut into small pieces, strips, or shred. Pre-freeze. Freeze-Dry.

Rehydrate: Put a pan of water on the stove and bring it to a boil. Place a colander over the pan and put the coconut in the colander. Let the coconut absorb the steam for a few minutes and then pull the coconut off and pat dry it with a towel.

Use: Great topping for desserts of all kinds.

Cranberries

Serving: 1 cup

Timing: 50-60 hours

Tip: Whole berries are difficult to dry. Cut or shred.

Prep: Remove stems and rinse.

Raw: Roughly chop or run through food processor. Pre-freeze. Freeze-Dry.

Rehydrate: 1/2 cup cranberries to 1/4 cup water.

Use: Toss into breads or pies. Blend or pulse and make into cranberry sauce.

Grapefruit

Serving: 140 grams (1/2 large)

Timing: 35-45+ hours

Tip: Remove all seeds to lessen batch time.

Prep: Rinse. Peel if desired.
Prep: Thinly slice or section the fruit. Spread on lined trays. Pre-freeze. Freeze-Dry.

Juice: Cut in half and scoop out flesh from segments. Squeeze fruit for juice. Peel and slice into pieces that are 1/4-1/2 inch thick. Blending them and pouring them into silicone molds. Pre-freeze. Remove from molds before freeze-drying.

Rehydrate: Juice: 1/8 cup powder to 1/2 cup water and sweeten to taste.

Use: Toss a slice into your water. Use powder to flavor baking items or toss peeled chunks into salads for a sweet, crunchy crouton.

Grapes

Serving: 140 grams (21 grapes or 1 cup)

Timing: 45-60+ hours

Tip: If they are still sticky or soft, they need more time!

Prep: Rinse and remove stems.
Raw: Cut grapes in half. Pre-freeze. Freeze-Dry.

Blanch: Drop in boiling water until they float (about 2 minutes.) Ice batch. Pre-freeze. Freeze-Dry. Blanching retains shape and saves batch time.

Rehydrate: Spritz a small amount of water on them. Place in a plastic bag and let it sit for 30-60 minutes.

Use: Perfect snack or tasty in smoothies and salads.

Honeydew

Serving: 150 grams (1/6 medium)

Timing: 30-40 hours

Tip: Wait until it is very ripe. That lets the sugars set.

Prep: Rinse, cut in half, scoop out seeds.

Raw: Cut into thin slices or cubes that are 1/2 inch thick.

Rehydrate: To use in a dessert add an equal amount of water.

Use: Delicious snack.

Kiwi, Golden

Serving: 140 grams (2 medium)

Timing: 40-50+ hours

Tip: Green kiwi tend to get really tart in the freeze-dryer.

Prep: Rinse and peel if desired.

Raw: Dice or thinly slice. Pre-freeze. Freeze-Dry.

Rehydrate: To use in a dessert add an equal amount of water.

Use: Excellent snack, smoothie bowl or granola topping.

Lemons

Serving: 55 grams (1 small)

Timing: 30-40+ hours

Tip: Removing seeds will lessen the batch time.

Prep: Remove peel if desired. Remove pith and seeds.

Raw: Slice into pieces that are 1/4-1/2 inch thick or blend with or without skin. Spread onto trays. Pre-freeze. Freeze-Dry.

Juice: Cut in half and scoop out flesh from segments. Squeeze fruit for juice. Blend and pour them into silicone molds. Pre-freeze. Remove from molds before freeze-drying.

Rehydrate: Juice: 1/8 cup powder to 1/2 cup water.

Use: Lemon water, lemonade, salad dressing, steak marinades, or lemon meringue.

Limes

Serving: 55 grams (1 small)

Timing: 30-40+ hours

Tip: 1 Lime = 2-3 Tbs juice.

Prep: Remove peel if desired. Remove pith and seeds.

Raw: Slice into 1/4 inches thick or blend with or without skin. Spread onto trays. Pre-freeze. Freeze-Dry.

Powder: Blend after freeze-drying for a fine powder.

Rehydrate: Juice: 1/8 cup powder to 1/2 cup water.

Use: Make lime water, key lime pie, salad dressing, guacamole, or salsa.

Mandarins

Serving: 55 grams (1 small)

Timing: 35-45+ hours

Tip: Freeze Dry the peel to use as zest or in cleaning products.

Prep: Remove peel if desired. Remove pith and seeds.

Raw: Slice into 1/4 inches thick or blend with or without skin. Spread onto trays. Pre-freeze. Freeze-Dry.

Powder: Blend again for a fine powder.

Rehydrate: Juice: 1/8 cup powder to 1/2 cup water and sweeten to taste.

Use: flavored water, salad dressing, steak marinades or tossed into summer salads.

Mangos

Serving: 140 grams (1/2 large)

Timing: 35-45+ hours

Tip: Store-bought frozen mango tends to not be ripe enough.

Prep: Rinse fresh, ripe mango. Cut on either side of the pit and remove the pit.

Raw: Peel and cut into small cubes. Pre-freeze. Freeze-Dry.

Rehydrate: To use in a dessert add an equal amount of water.

Use: Perfect for a healthy snack, smoothie addition, ice cream or yogurt topping.

Nectarines

Serving: 140 grams (1 medium)

Timing: 35-45+ hours

Tip: Nectarines are slightly soft when ripe.

Prep: Rinse. Remove the pith by cutting lengthwise around the pith and twist to separate halves.

Raw: Cut into 1/4 inch slices. To prevent browning, dip in lemon juice water. Pre-freeze. Freeze-Dry.

Rehydrate: Add 1 cup of nectarine to 1 cup of water and let it sit for 5-10 minutes until tender.

Use: Tasty as a snack or they work well in pies, cakes, smoothies, and muffins.

Oranges

Serving: 140 grams (1 medium)

Timing: 35-45+ hours

Tip: 1 cup juice becomes 1/4 cup powder.

Prep: Remove peel if desired. Remove pith and seeds.

Raw: Slice into 1/4 inches thick or blend with or without skin. Lay out or Spread onto trays. Pre-freeze. Freeze-Dry. Blend again for a fine powder.

Rehydrate: Mix 1/4 cup powder with 1 cup water for a glass of orange juice.

Use: throw a slice into water, sprinkle over salad, use in pies or cakes.

Peaches

Serving: 140 grams (1 medium)

Timing: 35-45+ hours

Tip: Use ripe peaches to keep it sweet.

Prep: Rinse. Peel if desired.

Blanch: Blanching will remove skins. Remove the pit by cutting the fruit lengthwise around the pit and twist to separate halves.

Raw: Cut into 1/4 inch slices. Pre-freeze. Freeze-Dry.

Rehydrate: Add 1 cup of peach to 1 cup of water and let it sit for 5-10 minutes until tender.

Use: Tasty as a snack or they work well in pies, cakes, smoothies, muffins.

Pears

Serving: 140 grams (1 medium)

Timing: 35-45+ hours

Tip: Lemon Water: 1 Tbs Lemon Juice and 1 cup Water.

Prep: Rinse. Cut it in half and remove the core.

Raw: Cut into 1/4 inch slices. To prevent browning, dip in lemon juice water. Pre-freeze. Freeze-Dry.

Rehydrate: Add 1 cup of pear to 1 cup of water and let it sit for 5-10 minutes until tender.

Use: Yummy snack, or they work well in pies, cobblers, breads, muffins, and smoothies.

Pineapple

Serving: 140 grams (2 medium slices)

Timing: 50-60+ hours

Tip: Make sure trays are lined with silicone or parchment!

Prep: Rinse, discard crown and bottom end. Remove the rind from top to bottom. Slice and core as desired.

Raw: Approximately 1/4 inch thick chunks, optional double layer using silicone mesh. Pre-freeze. Freeze-Dry.

Rehydrate: Add 1 cup pineapple to 1 cup of water and let it sit for 5-10 minutes until tender.

Use: Works well in pies, cakes, and smoothies.

Plums

Serving: 140 grams (1 medium)

Timing: 35-45 hours

Tip: Remove the skin to avoid tartness.

Prep: Cut in half. Remove the pit. Peel if desired.

Raw: Cut into 1/4 inch slices. Pre-freeze. Freeze-Dry.

Rehydrate: Add 1 cup plum slices to 1 cup of water.

Use: Make muffins, cakes, pies, and smoothies.

Pomegranate

Serving: 77 grams (1/2 fruit)

Timing: 50-60+ hours

Tip: Dilute puree 50:50.

Prep: Slit skin and carefully pull away skin and remove pith.

Raw: Lay out on trays and Pre-freeze. Freeze-Dry.

Powder: Blend seeds and strain to make juice. Dilute with water to avoid a foam explosion in your machine. Pour into your trays. Pre-freeze. Freeze-Dry.

Use: Perfect smoothie addition, ice cream or yogurt topping. Works great for a natural coloring in baking too.

Raspberries

Serving: 80 grams (1/2 cup)

Timing: 45-55 hours

Tip: Seeds make it tricky. When in doubt, add more time!

Prep: Gently rinse and pat dry.

Raw: Lay out on trays. Pre-freeze. Freeze-Dry.

Powder: You can use a juicer, or you can blend and strain to remove seeds.

Rehydrate: Add 3 tablespoons of water to 1 cup raspberries and let it sit for 5 minutes until tender.

Use: Works well in water, honey, muffins, cakes, smoothies, and popsicles. Try 2 freeze-dried lemon slices and a scoop of freeze-dried raspberry powder in water.

Rhubarb

Serving: 62 grams (1/2 cup)

Timing: 30-40 hours

Tip: Very sour. Mix with sweet fruits like strawberries.

Prep: Remove leaves, they are inedible and toxic. Rinse stalks well.

Raw: Dice. Pre-freeze. Freeze-Dry.

Rehydrate: Rehydrate 50:50 before adding to your sweet recipes.

Use: Rehydrates well to make jams or pie. Powdered makes a tasty drink flavor similar to lemonade.

Strawberries

Serving: 140 grams (7 medium or 1 cup)

Timing: 35-45+ hours

Tip: Seeds have a lot of moisture. Always add extra time.

Prep: Gently rinse, pat dry, then remove caps.

Raw: Slice 1/8–1/4 inches thick. Pre-freeze. Freeze-Dry.

Rehydrate: Add 1 cup strawberries to 1/2 cup of water and let it sit for 5 minutes.

Use: Use as a dry snack or in pies, cakes, smoothies, ice cream, muffins, and cheesecakes.

Tangerines

Serving: 140 grams (1 medium)

Timing: 30-40+ hours

Tip: Removing seeds will decrease the batch time.

Prep: Remove peel if desired. Remove pith and seeds.

Raw: Slice into 1/4 inches thick or blend with or without skin. Lay out or spread onto trays. Pre-freeze. Freeze-Dry. Blend again for a fine powder.

Rehydrate: Juice: 1/8 cup powder to 1/2 cup water and sweeten to taste.

Use: Throw a slice into water, use in pies or cakes.

Watermelon

Serving: 150 grams (1 cup diced)

Timing: 50-60+ hours

Tip: Remove seeds because they won't dry.

Prep: Rinse.

Raw: Cut melon into slices about 1/4 inches thick, small melon balls, or 1 inch cubes. Cut off the rind. Pre-freeze. Freeze-Dry.

Rehydrate: Rehydrate 50:50 before adding to your sweet recipes.

Use: Juice, smoothies, or sorbets.

Vegetables

Asparagus

Serving: 85 grams (10 medium spears)

Timing: 25-35 hours

Tip: Great as a blended soup or dry snack.

Prep: Rinse the spears. Remove the tough end of the stems. The spears can be chopped any size or left intact.

Roast: 425 °F. Very light oil. Season as desired. Depending on the thickness, roast in oven for 10-20 min until fork tender. Let it cool. Pre-freeze. Freeze-Dry.

Raw: Shred with a food processor or slice with a mandoline. Spread the weight limit on the tray. Pre-freeze. Freeze-Dry.

Blanch: Bring water to a boil. Drop vegetables in for 2-4 min. Shock in an ice bath. Pat dry. Pre-freeze. Freeze-Dry.

Sauté: Season as desired. Depending on the thickness, sauté with 1 tablespoon of water for 10-20 minutes until fork tender. Let cool. Pre-freeze. Freeze-Dry.

Rehydrate: Dip into water for 30 seconds. Sauté.

Use: You can eat them as is or add them to soups, casseroles, and chowders.

Beets

Serving: 72 grams (125 ml)

Timing: 30-40 hours

Tip: Boiling helps remove the skins & enhances sweetness.

Prep: Cut the stem off, leaving 1 inch. Rinse.

Raw: Shred with a food processor. Spread the weight limit on the tray. Pre-freeze. Freeze-Dry.

Boil: Boil for 20-40 minutes depending on the size until they are fork tender. Shock in an ice bath. Remove the skin, root, and stem. Roughly slice into 1/2 inch bits. Pre-freeze. Freeze-Dry.

Roast: Roast for 35 minutes at 375 °F. Remove skin, root, and stem. Cut into pieces and season as desired. Let it cool. Pre-freeze. Freeze-Dry.

Use: They work well as a natural coloring for baking. Great crunchy foods for snacks, or add them into stir-fries and smoothies.

Bok Choy

Serving: 90 grams (125 ml)

Timing: 30-40 hours

Tip: Ginger, garlic, and green onions are a boost of flavor.

Prep: Discard the outer, wilted leaves. After rinsing, split the head in half and take out the center.

Raw: Shred or cut into wedges. Pre-freeze. Freeze-Dry.

Cooked: Place the bok choy cut side down in a single layer in a pan. Cook until lightly browned, about 1 to 2 minutes. Flip cook the other side until lightly browned. Let cool. Season if desired. Pre-freeze. Freeze-Dry.

Use: Great to add to stir-fries, soups, or stews.

Broccoli

Serving: 85 grams (1 medium stalk)

Timing: 30-40 hours

Tip: great as a snack seasoned prior to freeze drying.

Prep: Rinse. Trim the main stem. Split into florets.

Boil: 15 minutes. Pre-freeze. Freeze-Dry.

Roast: Roast at 425 °F for 20 minutes. Pre-freeze. Freeze-Dry.

Blanch: Blanch for 3-5 minutes. Ice bath. Season or leave plain. Pre-freeze. Freeze-Dry.

Steam: 10 minutes. Pre-freeze. Freeze-Dry.

Rehydrate: Add 1/2 cup of water to one cup broccoli and let it sit for 5 to 10 minutes. Or toss into any meal.

Use: Fantastic in casseroles and soups. Delicious as a snack straight out of the bag.

Brussels Sprouts

Serving: 76 grams (4 sprouts)

Timing: 30-40 hours

Tip: Try shredding them through a food processor.

Prep: Rinse. Trim the stem ends. Cut into halves.

Blanch: Blanch for 3-5 minutes. Ice bath. Season as desired, or leave plain. Pre-freeze. Freeze-Dry.

Sauté: Sauté with salt and pepper until well-seared. Pre-freeze. Freeze-Dry.

Use: work wonderfully in stir-fries, soups, or even sautéed with onions and bacon.

Cabbage

Serving: 89 grams (1/8th med head)

Timing: 30–40 hours

Tip: Remove thick ridges to avoid bitterness.

Prep: Discard the outer, wilted leaves. Rinse. Remove the core by cutting the head in quarters lengthwise.

Raw: Shred or cut into chunks. Pre-freeze. Freeze-Dry.

Blanch: 3-5 minutes. Pre-freeze. Freeze-Dry.

Rehydrate: We do not recommend rehydrating cabbage for any "fresh" use, but instead to toss into soups or salads.

Use: Add it to a soup or stir-fry, or reconstitute with hot water and butter.

Carrots

Serving: 85 grams (1 medium carrot)

Timing: 25-35 hours

Tip: Smaller carrots will be sweeter.

Prep: Trim the stem and root ends. Rinse. Peel or scrub. Chop into 1/2-inch thick sticks, rounds, or shred. "Baby" carrots don't rehydrate well and are not recommended unless shredded.

Raw: Shred. Pre-freeze. Freeze-Dry.

Blanch: Blanch for 3-5 minutes. Ice bath. Season as desired, or leave plain. Pre-freeze. Freeze-Dry.

Rehydrate: Add 1/2 cup of water to 1 cup carrot.

Use: Throw them into soups whole or blend into carrot soup.

Cauliflower

Serving: 85 grams (1/6 of a med head)

Timing: 28-38 hours

Tip: Tasty if tossed with sauces prior to freeze-drying.

Prep: Rinse. Remove outer leaves and core. Cut into florets.

Blanch: Blanch for 3-5 minutes. Ice bath. Pat dry. Season as desired. Pre-freeze. Freeze-Dry.

Bake: Bake at 425°F for 20-25 minutes. Pre-freeze. Freeze-Dry.

Rehydrate: 1 cup water to 1 cup cauliflower. Let sit for 5 min.

Use: Fantastic in stews and soups. Delicious as a snack straight out of the bag.

Celery

Serving: 85 grams (1 large stalk)

Timing: 35–45 hours

Tip: Freeze dry the leaves too. They add great flavor.

Prep: Rinse the stalks well after separating them. Trim leaves, get rid of brown spots, dice, discard the bottom.

Raw: Pre-freeze. Freeze-Dry.

Rehydrate: Add 1/2 cup of water to 1 cup celery and let it sit for 5-10 minutes until tender.

Use: Add it to soups, stews, and broths. Powder it and use it as a seasoning for meat, poultry, and fish dishes.

Corn

Serving: 85 grams (Kernels from 1 med)

Timing: 30-40 hours

Tip: It tastes like candy when eaten dried.

Prep: Rinse after removing husks and silk.

Blanch: Blanch for 3-5 minutes followed by an ice bath. Cut the corn lengthwise, to remove the kernels. Pre-freeze. Freeze-Dry.

Frozen: Place onto the trays and straight into the freeze-dryer. Freeze-Dry.

Rehydrate: Add 1/2 cup of water to 1 cup corn and let it sit for 5-10 minutes until tender. Or toss into any dish.

Use: Great addition to soups, stews, or even adding a bit of nutrition to rice.

Cucumber

Serving: 85 grams (1/4 med or 1 mini)

Timing: 40-50+ hours

Tip: Tasty dry for a snack.

Prep: Rinse. Peel the skin if desired. Slice lengthwise and scoop out the seeds. Slice or chop into bite-size pieces.

Raw: Slices should be between 1/8-1/4 inches thick. Season if desired (ranch powder works great, as does dill and lemon pepper) Pre-freeze. Freeze-Dry.

Rehydrate: 1 cup chopped cucumber in 3/4 cup water and let it sit 10 minutes.

Use: Powder to make tzatziki sauce. Add slices to water. Rehydrate chunks and add to salads or smoothies.

Eggplant

Serving: 43 grams (125 ml)

Timing: 25-35 hours

Tip: Before sautéing, dip in seasoned bread crumbs.

Prep: Remove the stem. Peel if you like.

Sauté: Slice into 1/4 – 3/8 inch thick pieces. Before cooking, sprinkle with salt and allow it to rest for 30 to 60 minutes. Rinse and pat dry. Sauté until fork tender. Let cool. Spread onto trays. Pre-freeze. Freeze-Dry.

Rehydrate: Dip into water for 30 sec - 1 min on each side. Sauté normally.

Use: Crumble to make tasty faux meatballs or fritters. Add just enough water to get the right consistency. Or bake in casseroles!

Garlic

Serving: 3-6 grams (1–2 cloves)

Timing: 25-35 hours

Tip: Quick way to have garlic on hand with no hassle.

Prep: Loosen the bulb. Separate the cloves. Slightly crush each clove with the flat side of the blade. Peel.

Raw: Cut in halves or roughly chop. Pre-freeze. Freeze-Dry.

Rehydrate: Add 2 Tbs garlic halves to 1 Tbs water. It will rehydrate quickly.

Use: Toss into any dish that calls for garlic. Powder for an intense garlic powder or add equal parts garlic and salt for a tasty garlic salt.

Green Beans

Serving: 85 grams (20 medium beans)

Timing: 25-35 hours

Tip: These rehydrate better when cooked or blanched.

Prep: Rinse. Cut and discard the ends. Cut into bite sized pieces.

Blanch: Blanch for 3-5 minutes. Pre-freeze. Freeze-Dry.

Cooked or canned: Spread onto the trays. Season as desired. Pre-freeze. Freeze-Dry.

Rehydrate: Add 1 cup of water to 1 cup of beans and let it sit for 5 to 10 minutes until tender. Or toss into any dish.

Use: Works well in soups and stews. Quick green bean casserole too.

Kale

Serving: 71 grams (250 ml)

Timing: 25-35 hours

Tip: Blending with water allows more leafy greens per batch.

Prep: Rinse well, remove stems, and roughly chop.

Raw: Leave chopped or blend with a small amount of water to make a purée. Pre-freeze. Freeze-Dry.

Rehydrate: We don't recommend rehydrating greens like kale.

Use: Add powder to smoothies or add to soups, stews, and eggs.

Leeks

Serving: 47 grams (1/2 leek)

Timing: 25-35 hours

Tip: Thin slices can be a crunchy addition to salads.

Prep: Rinse well. Mince, chop, or slice.

Raw: Pre-freeze. Freeze-Dry.

Rehydrate: We don't recommend rehydrating leeks.

Use: Add to soups and stews.

Lettuce

Serving: 85 grams (2 cups; 1/4 head)

Timing: 25-35 hours

Tip: Blending with water allows more leafy greens per batch.

Prep: Wash well and discard root bottom. Roughly chop.

Raw: Leave roughly chopped or blend with a small amount of water to make a purée. Pre-freeze. Freeze-Dry.

Rehydrate: We don't recommend rehydrating greens like lettuce.

Use: Powders are a great way to get more nutrition in smoothies.

Mushrooms

Serving: 85 grams (5 medium)

Timing: 25-35 hours

Tip: Cooked mushrooms have more nutrients.

Prep: Rinse gently before use. Quarter or chop.

Sauté: 5-10 minutes. Pre-freeze. Freeze-Dry.

Rehydrate: Add 1/2 cup of water to 1 cup mushroom and let it sit for 5-10 minutes until tender. Or toss directly into any dish.

Use: Makes a great crispy snack or add them to stews, stir-fry, and pasta sauces.

Okra

Serving: 53 grams (125 ml)

Timing: 25-35 hours

Tip: Sprinkle with seasoning prior to freeze-drying.

Prep: Rinse. Remove the cap and tip and slice, unless blanching first.
Blanch: Blanch for 3 minutes. Remove the cap and tip. Slice into coins or slice lengthwise and place cut side up. Pre-freeze. Freeze-Dry.
Bake: Bake at 350°F for 20 minutes. Let it cool. Pre-freeze. Freeze-Dry.

Rehydrate: Add to soups, gumbo, casseroles, and stews directly. No need to rehydrate.

Use: Great to keep stocked as a delicious snack.

Onions

Serving: 85 grams (1/2 medium)

Timing: 25-35 hours

Tip: Use as a topping for pizzas, salads, and tacos.

Prep: Trim root and stem ends. Discard outer brittle leaves. Slice or chop.

Raw: Slice or chop. Pre-freeze. Freeze-Dry.

Rehydrate: Add 1/2 cup of water to 1 cup of onion and let sit 5 minutes until tender. Or toss into any dish. Pre-freeze. Freeze-Dry.
Use: Perfect and convenient for soups, stews, casseroles, sauces, and dressings, to add flavor and texture.

Parsnips

Serving: 70 grams (125 ml)

Timing: 25-35 hours

Tip: Add seasoning to make parsnip chips.

Prep: Trim off the root ends and the tops. Peel the skins. Shred or dice.
Raw: Pre-freeze. Freeze-Dry.

Blanch: Blanch for 3-5 minutes. Pre-freeze. Freeze-Dry.

Rehydrate: Add 1/2 cup parsnip to 1 cup of water.

Use: Add to stews and soups. Drizzle with maple syrup and brown sugar for a tasty treat.

Peas, Green

Serving: 77 grams (125 ml)

Timing: 25-35 hours

Tip: Easy to throw into any dish that needs veggies.

Prep: Shell the peas.
Raw: Pre-freeze. Freeze-Dry.
Blanch: Blanch for 2-3 minutes. Shock in an ice bath. Pre-freeze. Freeze-Dry.
Frozen: Place onto the trays and straight into the freeze-dryer.

Rehydrate: Add 1 cup dried peas to 1 cup of water. Soak in water. Warm up plain.

Use: Great as a snack as is. Delicious to eat in cold ham & pea salad.

Peas, Snap/Snow

Serving: 85 grams (125 ml)

Timing: 25-35 hours

Tip: Add crispy pieces to a salad for a healthy crunch.

Prep: Rinse, snap off ends.

Raw: Lay out on tray or cut into pieces. Pre-freeze. Freeze-Dry.

Rehydrate: Soak podded peas in half the amount of water for 5 minutes and drain.

Use: Great to add to stir-fries, pastas, and curries.

Peppers, Hot

Serving: 15 grams (1 pepper)

Timing: 25-35 hours

Tip: Freeze-dry and powder seeds for a powerful spice.

Prep: Rinse. Remove the stem, seeds, and pit. Wear gloves to avoid burning hands!

Raw: Cut into strips or dice. Pre-freeze. Freeze-Dry.

Rehydrate: Add 1/2 cup of water to 1 cup pepper and let it sit for 10 minutes until tender.

Use: Throw into chili, stews, sauces, and marinades.

Peppers, Sweet

Serving: 85 grams (1/2 medium)

Timing: 25-35 hours

Tip: Powder ripe peppers for a homemade paprika.

Prep: Rinse. Remove the stem, seeds, and pit.

Raw: Cut into strips or dice. Pre-freeze. Freeze-Dry.

Rehydrate: Add 1/2 cup of water to 1 cup pepper and let it sit for 10 minutes until tender.

Use: Toss into any dish including fajitas, soups, and salsas.

Potatoes

Serving: 110 grams (1 small)

Timing: 30-40+ hours

Tip: Raw potatoes must be blanched before they are freeze-dried, or they will turn black.

Prep: Scrub well. Peel and cut as desired, no more than 1/4 inches thick. Soak and rinse them several times to get as much starch out as possible.

Blanch: 3-5 minutes (Diced, sliced, or wedges) OR 1-3 minutes (Shredded). Ice bath. Pat dry. Pre-freeze. Freeze-Dry.

Mashed: Boil for 20-30 minutes. Strain. Mash with salt, pepper, and milk/water/broth. No butter. Pre-freeze. Freeze-Dry. Blend or crush into powder when dry.

Rehydrate: Add 1 cup of water to 1 cup potato and let it sit 5-10 minutes until tender.

Rehydrate mashed: Add 2 cups water to 2 cups mashed potato powder. Makes 3 cups. Stir, add butter, season as desired.

Use: Fry, mash, bake, or toss into soups, stews, or casseroles.

Pumpkins

Serving: 61 grams (125 ml)

Timing: 30-40 hours

Tip: Try using pumpkin in lieu of oil/fat in baking.

Prep: Cut in 2 halves, remove fibers and seeds.

Bake: Bake at 350 °F. Bake halves face down until they start to get soft. Once cooled, remove stem and peel. Cube or mash Pre-freeze. Freeze-Dry.

Rehydrate: 1 cup pumpkin purée to 1/4 cup water. 1 cup pumpkin chunks to 1/2 cup water.

Use: Use it diced in soups and stews, or reconstitute the powder for pies and breads.

Radish

Serving: 61 grams (125 ml)

Timing: 30-40 hours

Tip: Pickled radish are great to try too!

Prep: Trim stem and root ends.

Raw: Shred or dice. Pre-freeze. Freeze-Dry.

Rehydrate: We do not recommend rehydrating.

Use: Perfect as a salad topping.

Rutabaga

Serving: 74 grams (125 ml)

Timing: 25-35 hours

Tip: Great substitute for potatoes in soups.

Prep: Rinse and peel. Slice off the top and lay the flat surface down on the cutting board. Cut into small 1/2 inch sections.

Boil: Boil for 15 min. Let cool. Spread onto trays. Pre-freeze. Freeze-Dry.

Rehydrate: Add 1 cup cubes to 1 cup hot water. Let it sit for 10 minutes.

Use: Use in soups, roasts, or eat mashed.

Scallions

Serving: 15 grams (1 medium)

Timing: 25-35 hours

Tip: It's great to have them prepped and ready to use.

Prep: Rinse. Trim the roots.

Raw: Slice or dice. Pre-freeze. Freeze-Dry.

Rehydrate: Add 1/8 cup of water to 1/2 cup of scallions and let it sit for 2 minutes.

Use: Makes an awesome garnish. Toss into stir frys, soups, stews, salads, tuna salads no rehydration needed.

Spinach

Serving: 40 grams (1 cup)

Timing: 25-35 hours

Tip: 2 tablespoons is roughly 1 serving of spinach.

Prep: Rinse and roughly chop.
Raw: Pack in to the trays Pre-freeze. Freeze-Dry.
Powder: Purée with a little water, pour in trays. Pre-freeze. Freeze-Dry.
Rehydrate: Add 1/4 cup of water to 1 cup of spinach. Stir and cover for 3-5 minutes. Sauté with butter.
Use: Add pieces into casseroles, quiches, and soups. Use the powder in sauces and smoothies. Easy way to sneak nutrition into any dish such as: soups, stews, spaghetti sauce, chip dip, and egg casseroles.

Squash, Butternut

Serving: 205 grams (1 cup)

Timing: 30-40 hours

Tip: This squash can also be eaten raw.

Prep: Rinse. Cut the squash in half. Remove fibers and peel. Cut into cubes or slices.
Raw: Cut into slices or bite-sized chunks. Pat dry. Pre-freeze. Freeze-Dry.
Bake: At 350°F. Season as desired and bake cubes for 20-30 minutes until fork tender. Pre-freeze. Freeze-Dry.
Powder: Blend into a purée. Spread onto a lined tray. Pre-freeze. Freeze-Dry.
Rehydrate: Add 1/2 a cup of water to 1 cup of squash and let it sit for 5-10 minutes until tender. Or toss into any dish.
Use: Great soup thickener, sautee with butter, blended soup.

Squash, Spaghetti

Serving: 1 cup

Timing: 40-50 hours

Tip: To use as flour, add 1 part squash pwd. to 2 parts flour.

Prep: Cut in half lengthwise, and scoop out seeds. Salt and pepper the inside of the squash and drizzle it with olive oil.
Bake: Place on baking sheet, cut side down, poke holes with a fork. Bake at 400°F for 30 - 40 minutes, Let cool. Use a fork to scrape the strands. Pre-freeze. Freeze-Dry.
Rehydrate: Add 1/2 cup of water to 1 cup spaghetti squash and let it sit for 3-5 minutes until tender.
Use: Crush dry to make faux meatballs or fritters. Add just enough water to get the right consistency. Great soup thickener. Sautée with a small amount of water & butter.

Squash, Yellow

Serving: 69 grams (125 ml)

Timing: 25-35 hours

Tip: Tasty baked and topped with parmesan and salt.

Prep: Rinse. Cut in half. Remove seeds and stringy fiber if large. Peel if desired.

Raw: Cut into bite-sized 1-inch chunks. Pat dry. Pre-freeze. Freeze-Dry.

Bake: Finely slice. Bake until lightly browned. Let it cool. Pre-freeze. Freeze-Dry.

Rehydrate: Add 1/2 cup of water to 1 cup squash and let it sit for 5-10 minutes.

Use: Easy addition to casseroles, soups and stews.

Squash, Zucchini

Serving: 85 grams (1/2 medium)

Timing: 25-35 hours

Tip: To use as flour, add 1 part powder to 2 parts flour.

Prep: Rinse, remove ends, peel if desired. Slice, cube, shred, or cut into sticks. If larger zucchini, remove seeds.
Raw: Cut into sticks and season with your favorite spices. Garlic and salt work well for a snack. Dice for soups, casseroles, and eggs.
Bake: Finely slice and bake until lightly browned. Makes tasty chips.
Powder: Slice, shred, squeeze, and pat dry. Lay out onto trays. Pre-freeze. Freeze-Dry.
Rehydrate: Add 1/2 cup of water to 1 cup zucchini and let it sit for 5 minutes until tender. Or toss into any dish.
Use: Zucchini Powder is great in baking, breads, and adding extra nutrition.

Sweet Potatoes

Serving: 110 grams (1/2 medium)

Timing: 30-40 hours

Tip: Sweet potato chips with cinnamon are a great snack.

Prep: Scrub well. Peel and cut as desired, no more than 1/4 inches thick. Slice, shred, dice, or mash. Soak and rinse them several times to get as much starch out as possible.

Blanch: Blanch for 3-5 minutes for diced, sliced, or sweet potato wedges. Throw into an ice bath. Pat dry. Pre-freeze. Freeze-Dry.

Blanch Shredded: Blanch 1-3 minutes for shredded sweet potato. Throw into an ice bath. Pat dry. Pre-freeze. Freeze-Dry.

Mashed: Boil for 20-30 minutes. Strain. Mash with salt, pepper, and milk, water, or broth. Don't use butter. Pre-freeze. Freeze-Dry. Blend into powder when dry.

Rehydrate: Add 1 cup sweet potato to 1 cup of water. Let it sit for 5-10 minutes.

Rehydrate mashed: Add 2 1/2 cups water to 2 cups powder. Stir, add butter, and season as desired. This makes 3 cups.

Use: Toss into soups, stews, or casseroles. Eat mashed or dry.

Swiss Chard

Serving: 93 grams (125 ml boiled)

Timing: 25-35 hours

Tip: If the chard is bitter cook it longer.

Prep: Wash thoroughly.

Raw: Chop or purée with a little water & pour into trays. Pre-freeze. Freeze-Dry.

Blanch: Blanch leaves for 2-3 minutes. Pat dry to remove excess water. Leave whole or cut into bite-size pieces. Pre-freeze. Freeze-Dry.

Rehydrate: Add in small amounts of boiling water and butter to leaves until desired consistency is reached. Sauté for 2-3 minutes.

Use: Add pieces into casseroles or soups. Use the powder in smoothies.

Tomatoes

Serving: 85 grams (1/2 small; 1/3 med)

Timing: 35-45+ hours

Tip: Removing the seeds will reduce the drying time.

Prep: Rinse and discard stem.

Raw: Quarter the tomatoes with the peel on, squeeze, and drain as much liquid as you can. Remove seeds. Or Thinly slice and layer. Pre-freeze. Freeze-Dry.

Blanch: Score an X on the bottom. Place them into boiling water for 90 seconds each. Drop them into ice water. Peel slips off. Quarter, squeeze, and drain as much liquid and seeds as you can. Pre-freeze. Freeze-Dry.

Cooked: Remove skins if desired. Simmer with water on low-medium heat for several hours. Blend them with an immersion blender. Season if desired. Spread on trays.

Rehydrate: Sauce: Add 2/3 cup powder to 2 cups of water = 15 ounce can.
Juice: Add 1 cup powder to 8 cups of water = 64ounce bottle.

Use: Slices work well placed onto burgers. The burger rehydrates it slightly. Chunks can be tossed into soups and stews. Powdered great for sauces, soup or chili thickener.

Turnips

Serving: 125ml (1/2 cup)

Timing: 25-35 hours

Tip: If bitter, stir in a small bit of baking soda while boiling.

Prep: Rinse. Peel. Slice or cube into pieces that are 1/4 to 1/2 inch thick.

Boil: Boil for 20-40 minutes depending on size until they are fork tender, shock in an ice bath. Remove the skin, root, and stem. Roughly slice into 1/2 inch bits, or mash. Pre-freeze. Freeze-Dry.

Roast: Roast at 375°F for 35 minutes. Remove skin, root, and stem. Cut, and season as desired. Pre-freeze. Freeze-Dry.

Use: Toss into stews or soups.

Yams

Serving: 72 grams (125 ml)

Timing: 30-40 hours

Tip: Has lots of fiber, potassium, vit C, vit B6, and vit E.

Prep: Scrub yams well.

Boil: Peel and cube into 1/4 to 1/2 inches thick, boil for 10-20 minutes until fork tender. Drain. Let cool. Pre-freeze. Freeze-Dry.

Roast: Peel and cube or finely slice. Season as desired. Roast at 425°F for 30 minutes. Pre-freeze. Freeze-Dry.

Rehydrate: Add 1 cup cubes to 1 cup hot water. Let it sit for 10 minutes.

Bake: 350°F for 45 minutes. Scrape out of the peel and mash. Let cool and spread onto trays. Pre-freeze. Freeze-Dry.

Use: Toss into soups, stews, or casseroles. Eat mashed with butter.

Meats

Deli Meats

Serving: 3 ounces

Timing: 20-30 hours

Tip: Soon to expire meats can be purchased at a reduced rate.

Prep: Remove deli meats from packaging. Depending on the type of meat and thickness, roll two or three slices up. Spread evenly over the tray. Pre-freeze. Freeze-Dry

Rehydrate: Dip rolls into shallow water for a few seconds. You will be able to restore it to its original condition.

Use: Crispy meat chips, crumble as a salad topping, rehydrate for tortilla wraps, and even add to egg scrambles.

Beef

Ground

Serving: 3 ounces

Timing: 25-35 hours

Tip: Adding breadcrumbs post rinse can help rehydration.

These apply to other red meats, such as: Bison, Elk, Goat, Lamb, and Venison

Raw: 97% lean only. Spread out onto trays. Section with dividers if desired. Pre-freeze. Freeze-Dry.

Fry: Cook until browned and remove excess fat. Cover with water or beef stock and refrigerate overnight. Remove the fat cap the next morning. Drain any liquids. Pre-freeze. Freeze-Dry.

Boil: Simmer ground beef in a pot of boiling water until fully cooked. Refrigerate overnight. Remove the fat cap the next morning, drain liquid, pat dry, and place on trays. Pre-freeze. Freeze-Dry.

Rehydrate: Soak in water until fully rehydrated. Use excess water as a broth.

Use: add to soups, stews, stir-fries, tacos, or casseroles.

Filets

Serving: 3 ounces

Timing: 30-40 hours

Tip: If you want it to stay rare, use cool water to rehydrate.

Raw: Cut off visible fat. Fill trays. Pre-freeze. Freeze-Dry.

Prep: Cook until desired doneness. Cover with 1 in of water. Refrigerate overnight. Remove the fat cap the next morning, drain liquid, pat dry, and place on trays. Pre-freeze. Freeze-Dry.

Rehydrate: Soak RAW meat in cold water in the fridge over night. For Cooked, use very hot water and soak for 15-20 min.

Use: Rehydrate and grill this up for a gourmet freeze-dried meal.

Meatballs

Serving: 3 ounces

Timing: 25-35 hours

Tip: Mix with breadcrumbs or it may not rehydrate properly.

Pre-cooked frozen: Quarter, then place a layer of paper towel to absorb the grease. Pre-freeze. Freeze-Dry.

Bake: Make your meatballs on the smaller side. Rinse them well after cooking. Place a paper towel under. Pre-freeze. Freeze-Dry.

Rehydrate: Soak in water for 30-60 minutes, or throw them dried into sauces and soups.

Use: Toss into soups or sauces, or rehydrate and heat.

Patties

Serving: 3 oz patty

Timing: 25-35 hours

Tip: Use a bit of Worcestershire sauce when rehydrating.

Raw: Form lean beef into patties. place on the trays. Pre-freeze. Freeze-Dry.

Prep: Cook, drain off the water, and rinse the patties in hot water. Pat dry with paper towels and then season, if desired. Place a layer of paper towel on the trays to absorb the grease. Pre-freeze. Freeze-Dry.

Rehydrate: Thoroughly soak them so that the middle gets some water. Let it sit for 5 minutes. Microwave for 20-30 seconds each or heat in a pan for 1–2 minutes. If raw, use cool water. Worcestershire sauce is optional. replace with all water or broth.

Use: Rehydrate for tasty burgers.

Roast

Serving: 3 ounces

Timing: 25-35 hours

Tip: Trim excess fat before cooking or freeze-drying.

Prep: Cook and remove excess fat. Thinly slice or shred, removing any additional fat. Cover with water or beef stock and refrigerate overnight. Remove the fat cap the next morning. Drain any liquids and pat dry. Place a layer of paper towel on the trays to absorb the grease. spread meat. Pre-freeze. Freeze-Dry.

Slow Cook: Cover and cook on high until the roast shreds easily with a fork. Allow it to cook for 5-6 hours. Cover with water or broth. Place in the fridge overnight. Remove the fat cap in the morning. Drain liquid. Pre-freeze. Freeze-Dry.

Pressure Cook: Add 1 cup of water. Cook on medium/high for 70 minutes. Cover with water or broth. Place in the fridge overnight. Remove the fat cap in the morning. Drain liquid. Pre-freeze. Freeze-Dry.

Rehydrate: Add 1 cup powder to 1/2 cup of water. Let it sit for five minutes.

Use: Throw into soups, casseroles, enchiladas, tacos, or stews.

Steak

Serving: 3 ounces

Timing: 25-35 hours

Tip: Sear bite-sized chunks in garlic butter for a treat.

Raw: Cut off visible fat. Pre-freeze. Freeze-Dry.

Grill: Grill at 425°F for 2 minutes on each side, then rinse off with hot water. Season as desired. Pre-freeze. Freeze-Dry.

Rehydrate: Soak RAW meat in cold water in the fridge over night. For Cooked, use very hot water and soak for 15-20 min.

Use: Rehydrate and grill this steak up for a hearty meal.

Stew Meat

Serving: 3 ounces

Timing: 25-35 hours

Tip: Add diced veggies and herbs to create a delicious stew.

Leftovers: Use leftover chicken or steak, cut it into small portions, and season as desired. Pre-freeze. Freeze-Dry.

Fresh: Slice or dice into smaller pieces. Remove excess fat. Fry or boil. Drain. Season as desired. Pre-freeze. Freeze-Dry.

Rehydrate: Use very hot water and soak. It can take 12-24 hours to fully rehydrate.

Use: Toss into chili, soup, and stew or make a scrumptious gravy.

Pork

Bacon

Serving: 3 ounces

Timing: 25-35 hours

Tip: High fat items like bacon only last 6-12 months.

These apply to other meats, such as: Boar and Javelina

Bake: Bake in the oven on a grate with a pan below to catch the grease. Remove and cover with paper towels. Allow the bacon to cool. Place a layer of paper towel on the trays to absorb the grease. Pre-freeze. Freeze-Dry.

Fry: Fry in a pan. Put it on a paper towel to drain. Place on new paper towels to remove any remaining grease. Let cool. Place a layer of paper towel on the trays to absorb the grease. Pre-freeze. Freeze-Dry.

Rehydrate: We don't recommend rehydrating bacon.

Use: Add to soups, casseroles, mac and cheese, or on salads. Add to sandwiches dry.

Ham

Serving: 3 ounces

Timing: 25-35 hours

Tip: Ham is one of the best pork items to freeze-dry.

Prep: Pre-freeze. Freeze-Dry.

Fry: Fry in a pan. Put it on a paper towel to drain. Place on new paper towels to remove any remaining grease. Allow to cool. Pre-freeze. Freeze-Dry.

Rehydrate: Use very hot water and soak. It can take 12-24 hours to fully rehydrate.

Use: Perfect for cold salads, eggs or quick soups.

Roast

Serving: 3 ounces

Timing: 25-35 hours

Tip: Roast decreases in weight by 50% when cooked.

Prep: Trim excess fat. Season as desired.

Slow Cook: Cover and cook on high for 5-6 hours until the roast shreds easily with a fork. Cover with water or broth. Place int the fridge overnight. Remove the fat cap in the morning. Drain liquid. Pre-freeze. Freeze-Dry.

Pressure Cook: Place pork into a pressure cooker with a cup of water. Cook on medium/high for 70 minutes. Cover with water or broth. Place int the fridge overnight. Remove the fat cap in the morning. Drain liquid. Pre-freeze. Freeze-Dry.

Rehydrate: Add 1/2 c hot water to 1 c pork. Stir and let it sit covered for 15-20 min.

Use: Throw into soups, casseroles, enchiladas, tacos, or stews.

Poultry

These also apply to Rabbit, Duck, Goose, Pheasant, and Quail

Ground

Serving: 3-4 ounces

Timing: 25-35 hours

Tip: A great substitute to beef.

Raw: 97% lean only. Spread out onto trays. Section with dividers if desired. Pre-freeze. Freeze-Dry.

Fry: Brown the ground turkey and remove as much fat as you can. Cover in water or stock, and refrigerate overnight. Remove any fat cap in the morning. Drain liquid. Pat dry and load trays. Pre-freeze. Freeze-Dry.

Boil: Place ground turkey in a pot. Cover with water. Boil until done and drain. Then cover it with 1-2 inches of water and refrigerate overnight. Remove the fat cap in the morning. Pat dry and place on trays. Pre-freeze. Freeze-Dry.

Rehydrate: Soak in water until fully rehydrated. Use excess water as a broth.

Use: Toss into tacos, casseroles, and soups.

Roasted

Serving: 3 ounces

Timing: 25-35 hours

Tip: A deboned chicken weighs about 2 1/2 lbs.

Bake: Bake chicken in the oven until 165°F internal temperature. Trim fat and let it cool. Chop or leave it whole. Pre-freeze. Freeze-Dry.

Grill: Grill chicken on the stove or grill until 165°F internal temperature. Trim fat and let it cool. Lay out 6-12 breasts per tray. Pre-freeze. Freeze-Dry.

Rehydrate: Add 1/2 c hot water or broth to 1/2 c chicken. Cover let sit 10-20 minutes.

Use: Toss into soup, stew, tacos, and stir-fries.
Use the bones to make bone broth.

Turkey Bacon

Serving: 3 ounces

Timing: 25-35 hours

Tip: Ensure it is fully cooked for best results.

Bake: Preheat oven to 400°F. Line baking sheet with foil and place wire rack on top. Arrange on the rack in a single layer. Bake for 10 minutes, flip and cook for 5-10 more. Remove, dab with paper towels. Once clean, pre-freeze. Freeze-Dry.

Fry: Fry in a pan. Put it on a paper towel to drain. Place on new paper towels to remove any remaining grease. Allow to cool. Pre-freeze. Freeze-Dry.

Rehydrate: We don't recommend rehydrating bacon.

Use: Throw into soups, casseroles, mac and cheese, potatoes, or on salads.

Seafood

These apply to many kinds of Fish and Shellfish

White Fish

Serving: 3-4 ounces

Timing: 25-35 hours

Tip: White fish becomes super flaky when dry.

Prep: Select quality white fish, such as: Tilapia, Catfish, Perch, Bass, or Snapper.
Raw: Cut to max 3/4" thickness. Place on trays. Pre-freeze. Freeze-Dry.
Sauté: Preheat pan to medium/high heat. 10 minutes per 1 inch of fish. Add water instead of oil. Allow it to cool. Pre-freeze. Freeze-Dry.
Rehydrate: Use cold water and place it in the refrigerator to rehydrate. This will keep the fish from becoming rubbery.
Use: Raw fish can be used normally. Cooked fish can be added to casseroles, tacos, and soups.

Oily fish

Serving: 3-4 ounces

Timing: 25-35 hours

Tip: Make sure to not over-cook your fish.

Prep: Select quality, firm, oily fish, such as: Salmon, Tuna, Trout, or Swordfish.
Raw: Cut to max 3/4" thickness. Place on trays. Pre-freeze. Freeze-Dry.
Bake: Preheat oven, bake for a few minutes until done, 10 minutes per 1 inch of fish. Allow it to cool. Pre-freeze. Freeze-Dry.
Rehydrate: Soak fish in cold water and place it in the refrigerator overnight. This will keep the fish from becoming rubbery.
Use: Raw fish can be cooked like normal. Cooked fish can be added to casseroles, tacos, and soups.

Shellfish

Serving: 3-4 ounces

Timing: 25-35 hours

Tip: Keep fresh shellfish chilled to avoid bacteria.

Prep: Select quality shellfish, such as: Clams, Crab, Lobster, Mussels, Octopus, Oysters, Scallops, and Shrimp.
Boil: Place Shellfish in large pot and boil 2-5 minutes. Cool. Remove shells. Pre-freeze. Freeze-dry.
Rehydrate: Soak shellfish in cold water and place it in the refrigerator overnight. This will keep the shellfish from becoming rubbery.
Use: Raw Shellfish can be cooked like normal. Cooked shellfish can be added to soups, stirfries, and salads.

Dairy

Cottage Cheese

Serving: 3 Tbs

Timing: 20-30 hours

Tip: Ricotta is similar in method.

Prep: Measure the weight for the tray. Line the tray with a silicone mat and spread. Pre-freeze. Freeze-Dry.

Rehydrate: Add 1/2 cup powder to 1/4 cup of water. Add water slowly. Stir and let it sit for a few minutes before gently stirring again. Best to let it sit overnight in the refrigerator.

Use: dips, spreads, sauces. Tasty as a crunchy salad topping too.

Cream Cheese

Serving: 2 Tbs

Timing: 20-30 hours

Tip: If grainy, use an immersion blender or hand mixer on it.

Prep: Cut into slices about 1/2 inch thick. Measure the weight for the tray. Line the tray with a silicone mat. Pre-freeze. Freeze-Dry.

Rehydrate: 3 parts cream cheese to 1 part water, cover it and place in the refrigerator for 2-3 hours. You can use it right away if needed.

Use: As you normally would. Top bagels, make frosting, and cheesecake.

Hard Cheeses

Serving: 1.5 ounces

Timing: 20-30 hours

Tip: Place paper towels under cheeses to soak up oils.

Prep: Select a hard cheese, such as: cheddar, mozzarella, Swiss, or Parmesan.

Shredded: Shred cheese on a grater or food processor. Lay a paper towel onto your trays. Spread cheese to desired weight. Pre-freeze. Freeze-Dry.

Sliced or Cubed: Cut or slice to desired thickness between 1/4 in and 3/4 in. Lay a paper towel onto your trays. Spread cheese to desired weight. Pre-freeze. Freeze-Dry.

Rehydrate: Spritz shreds with water and flip. Soak slices and cubes in water and drain off the excess.

Use: Rehydrate to melt in dishes like pastas or casseroles.

Heavy Cream

Serving: 1/2 cup

Timing: 25-35 hours

Tip: Allow time to rehydrate and whisk well before using.

Prep: Place empty trays in the freezer first. Make sure they are level. Pour in the heavy cream. Put the lid on. Pre-freeze. Freeze-Dry.

Rehydrate: 1 part heavy cream to 3 parts water. Add water gradually while whisking until desired consistency.

Use: A rich and creamy addition to sauces, soups, stews, desserts, and baked goods.

Ice Cream

Serving: 1/2 cup

Timing: 20-30 hours

Tip: Give ice cream some space on the trays to expand.

Prep: Make sure the ice cream has been in the freezer for at least 12 hours. Cut or use a melon baller to get your ice cream in small bite sizes. Put the ice cream pieces on the trays and back into the freezer quickly. Let those freeze for at least 12 hours.

Freeze-dry: Turn on & start your freeze-dryer. Close drain valve & start the cycle, ignoring the prompt to load food. Wait until the temperature is close to 0°F before putting your trays into the freeze dryer to keep the ice cream from melting on the trays.

Rehydrate: Not recommended.

Use: Perfect snack, holiday gift, or midnight treat.

Milk

Serving: 8 ounce (1 cup)

Timing: 25-35 hours

Tip: 1 ounce of dried milk is an 8 ounce serving.

Prep: Place empty trays in the freezer first. Make sure they are level. Pour in the measured amount of milk. (Small: 3 cups, Medium: 4 cups, Large: 5.5 cups, X-Large: 10 cups.) Put the lid on. Pre-freeze. Freeze-Dry.

Rehydrate: Add 1/3 cup milk powder to 1 cup of water.

Use: Milk can be added dry to recipes or rehydrated to drink. We have found freeze-dried milk to taste normal, like fresh milk (not like dehydrated milk.)

Sour Cream

Serving: 2 Tbs

Timing: 20-30 hours

Tip: It is light and fluffy when dry.

Prep: Measure the weight for the tray. Line the tray with a silicone mat and spread. Pre-freeze. Freeze-Dry.

Rehydrate: Add room temperature water and use an immersion blender until well whipped. Best to sit overnight in the fridge, but it can be blended and used immediately.

Reconstitute: Add 1/2 cup powder to 1/4 cup of water. Add more until desired consistency.

Use: Stir in a tablespoon to add creaminess and tanginess to soups and stews. Use In dips, dressings, sauces, and toppings.

Whipped Cream

Serving: 2 Tbs

Timing: 15-25 hours

Tip: These can be close together, as they do not swell.

Prep: Pipe onto lined trays in small dollops.

Rehydrate: Not recommended.

Use: Delectable treat as is or drop a few into hot cocoa or coffee.

Yogurt

Serving: 1 cup

Timing: 22-32 hours

Tip: Always Pre-freeze to avoid spills in your freeze-dryer.

Prep: Measure the weight for the tray. Line the tray with a silicone mat. Place the trays in the freezer, before pouring in your yogurt. Pre-freeze. Freeze-Dry.

Rehydrate: Add room temperature water and use an immersion blender until well whipped.

Reconstitute: Add 1/2 cup powdered yogurt to 1/4 cup of water. Add more to reach the desired consistency. Chill for 30 minutes before serving.

Use: Great for smoothies! Add to your trail mix, oatmeal, or cereal. Crumble into a powder to add some extra flavor to your favorite dessert frostings.

Eggs

Serving: 1 egg or 2 egg whites

Timing: 25-35 hours

Tip: Pre-cooked scrambled eggs are not recommended. They become rubbery.

Raw: Crack eggs into a blender. Blend thoroughly. Put the empty tray in the freezer, making sure it's level. Then pour the eggs onto the tray. (Small: 3 cups, Medium: 4 cups, Large: 5.5 cups, X-Large: 10 cups.) Cover with the lid and add your next trays. Pre-freeze. Freeze-Dry.

Cooked Scrambles: Scramble slightly undercooked. Let cool. Place on the trays. Pre-freeze. Freeze-Dry.

Skillets & Casseroles: Cook as desired. Let cool. Place desired weight amount on the trays. Pre-freeze. Freeze-Dry.

Rehydrate: 1 Tbs eggs: 2 Tbs water. Whip well. Let sit for 5 min. Makes 1 Large egg.

Use: Make scrambled eggs or omelets. Use in baking to replace fresh eggs. Eat cooked ones out of the bag or rehydrate for a quick on the go or camping meal.

Grains

Breads

Serving: 1 ounce or 28 grams

Timing: 15-25 hours

Tip: Slice very thin to make crackers.

Prep: Cut the bread into thin, evenly-sized pieces. Lay onto the trays. Pre-freeze. Freeze-Dry.

Rehydrate: Dip into cool water for 10 seconds. Place on a hot frying pan for a few minutes.

Use: Cube and season to make croutons for salads or easily crush for breadcrumbs.

Cake

Serving: 3 square inches

Timing: 15-25 hours

Tip: Can become fragile or crumbly after rehydrating.

Prep: Cut the cake into thin, evenly-sized pieces. Lay onto the trays. Pre-freeze. Freeze-Dry.

Rehydrate: Dip into cool water for 10 seconds. Place on a hot frying pan for a few minutes.

Use: Tasty biscotti-like cracker. Perfect with milk, coffee, tea, or hot cocoa.

Pasta

Serving: 1 cup (140g) of cooked pasta

Timing: 25-45 hours (sauces vary)

Tip: Most pasta lasts 2-5 years if stored properly.

Prep: Bring a large pot of water to a boil. Add the pasta to the boiling water and stir occasionally to prevent sticking. Cook the pasta until al dente. Cooking time will vary depending on the type of pasta, but most pasta takes about 8 to 12 minutes to cook. Drain the pasta. Let cool. Mix with sauce if desired. Pre-freeze. Freeze-Dry.

Rehydrate: Slowly pour 1 cup boiling water into 1 cup pasta. Let it soak for 5-10 minutes.
Use: Add to soups, baked dishes, or add a sauce.

Oats

Serving: 1 cup

Timing: 25-35 hours

Tip: These come out so light and airy.

Prep: Cook Oats of choice as desired. Stir in any toppings or sweetener. Let cool. Pre-freeze. Freeze-Dry.

Rehydrate: Works with cold or hot water almost instantly. Add 1 cup oats to 2/3 cup of water. Stir and let it sit for 1-3 minutes.

Use: Rehydrate for a quick breakfast. Also a favorite as dry bites with milk. We like steel cut oats made with almond milk and diced apples.

Quinoa

Serving: 1 cup

Timing: 25-35 hours

Tip: Has a tasty cereal "crunch" to it.

Prep: Combine quinoa and water. Bring to a boil and simmer for fifteen minutes. Let cool. Pre-freeze. Freeze-Dry.

Rehydrate: Slowly pour 1 cup boiling water into 1 cup quinoa. Let it soak for 5-10 minutes.

Use: Toss it straight into soups as a great protein-filled thickener. Powder to make a flour substitute.

Rice

Serving: 1 cup

Timing: 25-35 hours

Tip: White rice will store for 25 years without freeze-drying.

Prep: Combine rice and water. Bring to a boil. Simmer for 15 minutes with the lid on. Let cool. Pre-freeze. Freeze-Dry.

Rehydrate: 1 cup water to 1 cup rice. Boil water. Add rice, stir, then remove from heat and cover. Wait 2-5 minutes, or until the water has been absorbed, and then fluff with a fork.

Use: freeze-dried form on top of soups like a homemade sizzling rice. Use with stir-fries, sauces, or gravies. The only reason to freeze-dry it is if it is in something you want the ease of just adding water, or if you enjoy it freeze-dried.

Legumes

Beans, dry

Serving: 1/2 cup

Timing: 25-35 hours

Tip: These rehydrate so quickly.

Prep: Sort and wash the beans. Soak overnight. Drain.
Boil: Cover with fresh water. Simmer until tender. Drain. Pre-freeze. Freeze-Dry.

Canned: Rinse. Pat Dry. Pre-freeze. Freeze-Dry.

Rehydrate: 1 cup beans to 1/2 cup water let sit 1-3 min.

Use: Soups and stews, veggie burgers and meat substitutes, rice and grain bowls.

Chickpeas

Serving: 1 cup

Timing: 25-35 hours

Tip: This is the fastest way to make homemade hummus.

Prep: Rinse and sort. Soak for 8 hours or overnight. Drain and transfer to a saucepan. Add enough fresh water to cover 1-2 inches. Simmer until tender, typically 1 to 2 hours. Drain. Let cool. Season if desired. Pre-freeze. Freeze-Dry.

Canned: Drain can. Rinse. Pre-freeze. Freeze-Dry.

Rehydrate: 1 cup chickpeas to 1/2 cup water let sit 1-3 min.

Use: For snacks and to top salad and soups, like a nutritious crouton. Or powder for quick thickener for soups and stews. Even tasty crushed as a casserole topper.

Lentils

Serving: 1 cup

Timing: 25-35 hours

Tip: Makes a speedy meal in a pinch.

Cook: Combine lentils and water in a medium saucepan and bring to a boil. Cover, decrease heat, and simmer for 15 to 20 minutes, stirring periodically, or until soft. Drain excess water and allow to cool. Pre-freeze. Freeze-Dry.

Canned: Drain can. Rinse. Pre-freeze. Freeze-Dry.

Rehydrate: 1 cup lentils to 1/2 cup water let sit 1-3 min.

Use: Soups and stews, curries and Indian-style dishes, veggie burgers and meat substitutes, rice and grain bowls, pasta dishes, dip or spread (such as lentil hummus).

Soybeans

Serving: 3.5 ounces

Timing: 25-35 hours

Tip: They're very crunchy and taste great seasoned.

Prep: Shell beans.
Raw: Fill trays. Pre-freeze. Freeze-Dry.

Roasted: Preheat oven to 350°F. Spread in a single layer on a baking sheet. Roast for 15-20 minutes, until golden brown and crunchy. Let cool. Fill trays. Pre-freeze. Freeze-Dry.

Rehydrate: 1 cup soybeans to 1/2 cup water let sit 1-3 min.

Use: Yummy crunchy snack.

Sprouts

Serving: 1 cup

Timing: 25-35 hours

Tip: Lower temp to 95°F to preserve nutrients.

Prep: Rinse.

Raw: Place on trays as is or blend with a small amount of water and blend. Pre-freeze. Freeze-Dry.

Rehydrate: We don't recommend rehydrating sprouts.

Use: Toss into soups and sandwiches dry. Use the powder to sneak nutrition in anywhere you can or even encapsulate them.

APPENDIX TWO: 40 EASY RECIPES

The following recipes work well in a freeze-dryer and are fairly simple. Individual experiences will vary. Please use common sense and follow cleanliness and safety practices. All freeze-dry times, shelf life years, and rehydration information are estimates and will depend on your ingredients, environment, packaging, and methods. Recipe categories include:

RECIPES

Cinnamon Applesauce

*This spiced Applesauce is sure to delight the senses.
Serve it as a tasty and nutritious snack or mouthwatering dessert.*

Cups: 9	**Servings:** 18	**Serving Size:** ½ cup	**Calories:** 149
Prep/Cook Time: 45 min	**Freeze-Dry Time:** 25-35 hrs	**Shelf-Life:** 20-25 yrs	

Ingredients:

18	ea	Apples, peeled, cored, chopped, 6lbs
3	cups	Water
1	cup	Sugar
2	Tbs	Lemon Juice
1	Tbs	Cinnamon, ground
1	tsp	Nutmeg, ground
1	tsp	Ginger, ground

Directions:

Peel, core, and chop the apples into ½" pieces (or ¼" slices.)

Place apples in a large saucepan and stir in the other ingredients.

Cover and cook over medium heat, stirring occasionally, for 20-25 minutes or until apples are tender.

Cool. Then puree in a blender or mash until the consistency is as you like.

Spread evenly onto trays, watching the weight limits for your size tray, and pre-freeze.

Freeze-dry the Cinnamon Applesauce on normal settings for 25-35 hours. Do a weight check and run Extra Dry Time until the weight doesn't change.

Seal in 7-mil mylar or a canning jar with an oxygen absorber and store in a cool, dry location.

Rehydration:

1	cup	FD Applesauce
¾	cup	Water

To rehydrate, add ¾ c water to 1 cup freeze-dried applesauce. Add more or less as needed.

Tips:

You can also use home-canned or applesauce from the store.

Try adding freeze-dried powders, such as strawberry and blueberry, instead of spices for more delicious options.

Fruit Crisps

A sweet and healthy treat for any time of the day.
Add a variety of options to make different flavors.

Pieces: 432	**Servings:** 18	**Serving Size:** 24 crisps	**Calories:** 103
Prep/Cook Time: 30 min	**Freeze-Dry Time:** 30-40 hrs	**Shelf-Life:** 20-25 yrs

Ingredients:

9	ea	Apples, peeled, cored, sliced, 3lbs
9	ea	Pears, peeled, cored, sliced, 3lbs
		Lemon Juice
		Water

Variations:
Sprinkle with Cinnamon & Sugar
Drizzle with Caramel Sauce
Sprinkle with Brown Sugar & Oats
Sprinkle with freeze-dried Fruit Powders
Experiment with spices like Ginger, Clove, & Nutmeg

Directions:

Cut fruits in half, core them, and then cut into ¼"
slices. Dip fruit slices into a solution of 1 Tbs
lemon juice and 1 cup of water to avoid browning.
Lay the sliced fruit out on the trays, watching the
weight limits for your size tray, and season, if
desired.
If seasoning, spritz the fruit with water and
sprinkle with the seasoning. Pre-freeze.
Freeze-dry the Fruit Crisps on normal settings for
30-40 hours. Do a weight check and run Extra Dry
Time until the weight doesn't change.
Seal in 7-mil mylar or a canning jar with an oxygen
absorber and store in a cool, dry location.

Rehydration:

The Fruit Crips are best as a
crunchy snack so we do not
recommend rehydrating them,
unless they'll be used in a dessert
(use 1:1.)

Tips:

You can try a variety of fruits,
including peaches, plums,
starfruit, and mango.

Fruit Pudding

This fruit pudding is the ideal way to finish off a delicious meal.
It's a favorite treat for birthday parties!

Cups: 16	**Servings:** 21	**Serving Size:** ¾ cup	**Calories:** 133
Prep/Cook Time: 20 min	**Freeze-Dry Time:** 45-55 hrs		**Shelf-Life:** 5-10 yrs

---

Ingredients:

2	cans	Crushed Pineapple, 20 oz
1	lb	Grapes, thinly sliced or diced
4	ea	Bananas, sliced
2	ea	Green Apples, cored & diced
1	can	Sliced Peaches, drained, 15 oz
2	pkg	Vanilla Pudding, 3.4 oz
3	cups	Milk

Directions:

Pour the juice of one of the pineapple cans into a large mixing bowl. Pour in the milk and stir the pudding mix into the bowl.

Discard the remaining juices. To the pudding mixture, add all of the cut-up fruit and gently mix everything together.

Pour onto the freeze-drying trays, watching the weight limits for your size tray, and pre-freeze. Freeze-dry the Fruit Pudding on normal settings for 45-55 hours. Do a weight check and run Extra Dry Time until the weight doesn't change.

Seal in 7-mil mylar or a canning jar with an oxygen absorber and store in a cool, dry location.

Rehydration:

1	cup	FD Fruit Pudding
½	cup	Water

To each cup of freeze-dried Fruit Pudding add ½ cup of water and stir. Allow it to sit in the fridge for 15 min.

This is a fabulous crunchy snack.

Tips:

Strawberries & mandarin oranges also go well in this pudding. The freeze-drying time increases when adding citrus or berries with seeds.

Mixed Fruit Salad

Such an easy and fresh-tasting fruit salad that is perfect for any time of the year.
Eat it plain or add the tangy sauce to add some zip.

Cups: 20	**Servings:** 20	**Serving Size:** 1 cup	**Calories:** 131
Prep/Cook Time: 20 min	**Freeze-Dry Time:** 40-50 hrs	**Shelf-Life:** 20-25 yrs	

Ingredients:

2½	cups	Pineapple, peeled, cored, cubed (1 large)
4½	cups	Strawberries, hulled, sliced (2 lbs)
5	cups	Mandarin Oranges, peeled, segmented (6 med)
5	cups	Mangoes, peeled, diced (4 med)
4	cups	Golden Kiwi, peeled, sliced (8 med)
4	cups	Blueberries (1½ lbs)
4	cups	Grapes (2 lbs)

To serve fresh, add ¾ tsp Lime Juice and ¾ tsp Honey to each cup of fresh Fruit Salad. Kiwi can sometimes become quite tart after it is freeze-dried. Substitute 4 cups of chopped Apples (3 med) for the kiwi to keep the recipe sweet.

Directions:

Wash, peel, and cut the fruits into bite-sized slices or chunks. Puncture or cut the grapes and blueberries. We like to cut them in half. Gently toss everything together. Spread the fruits out on the trays, watching the weight limits for your size tray, and pre-freeze. Freeze-dry the Fruit Salad on normal settings for 40-50 hours. (The pineapple may cause it to go longer.) Do a weight check and run Extra Dry Time until the weight doesn't change. Seal in 7-mil mylar or a canning jar with an oxygen absorber and store in a cool, dry location.

Rehydration:

1	cup	FD Fruit Salad
¾	cup	Water
¾	tsp	Lime Juice
¾	tsp	Honey

Stir a mixture of ¾ cup water, ¾ tsp Lime Juice, and ¾ tsp Honey into each cup of freeze-dried Fruit Salad. Add more or less to reach desired texture.

Tips:

Using silicone mats when freeze-drying fruits will help with cleanup.

Nilla Wafer Tarts

These little tarts are so tasty and so adorable at the same time!
They are perfect for a celebration or anytime you need a delightful treat.

Pieces: 80   **Servings:** 20   **Serving Size:** 4 tarts   **Calories:** 151

Prep/Cook Time: 3 hrs   **Freeze-Dry Time:** 30-40 hrs   **Shelf-Life:** 5-10 yrs

---

Ingredients:

1	box	Nilla Wafers, 11oz
1	cup	Strawberries, sliced
1	cup	Blueberries, pierced
Filling		
2	cups	Whole Milk
1	cup	Granulated Sugar
6	ea	Egg Yolks
¼	cup	Cornstarch
¼	tsp	Salt
1	tsp	Vanilla Extract

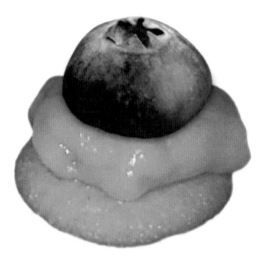

Directions:

Heat milk in a medium saucepan over medium heat, stirring constantly, for about 8 minutes. Whisk egg yolks and sugar together in a large bowl. Whisk in salt and cornstarch. Pour in half of the hot milk while stirring constantly.
Pour this mixture into the pot with the remaining hot milk and constantly whisk while cooking over medium heat for 5-8 minutes. Add the vanilla and pour the mixture into a bowl. Cover filling with plastic wrap and refrigerate for at least 2 hours.
Lay out the Nilla Wafers on the freeze-drying trays, flat side down.
Once filling is chilled, spoon it into an icing bag (or a zip-sealed bag with the tip cut off) and pipe a dollop directly onto the wafers (1/2 Tbs.) Add the pierced fresh fruit on top of the filling. Check the weight for your size tray, and pre-freeze.

Freeze-dry the Nilla Wafer Tarts on normal settings for 30-40 hours. Do a weight check and run Extra Dry Time until the weight doesn't change.
Seal in 7-mil mylar or a canning jar with an oxygen absorber and store in a cool, dry location.

Rehydration:

We do not recommend rehydrating the Nilla Wafer Tarts. They are best as a crunchy treat.

Tips: You can replace the filling with your choice of pudding!
Also makes 240 Mini Nilla Wafer Tarts with 1/2 tsp of filling per tart.

Cauliflower Bites

These Cauliflower Bites are a crunchy, delicious low-carb alternative to snacks like potato or tortilla chips.

Cups: 12	**Servings:** 12	**Serving Size:** 1 cup	**Calories:** 75
Prep/Cook Time: 25 min	**Freeze-Dry Time:** 28-38 hrs		**Shelf-Life:** 10-15 yrs

---

Ingredients:

6	lbs	Cauliflower (3 lrg heads)
¼	cup	Olive Oil
1	tsp	Salt
½	tsp	Black Pepper
¾	cup	Buffalo-style Hot Sauce

Alternate Flavor: Garlic Parmesan
  1 cup finely shredded Parmesan cheese
  ¾ cup Panko bread crumbs
  1½ teaspoon dried thyme, crushed
  4 cloves garlic, minced (1 tsp pwd)
Use this IN PLACE OF the hot sauce.

Directions:

Preheat oven to 400°F. Cut cauliflower into medium florets (abt 12 cups.)

In a large bowl, toss the cauliflower with oil to coat evenly and season with salt and pepper. Spread the cauliflower on a baking sheet and bake until just tender, about 15 minutes.

Remove the cauliflower from the oven and turn the oven onto broil, or 500°F.

Put the sauce and cauliflower in a large bowl and stir until fully coated.

Transfer back to the baking sheet and broil until cooked, or 5 minutes.

Lay out evenly onto trays, watching the weight limits for your size tray, and pre-freeze.

Freeze-dry the Cauliflower Bites on normal settings for 28-38 hours. Do a weight check and run Extra Dry Time until the weight doesn't change. Seal in 7-mil mylar or a canning jar with an oxygen absorber and store in a cool, dry location.

Rehydration:

We do not recommend rehydrating the cauliflower bites. They are best as a crunchy snack.

Tips:

These go really well with the Ranch Dip.

Guacamole

This is a simple and fresh-tasting guacamole dip.
It can be served smooth or chunky, depending on your tastes.

Cups:	6	**Servings:**	24	**Serving Size:**	¼ cup	**Calories:**	129
Prep/Cook Time:	25 min	**Freeze-Dry Time:**	25-35 hrs			**Shelf-Life:**	5-10 yrs

Ingredients:

8	ea	Avocados, pitted and scooped out
2	ea	Limes, juiced
2	tsp	Salt
4	ea	Tomatoes, seeded and diced
1	cup	Onion, diced (1 large)
½	cup	Cilantro, chopped
1	Tbs	Garlic, minced

Directions:

In a large bowl, mash avocados, lime juice, and salt together.

Stir in tomatoes, onion, cilantro, and garlic. Blend until it is the consistency you prefer. Spread evenly onto trays, watching the weight limits for your size tray, and pre-freeze. Freeze-dry the Guacamole on normal settings for 25-35 hours. Do a weight check and run Extra Dry Time until the weight doesn't change. Seal in 7-mil mylar or a canning jar with an oxygen absorber and store in a cool, dry location.

Rehydration:

1	cup	FD Guacamole
¾	cup	Water

To each cup of freeze-dried Guacamole, add ¾ cup of Water while stirring. Add more as needed.

Tips:

You can substitute Parsley for the Cilantro.

Removing all the tomato seeds will shorten your freeze-dry time.

Refried Beans

This savory bean dip complements many types of dishes,
including tacos, fajitas, and various chip dips.

Cups: 10	**Servings:** 20	**Serving Size:** ½ cup	**Calories:** 106
Prep/Cook Time: 2 hr 15 min	**Freeze-Dry Time:** 25-35 hrs		**Shelf-Life:** 20-25 yrs

Ingredients:

8	cans	Pinto Beans (15 oz cans)
2	Tbs	Onion Powder (2 med, chopped)
2	Tbs	Chili Powder
3	tsp	Salt
2	tsp	Garlic Powder (4 cloves, minced)
1	tsp	Cumin Powder
2	ea	Bay Leaf

Directions:

Mix all ingredients in a large pot, bring to a boil, and simmer for 30 minutes.
Remove bay leaves, mash to desired consistency, and cool.
Spread evenly onto trays, watching the weight limits for your size tray, and pre-freeze.
Freeze-dry the Refried Beans on normal settings for 25-35 hours. Do a weight check and run Extra Dry Time until the weight doesn't change. Seal in 7-mil mylar or a canning jar with an oxygen absorber and store in a cool, dry location.

Rehydration:

1	cup	FD Refried Beans
¾	cup	Hot Water

Rehydrate by adding ¾ cup of hot Water to each 1 cup serving of freeze-dried Refried Beans. Add more water as needed.

Tips:

4 cans Pinto beans can be replaced with 2 cups dry Pinto Beans cooked in 6 cups of Water.

Salsa

This delicious salsa can be made as a fresh salsa or as a flavorful roasted salsa. It rehydrates easily and can be a quick after-school snack.

Cups:	12	**Servings:**	24	**Serving Size:**	½ cup	**Calories:**	44
Prep/Cook Time:	40 min	**Freeze-Dry Time:**	30-40 hrs	**Shelf-Life:**	20-25 yrs		

Ingredients:

8	cups	Tomatoes, peeled, seeded, quartered (7lbs, 8 large)
2½	cups	Onions, cut in quarters (3 large)
1½	cups	Bell Pepper, seeded & cut in half (3 large)
½	cup	Jalapeno Pepper, seeded & cut in half (6 large)
¼	cup	Fresh Parsley or Cilantro, chopped
2	Tbs	Garlic, minced (12 large cloves)
2	Tbs	Salt
2	tsp	Cumin powder
2	tsp	Pepper, ground
2	cups	Tomato Sauce (32 oz)
2	cups	Tomato Paste (32 oz)

*To serve fresh, add 1 tsp Vinegar to each cup of freshly made salsa.

Directions:

Wash and prepare the vegetables.
For the most flavor, place tomatoes, onions, and peppers on a baking sheet and roast in a 400° oven for 20 minutes. Cool for 10 minutes and then process with the rest of the ingredients in a food processor.
For a fresh salsa taste, simply process all of the ingredients in a food processor.
Spread evenly on trays and pre-freeze.
Freeze-dry your batch of salsa on normal settings for 30-40 hours. Do a weight check and run Extra Dry Time until the weight doesn't change.
Seal in 7-mil mylar or a canning jar with an oxygen absorber and store in a cool, dry location.

Rehydration:

1	cup	FD Salsa
¾	cup	Water
1	tsp	Vinegar

Add a mixture of ¾ cup water and 1 tsp Vinegar to each cup of freeze-dried Salsa while stirring. Add more or less to reach desired consistency.

Tips:

Removing all the seeds will shorten your freeze-dry time.

Veggie Chips & Sticks

Veggie Chips & Sticks are delicious & easy to make out of fresh vegetables. Different spice blends add to the selection of flavors.

Pieces: 384	**Servings:** 16	**Serving Size:** 24 chips	**Calories:** 18
Prep/Cook Time: 15 min	**Freeze-Dry Time:** 25-35 hrs		**Shelf-Life:** 20-25 yrs

Ingredients:

4	med	Zucchini Squash, 6"
4	med	Yellow Squash, 6"

Seasoning Options:

BBQ Powder

1	cup	Paprika
½	cup	Fine Salt
½	cup	Granulated Sugar
½	cup	Chili Powder
½	cup	Ground Cumin
½	cup	Granulated Garlic
¼	cup	Mustard Powder
¼	cup	Black Pepper
¼	cup	Cayenne Pepper

Chili Powder

1	cup	Garlic Powder
1	cup	Ground Cumin
½	cup	Cayenne Pepper
½	cup	Dried Oregano
½	cup	Paprika

Ranch Powder

1	cup	Buttermilk Powder
¾	cup	Dried Parsley
¼	cup	Dried Chives
¼	cup	Dill Weed
¼	cup	Onion Powder
¼	cup	Garlic Powder
¼	cup	Onion Flakes
2	Tbs	Black Pepper
2	Tbs	Fine Salt

French Onion Powder

2	cup	Dried Minced Onion
1½	cup	Dried Chopped Chives
½	cup	Onion Powder
½	cup	Garlic Powder
4	tsp	Fine Salt

Directions:

Cut the veggies into ⅛" slices. For smaller pieces, further cut the slices into ½" sticks. Lay the sliced vegetables out on the trays, use parchment or silicone racks to stack a second layer, watching the weight limits for your size tray, and season, if desired.

If seasoning, spritz the veggies with water and sprinkle on the seasoning. Pre-freeze. Freeze-dry the Veggie Chips on normal settings for 25-35 hours. Do a weight check and run Extra Dry Time until the weight doesn't change.

Seal in 7-mil mylar or a canning jar with an oxygen absorber and store in a cool, dry location.

Rehydration:

We do not recommend rehydrating the Veggie Chips or Sticks, they are best as a dry, crunchy snack.

Tips: Combine with sliced cheese or meat. You can also try these seasonings with broccoli, carrots, green beans, corn, mushrooms, cucumbers, and potatoes.

Chicken Gravy

This is a savory and creamy gravy that rehydrates well.
It is versatile and can be used over rice, noodles, or potatoes.

Cups: 14   **Servings:** 14   **Serving Size:** 1 cup   **Calories:** 173

Prep/Cook Time: 35 min   **Freeze-Dry Time:** 25-35 hrs   **Shelf-Life:** 5-7 yrs

---

Ingredients:

2	qts	Chicken Broth
½	cup	Flour
2	Tbs	Onion Powder
4	tsp	Salt
1	tsp	Pepper
1	ea	Chicken, cooked & deboned (3 lbs)

Options

Add a pound of mushrooms, sauteed (or 8 oz can) into the gravy.

Add 2 tsp Garlic or Cumin to change the flavor.

Directions:

Whisk flour into cold chicken broth, bring to a boil, and simmer 5 minutes.

Add seasonings, chicken, and any extras into the gravy and simmer for 10 minutes.

Carefully scoop onto trays, watching the liquid & weight limits for your size tray, and pre-freeze.

Freeze-dry the Chicken Gravy on normal settings for 25-35 hours. Do a weight check and run Extra Dry Time until the weight doesn't change.

Seal in 7-mil mylar or a canning jar with an oxygen absorber and store in a cool, dry location.

Rehydration:

1	cup	FD Chicken Gravy
¾	cup	Hot Water

To each cup of freeze-dried Chicken Gravy add 1 cup of hot water for instant gravy. For a thicker gravy, add less water.

Tips:

You can make enough chicken and broth for this recipe from cooking and deboning one chicken.

Fajita Meat

This fajita meat is versatile and delicious! Substitute chicken for another flavor.
Add Pico De Gallo, sour cream, or guacamole fresh or rehydrated.

Cups:	24	Servings:	16	Serving Size:	1½ cups	Calories:	393
Prep/Cook Time:	50 min	Freeze-Dry Time:	25-35 hrs			Shelf-Life:	15-20 yrs

Ingredients:

8	lbs	Skirt or Flank Steak
8	lrg	Bell Peppers
4	med	Onions

Rub

4	Tbs	Salt
8	tsp	Brown Sugar
4	tsp	Chili Powder
4	tsp	Ground Cumin
4	tsp	Garlic Powder
4	tsp	Paprika
4	tsp	Black Pepper

Fresh Pico De Gallo (optional)

3	lrg	Roma Tomatoes, chopped
1	lrg	Avocado, chopped
1	med	Jalepeno, seeded, chopped
½	cup	Onion, chopped
¼	cup	Cilantro, chopped
2	Tbs	Lime Juice
½	tsp	Salt

Directions:

Stir together the Rub ingredients.
Generously apply the rub to both sides of the steak and allow it to sit for at least 30 minutes.
Slice up the bell peppers and onions and saute them in water for 5-8 minutes. Lightly season with salt and pepper.
Slice the steak into ½" thick pieces. Sear steak until browned (3+min) on both sides.
Mix the bell peppers, onions, and steak together. Spread evenly onto trays, watching the weight limits for your size tray, and pre-freeze.
Freeze-dry the Fajita Mix (and Pico De Gallo) on normal settings for 25-35 hours. Do a weight check and run Extra Dry Time until the weight doesn't change.
Seal in 7-mil mylar or a canning jar with an oxygen absorber and store in a cool, dry location.

Rehydration:

1	cup	FD Fajita Mix
½	cup	Hot Water
1	Tbs	Butter or Oil

To every cup of freeze-dried Fajita Mix add ½ cup of Hot Water and 1 Tbs of Butter and stir.

Tips:

Serve with Pico de Gallo. Try adding mushrooms to the onions and peppers mix.

Pulled Pork

This crock pot pulled pork recipe is the BEST you'll ever make!
With minimal effort, you can produce the most scrumptious pork imaginable.

Cups: 18	**Servings:** 18	**Serving Size:** 1 cup	**Calories:** 349
Prep/Cook Time: 7 hrs	**Freeze-Dry Time:** 20-30 hrs	**Shelf-Life:** 10-15 yrs

---

Ingredients:

12	lbs	Raw Pork Shoulder
2	cups	Water
4	Tbs	Apple Cider Vinegar
2	Tbs	Salt
2	Tbs	Onion Powder
2	tsp	Dried Oregano
2	tsp	Cumin, ground
2	tsp	Chili Powder
1	tsp	Garlic Powder
½	tsp	Pepper, ground

To serve fresh, top with BBQ Sauce and Dill Pickles

Directions:

Rinse and pat dry the raw pork shoulder.
Mix the Apple Cider Vinegar with all the spices and rub it all over the raw pork.
Add 2 c water to a roasting pan. Cover tightly with foil and roast at 300°F for 6+ hours, turning every hour.
Remove foil. Roast 20 min to crisp. Sit 15 min.
Drain off oil. Shred. Remove sections of fat. Rinse cooked pork in a colander with hot water to remove as much fat as possible.
Spread evenly onto trays, watching the weight limits for your size tray, and pre-freeze.
Freeze-dry the Pulled Pork on normal settings for 20-30 hours. Do a weight check and run Extra Dry Time until the weight doesn't change.
Seal in 7-mil mylar or a canning jar with an oxygen absorber and store in a cool, dry location.

Rehydration:

1	cup	FD Pulled Pork
¾	cup	Water
2	Tbs	BBQ Sauce

Add a mixture of ¾ cup water and 2 Tablespoons of BBQ sauce to each cup of freeze-dried Pulled Pork and allow to sit.

Tips:

Pork shoulder will reduce by about 50% during cooking, so a 12 lb raw roast will become 6 lbs of cooked pulled pork.

Taco Meat

This flavorful Taco Meat is a surefire way to give your tacos, burritos, and nachos a serious upgrade!

Cups: 8	**Servings:** 16	**Serving Size:** ½ cup	**Calories:** 289
Prep/Cook Time: 35 min	**Freeze-Dry Time:** 40-50 hrs		**Shelf-Life:** 5-10 yrs

Ingredients:

4	lbs	Ground Beef
2	cups	Breadcrumbs (or ground oats)
4	Tbs	Onion Powder (2 med)
4	tsp	Cumin Powder
4	tsp	Chili Powder
4	tsp	Salt
1	tsp	Garlic Powder (4 cloves)
1	tsp	Pepper, ground

Directions:

Fry ground beef. Drain off the oil. Rinse cooked beef in a colander with hot water to remove as much fat as possible.

Add the breadcrumbs, stir, and cook for 5 min. The ground beef can be freeze-dried unseasoned at this point, if desired.

Add seasonings and mix well.

Spread evenly onto trays, watching the weight limits for your size tray, and pre-freeze.

Freeze-dry the Taco Meat on normal settings for 40-50 hours. Do a weight check and run Extra Dry Time until the weight doesn't change.

Seal in 7-mil mylar or a canning jar with an oxygen absorber and store in a cool, dry location.

Rehydration:

1	cup	FD Taco Meat
⅔	cup	Hot Water
½	tsp	Butter or Oil

To every cup of freeze-dried Taco Meat add a mixture of ⅔ cup hot Water and ½ tsp of Butter or oil.

Tips:

You can use the same seasonings for Chicken or Fish Tacos too.

Tuna Melt

This Tuna Melt mixture makes stellar grilled Cheese Tuna sandwiches but can also be used as a dip or enjoyed with cottage cheese.

Cups: 8	**Servings:** 16	**Serving Size:** ½ cup	**Calories:** 169
Prep/Cook Time: 25 min	**Freeze-Dry Time:** 25-35 hrs	**Shelf-Life:** 10-15 yrs

---

Ingredients:

1	cup	Cream Cheese, 8 oz
½	cup	Lemon Juice (1½ med)
½	tsp	Salt
¼	tsp	Ground Pepper
6	cans	Tuna in water, 6 oz
2	cups	Shredded Cheddar Cheese, ½ lb
1	cup	Celery, finely chopped, 3 stalks
½	cup	Red Onion, finely chopped (1 sm)
½	cup	Dill Pickle Relish

*To make healthy, green "Monster Melts" add 6-12 Tbs Spinach Powder.

Directions:

In a large mixing bowl, combine cream cheese, lemon juice, salt, and pepper.

Drain the tuna, break into flakes, and stir it into the cream cheese mixture.

Add in the celery, pickles, and red onion. Stir well.

Spread the Tuna Melt mixture out on the trays, watching the weight limits for your size tray, and pre-freeze.

Freeze-dry the Tuna Melt mixture on normal settings for 25-35 hours. Do a weight check and run Extra Dry Time until the weight doesn't change.

Seal in 7-mil mylar or a canning jar with an oxygen absorber and store in a cool, dry location.

Rehydration:

½	cup	FD Tuna Melt
¼	cup	Water

To each ½ cup serving of freeze-dried Tuna Melt add ¼ cup of water and stir. Let it sit for 5 minutes. Spread onto bread and pan-fry with butter.

Tips: These can also be freeze-dried after grilling and cutting into sandwich bites.

Perfect for traveling. Mix with water and eat cold with crackers, bread, or veggies.

Beef Chili

Made with ground beef, beans, and a simple homemade combination of chili seasonings, this recipe is reminiscent of the chili mom cooks.

Cups: 12	**Servings:** 12	**Serving Size:** 1 cup	**Calories:** 184
Prep/Cook Time: 1 hr	**Freeze-Dry Time:** 35-45 hrs		**Shelf-Life:** 5-10 yrs

Ingredients:

2	lbs	90% Lean Gound Beef
2	med	Yellow Onions, diced
1	lrg	Bell Pepper, chopped
5	Tbs	Chili Powder
4	Tbs	Cumin, ground
2	Tbs	Garlic Powder
1	Tbs	Salt
1	tsp	Black Pepper, ground
½	tsp	Cayenne Pepper (opt)
3	cups	Beef Broth
4	cans	Petite Diced Tomatoes, 15 oz
4	cans	Red Kidney Beans, 16 oz, drained & rinsed

Directions:

Fully cook ground beef, breaking into small pieces. Drain off fat and rinse in hot water. Combine all ingredients, except kidney beans, together in a large pot and stir. Bring to a boil and simmer for 20 min.

Add kidney beans & simmer for 15 min. Cool. Scoop the chili onto the trays, watching the weight and liquid limits for your size tray, and pre-freeze.

Freeze-dry the Chili on normal settings for 35-45 hours. Do a weight check and run Extra Dry Time until the weight doesn't change.

Seal in 7-mil mylar or a canning jar with an oxygen absorber and store in a cool, dry location.

Rehydration:

½	cup	FD Chili
1	cup	Water

Add 1 cup of hot Water to each 1 cup serving of freeze-dried Chili and stir.

Tips:

Tasty as-is or serve with cheese, crackers, and sour cream.

Chicken Creole

*Chicken Creole is a savory dish that is delicious
served over rice or noodles.*

Cups: 15   **Servings:** 15   **Serving Size:** 1 cup   **Calories:** 246

Prep/Cook Time: 45 min   **Freeze-Dry Time:** 30-40 hrs   **Shelf-Life:** 10-15 yrs

---

Ingredients:

2	lbs	Ground Chicken
2	Tbs	Onion Powder
2	Tbs	Salt
1	Tbs	Chili Powder
1	tsp	Pepper, ground
1	cup	Green Pepper (1 lrg)
1	cup	Celery (2 stalks)
4	cups	Tomatoes (8 med)
4	cans	Northern Beans, 14.5 oz
1	cup	Water
4	Tbs	Flour

Directions:

Brown the ground chicken with the spices. Add the vegetables and beans and stir. Simmer 20 minutes.

Combine the water and flour and then add that to the creole and stir while it thickens. Simmer for 5 minutes. Cool.

Scoop the Chicken Creole onto the trays, watching the weight and liquid limits for your size tray, and pre-freeze.

Freeze-dry the Chicken Creole on normal settings for 30-40 hours. Do a weight check and run Extra Dry Time until the weight doesn't change.

Seal in 7-mil mylar or a canning jar with an oxygen absorber and store in a cool, dry location.

Rehydration:

1	cup	FD Chicken Creole
¾	cup	Hot Water

To each cup of freeze-dried Chicken Creole add ¾ cup of Hot Water and stir well. Let it sit 10 min, stir and add more water if needed.

Tips:

The creole can be mixed with 8 cups of pre-cooked rice and freeze-dried as a casserole.

Chicken & Rice Soup

This chicken and rice soup is a family favorite and can easily be changed up by substituting potatoes or noodles.

Cups:	20	**Servings:**	20	**Serving Size:** 1 cup	**Calories:** 247
Prep/Cook Time: 1 hr		**Freeze-Dry Time:** 20-30 hrs			**Shelf-Life:** 5-10 yrs

Ingredients:

2	qts	Chicken Broth
4	cups	Water
2	cups	White Rice
3	ea	Carrots, chopped (2 cups)
2	ea	Celery Stalk, chopped (2 cups)
1	lrg	Onion, chopped (1 cup)
2	clove	Garlic, minced (1 tsp)
2	tsp	Salt
2	tsp	Dried Parsley
½	tsp	Black Pepper, ground
¼	tsp	Dried Thyme
3	lbs	Cooked Chicken

Directions:

Place all ingredients, except the chicken, in a large pot and simmer for 30 minutes, stirring regularly.

Add chicken and cook 10 minutes. Cool.

Scoop the soup onto the trays, watching the weight and liquid limits for your size tray, and pre-freeze.

Freeze-dry the Chicken & Rice Soup on normal settings for 20-30 hours. Do a weight check and run Extra Dry Time until the weight doesn't change.

Seal in 7-mil mylar or a canning jar with an oxygen absorber and store in a cool, dry location.

Rehydration:

1	cup	FD Chicken Soup
1	cup	Hot Water

To each cup of freeze-dried Chicken & Rice Soup add 1 cup or more of Water and stir.

Tips:

Instead of Rice, try 4 chopped potatoes or 4 cups noodles.

You can make enough chicken and broth for this recipe from cooking and deboning one chicken.

Sausage Gumbo

*This sausage gumbo is sure to satisfy even a picky eater
with its combination of veggies, sausage, and rice.*

Cups: 20	**Servings:** 20	**Serving Size:** 1 cup	**Calories:** 267
Prep/Cook Time: 1 hr	**Freeze-Dry Time:** 30-40 hrs	**Shelf-Life:** 2-5 yrs

Ingredients:

2	lb	Sausage
6	Tbs	Flour
6	Tbs	Onion Powder
2	Tbs	Garlic Powder
4	tsp	Cajun Seasoning
8	cups	Chopped Tomatoes
2	qrt	Chicken Broth, 32 oz
2	cups	Minced Okra, 4-6 oz
2	cups	White Rice

Cajun Seasoning

5	Tbs	Salt
2	Tbs	Dried Oregano
2	Tbs	Paprika
2	Tbs	Ground Pepper
2	tsp	Cayenne Pepper

Directions:

Fry sausage, chopping in small pieces. Drain off oil and rinse sausage in hot water.

Return sausage to pan. Add spices and flour and cook for 5 min.

Add the rest of the ingredients and simmer for 30 minutes, constantly stirring.

Scoop the Sausage Gumbo onto the trays, watching the weight and liquid limits for your size tray, and pre-freeze.

Freeze-dry the Sausage Gumbo on normal settings for 30-40 hours. Do a weight check and run Extra Dry Time until the weight doesn't change.

Seal in 7-mil mylar or a canning jar with an oxygen absorber and store in a cool, dry location.

Rehydration:

1	cup	FD Sausage Gumbo
1	cup	Hot Water

To each cup of freeze-dried Sausage Gumbo, add a cup of hot water and stir. Allow it to sit for 10-15 minutes and then stir again.

Tips:

This is a thick gumbo, so be careful not to burn it. Add water if you want it to be a soup.

Split Pea & Ham Soup

This warm and creamy soup leaves you feeling full and cozy.
Perfect for a cold winter evening.

Cups: 24	**Servings:** 24	**Serving Size:** 1 cup	**Calories:** 130
Prep/Cook Time: 1 hr 20 min	**Freeze-Dry Time:** 28-38 hrs		**Shelf-Life:** 15-20 yrs

---

Ingredients:

¼	cup	Water
1	cup	Onion, diced (1 med)
2	cups	Celery, diced (4 ribs)
1	cup	Carrots, diced (3 med)
2	Tbs	Garlic, minced (6 cloves)
16	cups	Chicken Stock (64 oz)
4	cups	Ham, diced (1.5 lbs)
2	ea	Bay Leaves
4	cups	Dried Split Peas (2 lbs)
1	Tbs	Salt
1	tsp	Pepper

Directions:

Saute onion, celery, carrot, and garlic in a quarter cup of water, for 5 minutes.

Stir in chicken stock, ham, bay leaves, split peas and seasonings. Bring to a boil and lower heat to a simmer for 1 hour, stirring occasionally. Remove bay leaves. Spread evenly onto trays, watching the weight limits for your size tray, and pre-freeze.

Freeze-dry the Split Pea Soup on normal settings for 28-38 hours. Do a weight check and run Extra Dry Time until the weight doesn't change.

Seal in 7-mil mylar or a canning jar with an oxygen absorber and store in a cool, dry location.

Rehydration:

½	cup	FD Split Pea Soup
1	cup	Hot Water

Rehydrate this soup instantly by adding 1 cup of hot water to each ½ cup of freeze-dried Split Pea Soup.

Tips:

You can add nutritious freeze-dried powders, such as a Tablespoon of Spinach, into a soup like this.

Bagel Dippers

*These Bagel Dippers are a fun and easy breakfast
and can be a tasty snack any time of day.*

Strips: 192	**Servings:** 24	**Serving Size:** 8+2 Tbs CC	**Calories:** 272
Prep/Cook Time: 10 min	**Freeze-Dry Time:** 20-30 hrs		**Shelf-Life:** 10-15 yrs

Ingredients:

12	lrg	Bagels, cut into strips
3	pkg	Cream Cheese, 8 oz

Powdered Fruit Flavor Ideas:
> Strawberry
> Blueberry
> Peach

For flavored cream cheese:
Whip fruit powders into the cream
cheese before spreading it on a tray
and freeze-drying.

Directions:

Slice the bagels into 1/4" thin strips. A 4" bagel
makes 16 dipper strips.

Lay out the bagel strips on your trays, noting
weight, and pre-freeze.

Line a tray with a silicone mat. Cut the cream
cheese blocks into 1/2" thick pieces.

Lay the cream cheese slices out on the trays,
watching the weight limits for your size tray,
and pre-freeze.

Freeze-dry the Bagel strips and Cream Cheese
together on normal settings for 20-30 hours. Do
a weight check and run Extra Dry Time until the
weight doesn't change.

Seal in 7-mil mylar or a canning jar with an
oxygen absorber and store in a cool, dry
location.

Rehydration:

2	Tbs	FD Cream Cheese Pwd
1	Tbs	Water

Stir 1 Tbs cool water into 2 Tbs of
freeze-dried Cream Cheese powder.
Add more until desired consistency.
Cover and refrigerate 2 hours. Serve
dry strips with cream cheese. Or, to
rehydrate strips, place in water for 3
seconds and fry on a hot pan for 2-3
minutes.

Tips:

A serving is ½ a Bagel (8 strips) with 2
Tbs (1 oz) of Cream Cheese.

Add freeze-dried fruit powder to the
cream cheese for a bright color and
fruity flavor.

Breakfast Casserole

This tasty breakfast casserole is a holiday favorite.
With such hearty ingredients, it is sure to satisfy.

Pieces: 12	**Servings:** 12	**Serving Size:** 1 piece	**Calories:** 210
Prep/Cook Time: 1 hr	**Freeze-Dry Time:** 25-35 hrs		**Shelf-Life:** 5-10 yrs

Ingredients:

½	lb	Pork Sausage or Bacon
12	oz	Hashbrowns, frozen
15	ea	Eggs
1	cup	Milk
4	ea	Green Onions, sliced
1	lrg	Bell Pepper, diced
1	cup	Shredded Cheddar Cheese
1	cup	Spinach
2	tsp	Salt
½	tsp	Pepper

Other Nice Additions: Mushrooms, Tomatoes, Olives

Directions:

Preheat oven to 350°F. Grease a 9x13 pan.
Cook sausage over medium heat until browned.
Drain off oil and rinse sausage in hot water.
Saute onion and pepper for 5 minutes, adding water as needed.
Put the hashbrowns in the pan. Evenly spread the rinsed sausage over the hashbrowns. Lay the cooked veggies on top of the sausage.
In a large bowl, whisk the eggs and milk. Stir in cheese, spinach, salt and pepper. Carefully pour the egg mixture over the rest.
Place the casserole in the oven and bake for 45-50 minutes, or until the sides are firm.
Cool. Cut into 12 pieces, or desired size. We like to cut it into bite size pieces.
Lay out on the trays, watching the weight limits for your size tray, and pre-freeze.
Freeze-dry the Breakfast Casserole on normal settings for 25-35 hours. Do a weight check & run Extra Dry Time until weight doesn't change.

Seal in 7-mil mylar or a canning jar, if in pieces, with an oxygen absorber and store in a cool, dry location.

Rehydration:

1	cup	FD Breakfast Casserole
¾	cup	Hot Water

To each cup of freeze-dried Breakfast Casserole crumble add ¾ cup hot water and stir. Cover and let it sit for 10-15 minutes.
OR - Place the 12 pieces back in a casserole dish, add 9 cups of water, cover with foil, and heat in a 350°F oven for 30 min.

Tips: For a vegetarian option, replace the meat with mushrooms.

We have found this to be an awesome dry and crunchy trail snack.

French Toast

This yummy and simple recipe works well with white, whole wheat, brioche, cinnamon-raisin, Italian, and french bread.

Slices: 16	**Servings:** 16	**Serving Size:** 1 slice	**Calories:** 113
Prep/Cook Time: 10 min	**Freeze-Dry Time:** 20-30 hrs	**Shelf-Life:** 10-15 yrs

Ingredients:

16	oz	Sliced Bread, 16 slices
1½	cups	Milk
6	lrg	Eggs
2	tsp	Vanilla Extract
¼	tsp	Cinnamon
⅛	tsp	Salt

Directions:

In a shallow dish, mix together milk, eggs, vanilla, cinnamon, and salt.

Soak the bread slices in the egg mixture on both sides. If enjoying fresh, fry on a skillet, flipping half way.

Place the uncooked French Toast slices on the freeze-dryer trays, noting the weight, and pre-freeze.

Freeze-dry the French Toast on normal settings for 20-30 hours. Do a weight check and run Extra Dry Time until the weight doesn't change.

Seal in 7-mil mylar or a canning jar, if in sticks, with an oxygen absorber and store in a cool, dry location.

Rehydration:

To rehydrate, soak in a shallow dish of water on each side for 30-45 seconds and fry as usual.

Tips:

The French Toast is processed with RAW eggs, so keep things clean and mark the package clearly.

The French Toast can be fried before freeze-drying. The slices will rehydrate the same way.

Fruity Oatmeal

This is a hearty & comforting oatmeal that can be enhanced with apples, bananas, or berries. This is a hit with kids when made into bites and eaten dry with milk!

Cups: 16	**Servings:** 21	**Serving Size:** ¾ cup	**Calories:** 89
Prep/Cook Time: 35 min	**Freeze-Dry Time:** 25-35 hrs	**Shelf-Life:** 15-20 yrs

Ingredients:

14	cups	Water
4	cups	Steel Cut Oats
1	cup	Maple Syrup
1	tsp	Salt
5	cups	Fruit

Fruit Options:
Add 5 cups of diced apples (4 med) and 2 Tablespoons cinnamon, or add 5 cups of diced strawberries, sliced bananas, frozen berries, or a combination.
Our favorite is 2 apples, 1 banana, 1 cup sliced strawberries, and 1 cup blueberries.

Directions:

In a large saucepan bring the water to a boil over high heat. We like to substitute 4 cups of Almond milk. *See tip 2.

Stir in the oats, maple syrup, and salt and bring to a steady boil. Lower heat and gently simmer for 20 minutes, stirring regularly.

Stir in the fruit and spices and simmer for another 5-10 minutes.

Spread evenly on trays and pre-freeze.

Freeze-dry Fruity Oatmeal on normal settings for 25-35 hours. Do a weight check and run Extra Dry Time until the weight doesn't change.

Seal in 7-mil mylar or a canning jar with an oxygen absorber and store in a cool, dry location.

Rehydration:

1	cup	FD Fruity Oatmeal
1	cup	Water

Add 1 cup water to each cup of freeze-dried Fruity Oatmeal and stir. Enjoy instantly!

Tips:

Make sure any berries have been punctured prior to freeze-drying.

Substitute milk for a portion of the water (up to 6 cups) for a more creamy texture.

Scrambled Eggs

The BEST tasting freeze-dried scrambled eggs are processed raw.
After rehydrating, add meat, veggies, and cheese for an omelet.

Cups: 3,4,5,10 **Servings:** 12,18,24,48 **Serving Size:** 1 egg   **Calories:** 72
Prep/Cook Time: 10 min **Freeze-Dry Time:** 35-45 hrs   **Shelf-Life:** 20-25 yrs

---

Ingredients:

12	Eggs	Small Freeze-dryer Tray, 3 cups
18	Eggs	Medium Freeze-dryer Tray, 4 cups
24	Eggs	Large Freeze-dryer Tray, 5 cups
48	Eggs	X-Large Freeze-dryer Tray, 10 cups

Directions:

Crack the raw eggs into a blender or large bowl and blend thoroughly.

Put an empty tray in the freezer, making sure it sits level.

Pour the eggs onto the tray and cover with a lid. Repeat with any additional trays.

Pre-freeze for 24 hours.

Freeze-dry the raw eggs on normal settings for 35-45 hours. Do a weight check and run Extra Dry Time until the weight doesn't change.

Seal in 7-mil mylar or a canning jar with an oxygen absorber and store in a cool, dry location.

Rehydration:

2	Tbs	FD Egg Powder
2	Tbs	Water

For one large egg: Mix 2 tablespoons of FD Egg Powder and 2 tablespoons of water, stir, and allow to sit 5-10 minutes.

Tips:

To make a perfectly sized omelet use ¼ cup FD Egg Powder with ¼ cup Water.

Cheese Crisps

The cheese crisps are light and crunchy and make a wonderful snack.
Add different spices for a variety of flavors.

Pieces: 384	**Servings:** 32	**Serving Size:** 12 crisps		**Calories:** 105
Prep/Cook Time: 20 min	**Freeze-Dry Time:** 20-30 hrs			**Shelf-Life:** 10-15 yrs

Ingredients:

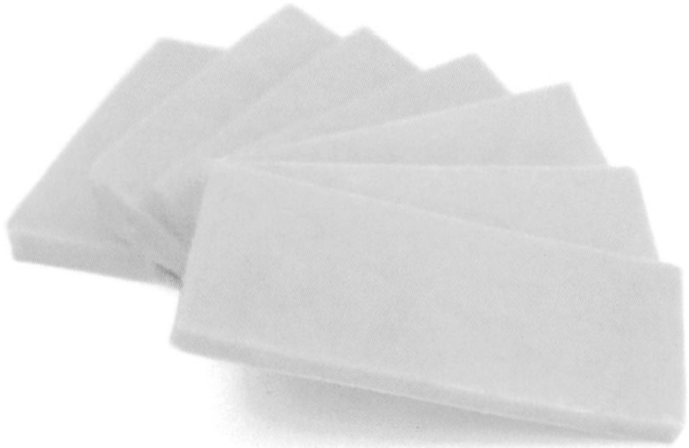

2   lbs   Cheddar Cheese (32 oz)

Seasoning Options:

BBQ Powder
1	cup	Paprika
½	cup	Fine Salt
½	cup	Granulated Sugar
½	cup	Chili Powder
½	cup	Ground Cumin
½	cup	Granulated Garlic
¼	cup	Mustard Powder
¼	cup	Black Pepper
¼	cup	Cayenne Pepper

Chili Powder
1	cup	Garlic Powder
1	cup	Ground Cumin
½	cup	Cayenne Pepper
½	cup	Dried Oregano
½	cup	Paprika

Ranch Powder
1	cup	Buttermilk Powder
¾	cup	Dried Parsley
¼	cup	Dried Chives
¼	cup	Dill Weed
¼	cup	Onion Powder
¼	cup	Garlic Powder
¼	cup	Onion Flakes
2	Tbs	Black Pepper
2	Tbs	Fine Salt

French Onion Powder
2	cup	Dried Minced Onion
1½	cup	Dried Chopped Chives
½	cup	Onion Powder
½	cup	Garlic Powder
4	tsp	Fine Salt

Directions:

Cut each pound of cheese into 48 slices. Further cut those slices into 4 pieces each. Lay the cheese pieces out on the trays, watching the weight limits for your size tray, and season, if desired.
If seasoning, spritz the cheese with water and sprinkle on the seasoning. Pre-freeze. Freeze-dry the Cheese Crisps on normal settings for 20-30 hours. Do a weight check and run Extra Dry Time until the weight doesn't change.

Seal in 7-mil mylar or a canning jar with an oxygen absorber and store in a cool, dry location.

Rehydration:

Gradually spritz with water until bendable. We do not recommend rehydrating the cheese crisps, but instead to eat them dry as a crunchy snack.

Tips:

You can use any type of cheese that can be sliced. Combine with sliced fruits or meats & crackers.

Cheese Ball & Spread

This simple and delicious appetizer is a combination of three favorite flavors: cream cheese, cheddar, and Ranch!

Cups: 5 ½	**Servings:** 44	**Serving Size:** 2 Tbs	**Calories:** 102
Prep/Cook Time: 15 min	**Freeze-Dry Time:** 25-35 hrs		**Shelf-Life:** 10-15 yrs

Ingredients:

32	oz	Cream Cheese
1½	cups	Shredded Cheddar Cheese
½	cup	Green Onion, chopped (opt)
¼	cup	Sour Cream
2	1-oz	Ranch Dressing Mix Packet
2	tsp	Worcestershire Sauce

Option:

To make a Cheese Ball: Place the spread into plastic wrap, shape, and chill for 4 hours.

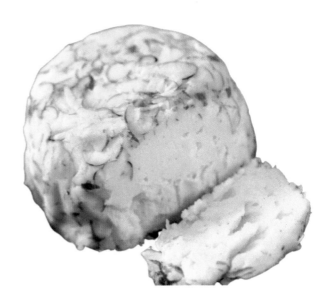

Directions:

Mix the cream cheese in a large bowl until smooth.

Stir in the other ingredients until thoroughly blended.

Spread evenly onto trays, watching the weight limits for your size tray, and pre-freeze.

Freeze-dry the Cheese Spread on normal settings for 25-35 hours. Do a weight check and run Extra Dry Time until the weight doesn't change.

Seal in 7-mil mylar or a canning jar with an oxygen absorber and store in a cool, dry location.

Rehydration:

For Cheese Spread
1	cup	FD Cheese Powder
1	cup	Water

For Cheese Ball
1	cup	FD Cheese Powder
¾	cup	Water

To every cup of freeze-dried Cheese Powder add 1 cup water for a spread and ¾ cup water for a ball and blend well.

Tips:

Coat the chilled cheese ball in nuts or bacon for an extra special touch.

Homemade Ice Cream

This is such a simple and sweet homemade ice cream. Make a big batch in an ice cream machine and freeze in ice cube trays for easy delicious treats.

Cups:	5	**Servings:**	10	**Serving Size:**	½ cup	**Calories:**	267
Prep/Cook Time:	20 min	**Freeze-Dry Time:**	25-35 hrs			**Shelf-Life:**	15-20 yrs

Ingredients:

2	cups	Milk
2	cups	Cream
1	cup	Sugar
2	tsp	Vanilla

Fun Options:
Add fresh or freeze-dried fruits.
Add freeze-dried powders for flavoring.

4	cups	Rock Salt
16	cups	Ice
1	ea	1-Gallon Zip Bag
1	ea	3-Gallon Zip Bag

Directions:

Combine milk, cream, sugar, and vanilla in a gallon-sized zip-sealed bag and seal tightly.
Combine rock salt and ice in a 3-gallon zip-sealed bag.
Place the sealed gallon bag of liquid ice cream inside the 3-gallon bag with the ice and seal the 3-gallon bag tightly.
Shake the bag vigorously for 10 minutes or until the ice cream has firmed up.
Remove the ice cream bag from the ice bag and clean off the opening (to avoid salt.)
Transfer the ice cream into silicone molds or ice cube trays and pre-freeze.
Pop out ice cream mold and place them evenly onto trays and put them back in the freezer until Freeze-Dryer is ready.
On the Customize screen, lower the Initial Freeze temperature down to -20°F.

Allow the chamber to cool for 60 minutes.
Freeze-dry the ice cream for 25-35 hours. Do a weight check and run Extra Dry Time until the weight doesn't change.
Seal in 7-mil mylar or a canning jar with an oxygen absorber and store in a cool, dry location.

Rehydration:

We do not recommend rehydrating ice cream. It is best as a crunchy snack.

Tips:

Add crumbled freeze-dried fruits or candies as a lovely decoration on top!

Ranch Dip & Dressing

This creamy dip is fantastic for crackers, veggies, chips, and more.
Add extra water and you can use it as a dressing.

Cups:	12	**Servings:**	48	**Serving Size:**	4 Tbs	**Calories:** 120
Prep/Cook Time:	30 min	**Freeze-Dry Time:**	30-40 hrs			**Shelf-Life:** 10-15 yrs

Ingredients:

96	oz	Sour Cream (12 cups)
4	Tbs	Italian Seasoning
4	tsp	Onion Powder
4	tsp	Garlic Powder
4	tsp	Salt

Options:

Mix 8 oz (1 cup) of diced crab, ham,
  chicken, or other meat with 8 oz of
  cream mix to make a savory salad.
Add 2 oz (1/4 cup) chopped black olives,
  scallions, or bacon to 8 oz of cream mix.
Add 4 oz of water to every 8 oz of cream
  to get a ranch dressing.

*Make Italian Seasoning
with 1 Tbs each of Marjoram,
Basil, Oregano, and Parsley
and 1 tsp each of Rosemary,
Thyme, and Sage.

Directions:

Mix seasonings into sour cream. Add additions,
such as crab and black olives for more of a salad.
Spread evenly onto trays, watching the weight
limits for your size tray, and pre-freeze.
Freeze-dry your batch of ranch dip on normal
settings for 30-40 hours. Do a weight check and
run Extra Dry Time until the weight doesn't
change.
Seal in 7-mil mylar or a canning jar with an
oxygen absorber and store in a cool, dry location.

Rehydration:

For Ranch Dip
  1   cup   FD Ranch Powder
  ¾   cup   Water
For Ranch Dressing
  1   cup   FD Ranch Powder
  1   cup   Water
To every cup of freeze-dried
Ranch Powder add ¾ cup water
for a dip or 1 cup water for a
dressing.

Tips:

The sour cream can be
substituted with yogurt.

Yogurt Drops

This is a super simple, super healthy snack. The kiddos can eat these as finger food, and you can easily add them to your smoothies.

| **Pieces:** 450 | **Servings:** 10 | **Serving Size:** 45 drops | **Calories:** 143 |
| **Prep/Cook Time:** 30 min | **Freeze-Dry Time:** 20-30 hrs | **Shelf-Life:** 10-15 yrs | |

Ingredients:

| 80 | oz | Yogurt, nonfat, plain, Greek |
| 3 | Tbs | Tapioca Starch, as a binding agent |

Variations:

Add Fruit, chopped or punctured

Add Granola or Oats or Grape Nuts

Add Graham Cracker crumbs & chopped strawberries for a delightful strawberry shortcake yogurt.

Add Freeze-dried Powders for flavors!

Directions:

Line trays with parchment or silicone mats.

Stir the tapioca starch into the yogurt. Blend in any additional fruit, grains, or flavors.

Place yogurt into an icing bag (or a zip-sealed bag with the tip cut off) and slowly dispense the yogurt onto the tray in drops, similar to extra large chocolate chips.

Pre-freeze on trays.

Freeze-dry Yogurt Drops with the Dry Temp turned down to 90° (on the Customize screen) for 20-30 hours. Do a weight check and run Extra Dry Time until the weight doesn't change.

Seal in 7-mil mylar or a canning jar with an oxygen absorber and store in a cool, dry location.

Rehydration:

| 45 | ea | FD Yogurt Drops |
| ¾ | cup | Water |

To rehydrate into 1 cup of creamy yogurt add ¾ c water to 45 Yogurt Drops (1 cup Yogurt powder). Add more or less as needed.

Tips:

You can use any kind of yogurt, including any kind of flavor. More sugar will hold the shape better.

Each cup serving (8oz) of yogurt makes approximately 45 yogurt drops (1 tsp ea.)

Cold Brew Coffee

This easy-to-make coffee recipe is perfect for outdoor adventures. You can enjoy a delicious, fresh cup of coffee wherever your journey takes you.

Cups:	8	Servings:	8	Serving Size:	1 cup	Calories:	2.4
Prep/Cook Time:	12 hrs	Freeze-Dry Time:	35-45 hrs	Shelf-Life:	20-25 yrs		

Ingredients:

2   cups   Ground Coffee Beans
8   cups   Cold Water
          Pitcher or Jar
          Cheesecloth or Coffee Filter

Directions:

In a pitcher or jar, combine the ground coffee with cold water. Stir well.

Cover and let it steep in the refrigerator for at least 12 hours, or up to 24 hours.

Strain the mixture through a cheesecloth or coffee filter to remove the grounds.

Put an empty tray in the freezer, making sure it sits level.

Pour the coffee onto the tray and cover with a lid. Repeat with any additional trays and pre-freeze.

Freeze-dry the Coffee on normal settings for 35-45 hours. Do a weight check and run Extra Dry Time until the weight doesn't change.

Seal in 7-mil mylar or a canning jar with an oxygen absorber and store in a cool, dry location.

Rehydration:

1-3   tsp   FD Coffee Powder
1   cup   Boiling Water

Add 1-3 teaspoons of freeze-dried coffee powder to a cup of boiling water for hot coffee. For iced coffee use ¾ cup of cold water, stir, and add ½ cup of ice.

Tips:

You can also add milk, sweeteners, or flavors after rehydrating.

To maximize yield, ensure it is a strong brew.

Creamy Eggnog

This is the absolute BEST eggnog recipe ever!
Its rich, creamy flavor delights the senses.

Cups:	8	**Servings:**	16	**Serving Size:**	½ cup	**Calories:**	221
Prep/Cook Time:	25 min	**Freeze-Dry Time:**	35-45 hrs			**Shelf-Life:**	10-15 yrs

Ingredients:

12	ea	Large Egg Yolks
1	cup	Granulated Sugar
2	cups	Heavy Whipping Cream
4⅓	cups	Whole Milk
1	tsp	Nutmeg, ground
1	tsp	Vanilla Extract
		Ground Cinnamon, for topping

Directions:

Whisk the egg yolks and sugar together in a medium bowl until light and creamy.
In a saucepan over medium-high heat, combine the cream, milk, and nutmeg. Stir often until mixture reaches a bare simmer. Do not Boil.
To temper the eggs, add a big spoonful of the hot milk to the egg mixture while whisking vigorously. Repeat, until most has been added. Pour the mixture back into the saucepan and heat, while constantly whisking, for 5 minutes. Remove from heat and stir in the vanilla. Refrigerate until chilled. It will thicken as it cools. Serve with cinnamon on top.
Put an empty tray in the freezer, making sure it sits level. Pour the Eggnog onto the tray and cover with a lid. Repeat with any additional trays and pre-freeze.
Freeze-dry the Eggnog on normal settings for 35-45 hours. Do a weight check and run Extra Dry Time until the weight doesn't change.
Seal in 7-mil mylar or a canning jar with an oxygen absorber and store in a cool, dry location.

Rehydration:

½	cup	FD Eggnog Powder
½	cup	Water

To each ½ cup serving of freeze-dried Eggnog powder add ½ cup of Water and stir. It will thicken. Add more water to get the desired consistency.

Tips:

Add 1 ounce of alcohol to a serving of freeze-dried Eggnog. Good Alcohol Choices: Rum, Brandy, Bourbon, or Whiskey. Alcohol doesn't freeze-dry, it evaporates, so alcohol should not be processed, and instead be added just before drinking.

Pineapple Coconut Slushie

The pineapple coconut slushie is a refreshing tropical burst of flavor. It's simple yet satisfying.

Cups: 8	**Servings:** 8	**Serving Size:** 1 cup	**Calories:** 70
Prep/Cook Time: 5 min	**Freeze-Dry Time:** 35-45 hrs		**Shelf-Life:** 10-15 yrs

Ingredients:

6   cups   Pineapple Chunks, frozen
2   cups   Coconut Water or Fruit Juice

Optional Flavors:
Substitute for all or part of the pineapple.
     Banana Chunks, frozen
     Mango Chunks, frozen
     Mixed Berries, frozen
     Peach Chunks, frozen
     Watermelon Chunks, frozen

Directions:

Place all the ingredients in a high-powered blender and blend until smooth. Add more liquid if needed.

Put an empty tray in the freezer, making sure it sits level.

Pour the Slushie onto the tray and cover with a lid. Repeat with any additional trays and pre-freeze.

Freeze-dry the Slushie on normal settings for 35-45 hours. Do a weight check and run Extra Dry Time until the weight doesn't change.

Seal in 7-mil mylar or a canning jar with an oxygen absorber and store in a cool, dry location.

Rehydration:

1   cup   FD Slushie Powder
¾   cup   Water
1   cup   Crushed Ice

To each cup of freeze-dried Slushie powder add ¾ cup water, stir, and add 1 cup Crushed Ice

Tips:

Add 1 oz alcohol, such as Rum, to a serving of freeze-dried Slushie. Alcohol doesn't freeze-dry, it evaporates, so alcohol should not be processed, and instead be added just before drinking.

Raspberry Protein Shake

*This shake will make your morning brighter
with its sweet and hearty ingredients.*

Cups: 5	**Servings:** 5	**Serving Size:** 1 cup		**Calories:** 157
Prep/Cook Time: 10 min	**Freeze-Dry Time:** 25-35 hrs			**Shelf-Life:** 10-15 yrs

Ingredients:

2	cups	Raspberries, frozen
2	lrg	Ripe Banana, fresh or frozen
2	cups	Almond Milk
2	Tbs	Chia Seeds
4	Tbs	Vanilla Protein Powder
2	Tbs	Maple Syrup

Directions:

Place all the ingredients in a high-powered blender and blend until smooth.

Taste and adjust according to preferences, such as adding more maple syrup or fruit for additional sweetness.

Put an empty tray in the freezer, making sure it sits level.

Pour the shake onto the tray and cover with a lid. Repeat with any additional trays and pre-freeze.

Freeze-dry the Protein Shake on normal settings for 25-35 hours. Do a weight check and run Extra Dry Time until the weight doesn't change.

Seal in 7-mil mylar or a canning jar with an oxygen absorber and store in a cool, dry location.

Rehydration:

1	cup	FD Protein Powder
¾	cup	Water
½	cup	Crushed Ice

To each cup of freeze-dried powder, add ¾ cup of water & blend well, then add crushed ice.

Tips:

Add more milk for a thinner consistency.

If on the go, skip the ice & use 1 cup of water in a blender bottle.

Strawberry Mint Smoothie

This smoothie is cool and refreshing with just a hint of mint.
Enjoy as a breakfast addition or a healthy treat anytime.

Cups: 8	**Servings:** 8	**Serving Size:** 1 cup	**Calories:** 107
Prep/Cook Time: 10 min	**Freeze-Dry Time:** 25-35 hrs	**Shelf-Life:** 10-15 yrs

---

Ingredients:

5	cups	Strawberries, 2 lbs, fresh or frozen
2	lrg	Ripe Bananas, fresh or frozen
10	ea	Ice Cubes - if using FRESH fruit
12	ea	Fresh Mint Leaves
2	cups	2% Milk
2	Tbs	Honey (opt)

Directions:

Place all the ingredients in a high-powered blender and blend until smooth.

Taste and adjust according to preferences, such as adding more honey or fruit for additional sweetness.

Put an empty tray in the freezer, making sure it sits level.

Pour the Smoothie onto the tray and cover with a lid. Repeat with any additional trays and pre-freeze.

Freeze-dry the Smoothie on normal settings for 25-35 hours. Do a weight check and run Extra Dry Time until the weight doesn't change.

Seal in 7-mil mylar or a canning jar with an oxygen absorber and store in a cool, dry location.

Rehydration:

1	cup	FD Smoothie Powder
¾	cup	Water
½	cup	Crushed ice

To each cup of freeze-dried powder, add ¾ cup of water & blend well, then add ice. If on the go, skip the ice & use 1 cup of water in a blender bottle.

Tips:

Add more milk for a thinner consistency.

Substitute almond milk for a vegan version.

Banana Bread Bites

This classic banana bread recipe makes tasty bites of goodness you'll love any time of day.

Pieces: 288	**Servings:** 24	**Serving Size:** 12 bites	**Calories:** 197
Prep/Cook Time: 1 hr 15 min	**Freeze-Dry Time:** 25-35 hrs	**Shelf-Life:** 15-20 yrs	

Ingredients:

4	cups	Flour
2	tsp	Baking Soda
1	tsp	Salt
1	tsp	Cinnamon
1	cup	Butter (2 sticks)
1	cup	Brown Sugar
½	cup	Granulated Sugar
4	lrg	Eggs
2	tsp	Vanilla Extract
3	cups	Bananas, mashed (4 med)

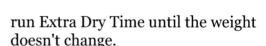

Directions:

Preheat oven to 350°. Prepare two 8-by-4-inch loaf pans by greasing & flouring or lining with parchment paper.

In a small bowl, whisk together the flour, baking soda, salt, and cinnamon.

Using a hand mixer set to medium speed, cream together the butter and sugars in a medium bowl until light and fluffy.

Combine the eggs and vanilla extract. Mix in mashed bananas.

Stir together the dry and wet ingredients. Pour into the pan and bake for 50–60 minutes, or until a toothpick inserted in the center comes out clean.

Leave the pan to cool for 5 minutes. Take the bread out of the pans and cool on a rack.

Slice ¾" thick. Cut each slice into 12 bite-sized pieces. Put on trays and pre-freeze.

Freeze-dry your Banana Bread Bites on normal settings for 25-35 hours. Do a weight check and run Extra Dry Time until the weight doesn't change.

Seal in 7-mil mylar or a canning jar with an oxygen absorber and store in a cool, dry location.

Rehydration:

We highly recommend eating this treat dry and crunchy.

To rehydrate, place several bites in a zip sealed bag with a moist paper towel and allow it to sit for 20 minutes.

Tips:

This technique will work with any of these types of sweet breads.

Berry Cobbler

*This delectable cobbler is delicious for breakfast
or a sweet and satisfying dessert any time.*

Cups:	8	**Servings:**	8	**Serving Size:**	1 cup	**Calories:**	118
Prep/Cook Time:	45 min	**Freeze-Dry Time:**	35-45 hrs			**Shelf-Life:**	15-20 yrs

Ingredients:

Filling

6	cups	Berries, fresh or frozen
2	Tbs	Maple Syrup
4	Tbs	Lemon Juice (1 med)
⅛	tsp	Fine Salt

Topping

2	cups	Rolled Oats
2	Tbs	Ground Flax, Chia, or Hemp Seeds
1	Tbs	Ground Cinnamon
⅛	tsp	Fine Salt
½	cup	Applesauce
2	Tbs	Maple Syrup
⅛	cup	Slivered almonds

Directions:

Preheat oven to 350°F. In a medium bowl, mix berries with maple syrup and lemon juice. Lightly mash to ensure the berries have all been pierced. Pour into 9x11 baking dish.
In a separate mixing bowl. Stir oats, ground seeds, cinnamon, and salt until combined. Mix in applesauce and maple syrup.
Spread the topping evenly over the filling. Sprinkle almonds on top. Bake for 25-30 minutes. Let cool.
Scoop onto freeze-dryer trays, watching the weight limits for your size tray, and pre-freeze. Freeze-dry the Berry Cobbler on normal settings for 35-45 hours. Do a weight check and run Extra Dry Time until the weight doesn't change.

Seal in 7-mil mylar or a canning jar with an oxygen absorber and store in a cool, dry location.

Rehydration:

1	cup	FD Berry Cobbler
1	cup	Water

To each cup of FD Berry Cobbler add 1 cup of water and stir.

Tips:

We like to warm this up and eat it with ice cream!

Pumpkin Pie Drops

The Pumpkin pie drops are a crunchy, flavorful snack, that goes great with a glass of milk. This is an excellent twist on a classic desert.

Pieces: 240	**Servings:** 10	**Serving Size:** 24 drops	**Calories:** 298
Prep/Cook Time: 20 min	**Freeze-Dry Time:** 25-35 hrs		**Shelf-Life:** 10-15 yrs

Ingredients:

2	cans	Pumpkin Puree, 15 oz
2	cups	Whipped Cream, 32 oz
½	cup	Maple Syrup
2	tsp	Pumpkin Pie Spice

Each ½ cup serving of Pumpkin dessert will make approximately 24 nickle-sized dollops (1 tsp each.)

Directions:

Line trays with parchment or silicone mats. Blend or stir ingredients together until creamy and smooth.

Place the pumpkin mixture into an icing bag (or a zip-sealed bag with the tip cut off) and slowly dispense onto the tray in drops, similar to extra large chocolate chips. Place quarter-sized dollops evenly onto the trays and pre-freeze.

(You can spread the pumpkin pie dessert on the trays if you'd rather create a powder.)

Freeze-dry the Pumpkin Pie Drops on normal settings for 25-35 hours. Do a weight check and run Extra Dry Time until the weight doesn't change.

Seal in 7-mil mylar or a canning jar with an oxygen absorber and store in a cool, dry location.

Rehydration:

½	cup	FD Pumpkin Powder
¼	cup	Water

To rehydrate into a creamy pumpkin dessert add ¼ c water to ½ cup Pumpkin Powder (24 drops). Add more or less as needed. We don't rehydrate Pumpkin Pie Drops because we love them as a crunchy snack.

Tips:

Use the powder as a topping for desserts, mix it into ice cream, add to sweet bread, or stir it into coffee.

Snickerdoodle Cookies

These cookies are our favorite because they are incredibly soft and packed with cinnamon. Once freeze-dried, they are a perfect crunchy treat.

Cookies: 36	**Servings:**	36	**Serving Size:**	1 cookie	**Calories:** 122
Prep/Cook Time: 25 min	**Freeze-Dry Time:**		20-30 hrs		**Shelf-Life:** 15-20 yrs

Ingredients:

2¾	cups	All-purpose Flour
2	tsp	Cream of Tartar
1	tsp	Baking Soda
½	tsp	Fine Salt
1	cup	Unsalted Butter, softened
1½	cups	Granulated Sugar
2	lrg	Eggs
1	tsp	Vanilla Extract

Coating

⅓	cup	Granulated Sugar
2	Tbs	Cinnamon

Directions:

Preheat oven to 350°F. In a large mixing bowl blend together butter and sugar. Stir in the eggs and vanilla.

Combine flour, cream of tartar, baking soda, and salt. Mix the dry and wet components.

In a small bowl, combine the cinnamon and sugar coating mixture.

Scoop out dough, make a 1" ball, and roll in the cinnamon and sugar mixture.

Bake on ungreased cookie sheet for 8-10 minutes. Allow to sit 2 min before placing on cooling rack. Cool.

Place cookies on trays and pre-freeze.

Freeze-dry the Snickerdoodles on normal settings for 20-30 hours. Do a weight check and run Extra Dry Time until the weight doesn't change.

Seal in 7-mil mylar or a canning jar with an oxygen absorber and store in a cool, dry location.

Rehydration:

We do not recommend rehydrating cookies. They are best as a crunchy snack.

If you wish to rehydrate, wrap each cookie in a moist paper towel and put in a zip sealed bag.

Tips:

To make Cookie Bites, cut cookies in quarters after they have been cooked.

Strawberry Shortcake

Strawberry shortcake is a classic dessert consisting of two layers of fluffy cake, with juicy strawberries & whipped cream. It is sure to satisfy any sweet tooth.

Pieces: 48	**Servings:** 24	**Serving Size:** 2 pieces	**Calories:** 389
Prep/Cook Time: 40 min	**Freeze-Dry Time:** 45-55 hrs	**Shelf-Life:** 10-15 yrs

Ingredients:

Cake

3	cups	All-purpose Flour
4	tsp	Baking Powder
½	tsp	Fine Salt
½	cup	Unsalted Butter, softened
1⅓	cups	Granulated Sugar
2	lrg	Eggs, room temperature
2½	tsp	Vanilla Extract
1	cup	Milk, room temperature

Sauce

¼	cup	Granulated Sugar
3	lbs	Fresh Strawberries, sliced

Cream

1½	cups	Whipping Cream
3	Tbs	Confectioners' Sugar (pwd)
½	tsp	Vanilla Extract

Directions:

Preheat oven to 350°F. Grease a 9x13 pan and line it with parchment to make handles.
Combine flour, baking powder, and salt.
Cream butter and sugar. Add eggs and vanilla and beat well.
Alternate adding the flour mixture and milk until thoroughly mixed with the egg mixture and pour into pan. Bake 20 minutes and cool.
The sauce: Cook strawberries and sugar in a medium saucepan over medium heat and stir gently until the sugar is dissolved. Cool.
The cream: Whip cream, powdered sugar, and vanilla together until soft peaks form.
Remove cake from pan, slice in half horizontally, & place the bottom in the pan.
Spread half the strawberries over the cake, spread on half the cream, & lay down the top of the cake. Repeat the strawberries & cream.

Refrigerate 2 hours. Cut into 48 Pieces, lay out on trays, watching the weight limits for your size tray, and pre-freeze. Freeze-dry the Strawberry Shortcake on normal settings for 45-55 hours. Do a weight check and run Extra Dry Time until the weight doesn't change.
Seal in 7-mil mylar or a canning jar, if in small pieces, with an oxygen absorber and store in a cool, dry location.

Rehydration:

We do not recommend rehydrating the Strawberry Shortcake dessert bites. They are best enjoyed as a crunchy snack.

Tips: 7 cups freeze-dried sliced strawberries+5 cups water=3lbs fresh.

APPENDIX THREE: 18 PRINTABLE WORKSHEETS

The worksheets included here are intended to aid you in your freeze-drying adventure. There are information pages, reminders, logs, and checklists to help your journey be smooth. The pages can be printed and kept in a 3-ring binder for ease of organization. The workbook is also available on Amazon. The worksheets include:

Scan the QR code for a printable PDF or visit: BFDPDF.2MHE.COM

WORKSHEETS

Quick Start Worksheets

Kitchen Worksheets

Foods You Cannot Freeze-Dry

Foods You Can Freeze-Dry

Information Worksheets

Record Keeping Worksheets

GETTING STARTED CHECKLIST

Approve & Inspect Items in Your Order

- ☐ Inspect for Damage (HR: 801-386-8960)
- ☐ Harvest Right Freeze-dryer
- ☐ Shelving unit (inside the appliance)
- ☐ 6' power cord (black)
- ☐ Drain line tubing (clear)
- ☐ Vacuum pump
- ☐ Vacuum hose (black)
- ☐ Vacuum pump oil (unless oil-free)
- ☐ Oil filter (unless oil-free)
- ☐ Impulse sealer
- ☐ Stainless steel trays (S: 3, M: 4, L: 5, XL: 6)
- ☐ Package of Mylar bags
- ☐ Package of oxygen absorbers (OA)
- ☐ Harvest Right owner's manual
- ☐ Harvest Right Guide to Freeze-drying
- ☐ Additional Accessories

Positioning your Machine

- ☐ Carefully Move into position
- ☐ Environment is Clean & Dry
- ☐ Room Temperature is Cool (45°F - 75°F)
- ☐ Adequate Ventilation on both sides
- ☐ Table, Cart, or Countertop
- ☐ Surface is stable and level

Tasks while you Wait

- ☐ Read the Harvest Right Owner's Manual.
- ☐ Open the door and ensure the shelving unit is connected and positioned correctly.
- ☐ Inspect the rubber gasket & acrylic door and wipe with warm water and a cotton cloth.
- ☐ Attach the drain hose to the fitting on the side of the appliance.
- ☐ Allow the vinyl hose to fall into a 5-gallon bucket while hanging loosely.
- ☐ Add the ⅜" Y fittings to your tubing by cutting the line & pushing the ends onto the fitting.
- ☐ Attach the power cord, but do not plug it in until the 24 hours have passed.
- ☐ Position the pump by placing it on the right side or below the freeze-dryer. (oil-free above)
- ☐ Add the included oil to your pump up to just above the centerline.
- ☐ Attach vacuum hose to fitting on right side & attach the other end to the pump.
- ☐ Plug the pump into the receptacle on the back of the freeze-dryer.
- ☐ Flip the vacuum pump switch to the ON position. (It won't turn on.)
- ☐ Place fans to blow directly on the vacuum pump and on the left side of the appliance.
- ☐ Find locations for your equipment: impulse sealer, food funnel, FoodSaver®, etc.
- ☐ Find a good storage place for your packaging materials: Mylar bags and oxygen absorbers.
- ☐ Store your accessories: silicone mats, molds, parchment, dividers, corner stackers, etc.

After the 24 hours

- ☐ Plug freeze-dryer into prepared outlet
- ☐ Close drain valve on side of freeze-dryer
- ☐ Close door in two turns & check seal
- ☐ Flip power switch to ON position
- ☐ Test the Freeze function (40 min)
- ☐ Test the Vacuum function (30 min)
- ☐ Set up the Interface (10 min)
- ☐ Complete the Bread Run (24 hours)

FREEZE-DRYING STEPS

Putting Food IN to your Freeze-Dryer

1. Prepare food to ½" - ¾" thickness or into pieces.

2. Pre-freeze for 24-48 hrs. This improves appliance efficiency & avoids messes.

3. Check the Oil in the Pump. It should be clear and between half-full and max.

4. Plug in the freeze-dryer, flip the Switch on, seat the Gasket, close the Door, check the Seal, and fully latch the Handle.

5. On the Customize Screen, set any changes in Temperature & Time.

6. Press Start to begin pre-cooling the chamber (minimum 15-90 min.)

7. Point a fan on the left side of the freeze-dryer.

8. Wait for the Prompt (after 15+ min,) and close the Drain Valve.

9. Weigh the trays. Put the food trays in, close the Door, check the Seal, and fully latch the Handle.

10. Press Continue and wait for 24-60+ hours. Start prepping the next batch.

Taking Food OUT of your Freeze-Dryer

1. When the three phases are complete Extra Dry Time starts. You can cancel anytime to check the food. Set Extra Dry Time to 24 hours. You can't overdry.

2. Ensure the drain hose is in an empty bucket, press Cancel, slowly open the Drain Valve & wait 5 min for pressure to release.

3. Open the Door, remove the food, & check for cold or soft spots. Weigh each tray.

4. Put trays back in. Set More Dry Time to 4+ hours and check the weight in 2 hours. Repeat as needed. When weight doesn't change it is fully dry & can be packaged.

5. Remove the food from the trays and put them immediately into proper storage. (7-mil Mylar bag heat sealed with OA or canning jar vacuum sealed with an OA.)

6. Add an Oxygen Absorber (OA). 100cc/quart, 300cc/gallon.

7. Remove excess oxygen. Seal the Mylar bag or canning jar.

8. Defrost the Chamber by opening the door (or select Defrost.)

9. Clean the freeze-dryer components with a soft cloth and warm water. Sterilize with isopropyl alcohol or Everclear.

10. Aim a fan directly in the chamber to help get it dry. Then start the next batch.

FREEZE-DRYER SCREENS

Harvest Right™ System Configuration
Appliance Log, Serial Number, Hours Running,
Number of Batches, Temperature °F to °C,
Set Time button, and Pump button.

Set Time: Date, Time, Alarm
Pump: Select Type, Reset Hours

Leaf: Functional Testing
Freeze, Vacuum, Heater, and Aux Relay

Customize: Freeze & Dry
Temperatures & Times

Customize Defaults:
   Initial freeze: -10°F
   Extra Freeze Time: 0:00
   Dry Mode Normal
   Dry Temp.: 125°F
   Extra Dry Time: 2:00
    (Recommended 12:00 - 24:00)

Start
Begins the process by Cooling the chamber

System Name
Your Choice of a Name

REHYDRATION INFORMATION

Rehydration is not always necessary.

If you want a crunchy snack, just eat it right out of the bag or jar.

If you are making soup add the freeze-dried food to the pot and add water as needed.

Fruits & vegetables best used dry can be blended into a powder & added to soups, sauces, or smoothies.

Some foods require much less water to rehydrate. Start with less (HALF) and add more slowly.

Rehydration General Rule of Thumb:

 + **1 cup Freeze-dried Food**

½ - 1 cup Water* (start with ½ cup)

*Add a small amount of water gradually, stir or turn items, and add the rest as needed.

Meals
5-20+ min

Add hot water, stir, and allow it to sit. Or, break it up in an oven-safe dish, add hot water, cover, and bake in the oven like a casserole.

Cooked Meats
5-60 min

Place the food in a dish and add just enough hot water to cover. Too much water can turn cooked meats into mush.

Fruits & Vegetables
1-10 min

Lay out food on a tray & spritz lightly with cold water. Flip or stir to get the other side. Allow it to soak in & then spritz more as needed.

Raw Meats
30 min - 3+ hrs

Place the raw meat in a dish, add cold water or broth, and place in the fridge overnight. Pat dry with paper towel and thoroughly cook.

Eggs
1-2 min

To reconstitute raw eggs add 2 Tablespoons egg powder to 2 Tablespoons cold water. Stir and allow it to sit. Use as you would a raw egg.

Powders
1-2 min

Add small amounts of cold water and stir. It is typically about 50:50 water to powder, regardless of what kind of powder.

Cheeses
5-15 min

Wrap cheese slices in moist paper towels & allow to sit. Spritz shredded cheese with cold water. Other cheeses are best dry or added to recipes.

Desserts
5-10 min

Place the treat & a moist paper towel inside a ziplock bag & allow to sit. Alternatively, wrap the treat in a moist paper towel. Or just eat crunchy!

*Note: Some foods will take considerably longer to rehydrate than others in the same category.

CONVERSIONS

Use these handy conversions to make life in the kitchen a little easier.

1 CUP =
16 tablespoons,
8 ounces
240 ml

1/2 CUP =
8 tablespoons
120 ml

1 PINT =
2 cups,
16 ounces
480 ml

1 GALLON =
4 quarts,
8 pints,
16 cups,
128 ounces
3.8 liters

1 QUART =
2 pints,
4 cups,
32 ounces,
950 ml

1 teaspoon = 5 ml
1 tablespoon = 3 teaspoons = 15 ml
2 tablespoons = 1 ounce = 30 ml
4 tablespoons = 1/4 cup = 60 ml
5 tablespoons + 1 teaspoon = 80 ml

oz	grams	lbs
1/2	14	
3/4	21	
1	28	
2	57	1/8
3	85	
4	113	1/4
5	142	
6	170	
7	198	
8	227	1/2
9	255	
10	284	
11	312	
12	340	3/4
13	369	
14	397	
15	425	
16	454	1
24	680	1.5
32	907	2
40	1134	2.5
48	1361	3
56	1588	3.5
64	1814	4
72	2041	4.5
80	2268	5

FOODS YOU CANNOT FREEZE-DRY

Oily or Fatty Foods and Sugary foods do not freeze-dry well.
Small amounts within prepared recipes generally work out fine.

Any meals or foods that contain oils should be used within
1-5 years due to the nature of fats, which go rancid over time.

FREEZE-DRYER NO'S

High Fat:

- Oils
- Butter
- Mayonnaise
- Pure Chocolate
- Nuts
- Nut Butters
- Nutella
- Peanut Butter

High Sugar:

- Honey
- Syrup
- Soda
- Jam
- Jelly
- Preserves

Treats:

- Twizzlers
- Licorice
- Oreos
- Candy Canes
- Swedish Fish
- Fruit Snacks
- Gum Drops
- Cinnamon Disks

Other:

- Bones
- Alcohol
- Vinegar
- Water (lol!)

GREAT FOODS TO FREEZE-DRY

Fruits

- Apples
- Apricots
- Avocado
- Bananas
- Blackberries
- Blueberries
- Cantaloupe
- Cherries
- Coconut
- Cranberry
- Currants
- Dewberries
- Elderberries
- Figs
- Goji Berries
- Gooseberries
- Grapefruit
- Grapes
- Ground cherries
- Honeydew
- Kiwifruit
- Lemons
- Limes
- Mandarins
- Mangos
- Mulberries
- Nectarines
- Oranges
- Passion Fruit
- Peaches
- Pears
- Pineapple
- Plums
- Pomegranate
- Raspberries
- Rhubarb
- Star Fruits
- Strawberries
- Tangerines
- Watermelon

Snacks

- Applesauce
- Breads
- Croutons
- Diluted BBQ Sauce
- Diluted Ketchup
- Diluted Mustard
- French Onion Dip
- Guacamole
- Nacho Cheese
- Pickles
- Pizza
- Ranch Dip
- Refried Beans
- Salsa
- Sourdough Starter
- Sweet Breads

GREAT FOODS TO FREEZE-DRY

Vegetables

- Asparagus
- Beets
- Bok Choy
- Broad Beans
- Broccoli
- Brussel Sprouts
- Cabbage
- Carrots
- Cauliflower
- Celery
- Corn
- Cucumber
- Eggplant
- Garlic
- Green beans
- Greens
- Kale
- Kohlrabi
- Leeks
- Lettuce
- Mushrooms
- Okra

- Onions
- Parsnips
- Peas, Green
- Peas, Snap
- Peppers, Hot
- Peppers, Sweet
- Potatoes
- Pumpkins
- Radish
- Rutabaga
- Scallions
- Spinach
- Squash, Butternut
- Squash, Spaghetti
- Squash, Yellow
- Squash, Zucchini
- Sweet potatoes
- Swiss chard
- Tomatillos
- Tomatoes
- Turnips
- Yams

*change dry temp to 90°F

Dairy

- Buttermilk
- Cheese Curds
- Condensed Milk
- Cottage Cheese
- Cow Milk
- Cream Cheese
- Custard
- Goat Milk

- Hard Cheeses
- Heavy Cream
- Ice Cream
- Kefir*
- Soft Cheeses
- Sour Cream
- Whipped Cream
- Yogurt*

GREAT FOODS TO FREEZE-DRY

Meats

Beef - Lean

- Cubed Steak
- Deli Meat
- Ground
- Filets
- Kabobs
- Meatballs
- Patties
- Roast
- Shredded
- Strips
- Steaks
- Stew Meats

Pork - Lean

- Bacon
- Chops
- Ham
- Loin
- Roast
- Shredded

Poultry

- Chopped
- Ground
- Roasted
- Shredded
- Sliced
- Turkey Bacon
- Game Fowl

Other

Bison, Boar, Elk, Deer, Goat, Rabbit, Sheep

Seafood

Freshwater

- Bass
- Bluegill
- Carp
- Catfish
- Perch
- Tilapia
- Trout
- Walleye

Saltwater

- Cod
- Flounder
- Redfish
- Snapper
- Salmon
- Sheepshead
- Swordfish
- Tuna

Shellfish

- Clam
- Crab
- Lobster
- Mussel
- Octopus
- Oyster
- Scallop
- Shrimp

GREAT FOODS TO FREEZE-DRY

Meals

- Beef stroganoff
- Breakfast Skillet
- Casseroles
- Cheese steak
- Chicken parmesan
- Chili
- Chow mein
- Creole
- Enchiladas
- Fajitas
- Goulash
- Gumbo
- Hamburger patties
- Hash browns
- Jambalaya
- Lasagna
- Macaroni & Cheese
- Mashed potatoes
- Meatballs
- Meat Loaf
- Oatmeal
- Pasta
- Pizza Casserole
- Roast Turkey Dinner
- Roast Beef Dinner
- Soups
- Spaghetti
- Stews
- Tacos
- Tuna Salad

Drinks

- Bone Broth
- Broth
- Carrot Juice
- Coconut Water
- Coffee
- Cow Milk
- Eggnog
- Fruit Juices
- Fruit Smoothies
- Goat Milk
- Grapefruit Juice
- Green Machine
- Greens Juices
- Hot Cocoa
- Lemon Juice
- Lime Juice
- Milkshakes
- Oat Milk
- Orange Juice
- Pineapple Juice
- Protein Shakes
- Prune Juice
- Rice Milks
- Smoothies
- Supplements
- Tomato Juice
- V8 & Fusions
- Vegetable Juices

GREAT FOODS TO FREEZE-DRY

Legumes & Grains

- Chickpeas
- Beans
- Lentils
- Peas
- Soybeans
- Sprouts

- Barley
- Oats
- Quinoa
- Rice
- Rye
- Wheat

- Bread
- Cake
- Cookies
- Crackers
- Granola
- Pasta

Desserts

- Cake
- Cheesecake
- Cookies
- Ice Cream
- Ice Cream Sandwiches
- Jell-O
- Lemon Bars

- Marshmallows
- Mousse
- Pie
- Pudding
- Shortcake
- Tarts
- Twinkies

*use Candy mode

*Candies**

Use Whole

- Candy Corn
- Caramel Apple Pops
- Caramel M&M's
- Gummy Bears
- Gummy Worms
- Junior Mints
- Lemonheads
- Life Saver Gummies
- Mamba
- Peach Rings
- Skittles
- Stuffed Puffs

Cut into Pieces

- Airheads (⅓)
- Bit 'O Honey (⅓)
- Caramels (½)
- Jolly Ranchers (⅓)
- Laffy Taffy (¼)
- Milk Duds (½)
- Mini Milky Way (½)
- Salt Water Taffy (¼)
- Mini Snickers (½)
- Starburst (¼)
- Tootsie Chews (½)
- Twix (¼)

GREAT FOODS TO FREEZE-DRY

Eggs

- Cooked
- Raw (Pre-freeze Solid)
- Scrambled
- Skillets
- Casseroles
- Quiche

*change dry temp to 90°F

*Herbs**

- Basil
- Chives
- Cilantro
- Comfrey
- Dill Weed
- Fennel
- Ginger
- Ginseng
- Horseradish
- Lemon Balm
- Marjoram
- Nettle
- Oregano
- Parsley
- Peppermint
- Rosemary
- Sage
- Spearmint
- Stevia
- Tarragon
- Thyme
- Turmeric

*change dry temp to 90°F

*Edible Flowers**

- Begonia
- Borage
- Calendula
- Carnations
- Chamomile
- Chrysanthemums
- Cornflowers
- Daisies
- Dandelion
- Dianthus
- French Marigolds
- Gladioli
- Hibiscus
- Hollyhock
- Honeysuckle
- Hostas
- Lavender
- Nasturtium
- Pansies
- Roses
- Snapdragons
- Sunflowers
- Tulips
- Violas

FREEZE-DRYER INFORMATION

Specifications		Small	Medium	Large	X-Large
Current Price	Color Stainless Steel	$2,495 $2,695	$3,195 $3,395	$3,895 $4,095	$5,095
Size	Width Depth Height	17.4" W x 21.5" D x 26.8" H	19" W x 25" D x 29" H	21.3" W x 27.5" D x 31.3" H	24.3" W x 37.4" D x 35.6" H
FD Weight		61 lbs SS 80 lbs	112 lbs SS 133 lbs	138 lbs SS 161 lbs	265 lbs
Premier Vacuum Pump Weight		32 lbs	32 lbs	32 lbs	33 lbs
Shipping Weight		139 lbs SS 150 lbs	212 lbs SS 221 lbs	253 lbs SS 274 lbs	370 lbs
Average Power Draw		9-10 amps/hr. Spikes to 16.	10-11 amps/hr. Spikes to 16.	10-12 amps/hr. Spikes to 16.	12-14 amps/hr. Spikes to 16.
Power Needs		110 Volt Outlet. Dedicated 20 amp circuit recommended. No GFCI.		110 Volt Outlet NEMA 5-20. Dedicated 20 amp circuit REQUIRED. No GFCI.	

Food Information		Small	Medium	Large	X-Large
Number of Trays		3	4	5	6
Tray Size	Width Length Height	7.75" W x 14" L x 0.75" H	7.5" W x 18" L x 0.75" H	9" W x 20.5" L x 0.75" H	10.9" W x 29.5" L x 0.75" H
Max Fresh per Tray	Cups Ounces Liters Pounds Kilograms	3 c 24 oz 0.8 L 2.3 lbs 1 kg	4 c 32 oz 1 L 2.5 lbs 1.1 kg	5.5 c 44 oz 1.4 L 3.2 lbs 1.5 kg	10 c 80 oz 2.5 L 5.8 lbs 2.6 kg
Max Fresh per Batch	Cups Ounces Liters Pounds Kilograms	9 c 72 oz 2.4 L 7 lbs 3 kg	16 c 128 oz 4 L 10 lbs 4.5 kg	27.5 c 220 oz 7 L 16 lbs 7.5 kg	60 c 480 oz 16 L 35 lbs 15.8 kg
Freeze-dried per Batch	Gallons	1-1.5 gal	1.5-2.5 gal	1-3.5 gal	8-10 gal
Average Annual Batches		200+	200+	200+	200+
Average Pounds		4.2 lbs	7.25 lbs	12.5 lbs	25 lbs
Average Annual Fresh		840 lbs	1,450 lbs	2,500 lbs	5,000 lbs
Average Annual Freeze-dried		195 gal	312 gal	546 gal	1200 gal

CAPACITY

X-Large Freeze-Dryer

Dimensions:
Black: 265 lbs
24.3" W x 37.4" D x 35.6" H

Freeze-dryer Trays
6 Trays: 10.9" W x 29.5" D x 0.75" H

Max Fresh Food per Tray:
10 cups, 80 oz, 2.5 L, 5.8 lbs, 2.6 kg

Max Fresh Food per Batch:
60 cups, 480 oz, 16 L, 35 lbs, 15.8 kg

Freeze-Dried per Batch:
Average: 8-10 gallons freeze-dried

Annual Batches:
200 batches @ 25 lbs
= 5,000 lbs fresh
= 1,200 gal FD

CAPACITY

Large Freeze-Dryer

Dimensions:
Black/White: 138 lbs, Stainless Steel: 161 lbs
21.3" W x 27.5" D x 31.3" H

Freeze-dryer Trays
5 Trays: 9" W x 20.5" D x 0.75" H

Max Fresh Food per Tray:
5.5 cups, 44 oz, 1.4 L, 3.2 lbs, 1.5 kg

Max Fresh Food per Batch:
27.5 cups, 220 oz, 7 L, 16 lbs, 7.5 kg

Freeze-Dried per Batch:
Average: 2-3.5 gallons freeze-dried

Annual Batches:
200 batches @ 12.5 lbs
= 2,500 lbs fresh
= 546 gal FD

CAPACITY

Medium Freeze-Dryer

Dimensions:
Black/White: 112 lbs, Stainless Steel: 133 lbs
18" W x 21.25" D x 28.5" H

Freeze-dryer Trays
4 Trays: 7.5" W x 18" D x 0.75" H

Max Fresh Food per Tray:
4 cups, 32 oz, 1 L, 2.5 lbs, 1.1 kg

Max Fresh Food per Batch:
16 cups, 128 oz, 4 L, 10 lbs, 4.5 kg

Freeze-Dried per Batch:
Average: 1.5-2.5 gallons freeze-dried

Annual Batches:
200 batches @ 7.25 lbs
= 1,450 lbs fresh
= 312 gal FD

CAPACITY

Small Freeze-Dryer

Dimensions:
Black: 61 lbs, Stainless Steel: 80 lbs
16.5" W x 18.5" D x 25" H

Freeze-dryer Trays
3 Trays: 7.75" W x 14" D x 0.75" H

Max Fresh Food per Tray:
3 cups, 24 oz, 0.8 L, 2.3 lbs, 1 kg

Max Fresh Food per Batch:
9 cups, 72 oz, 2.4 L, 7 lbs, 3 kg

Freeze-Dried per Batch:
Average: 1-1.5 gallons freeze-dried

Annual Batches:
200 batches @ 4.2 lbs
= 840 lbs fresh
= 195 gal FD

X-L   FREEZE-DRYER BATCH LOGS   PAGE#

Keep track of how the foods process in your freeze-dryer.

Batch #		Start Cooling		Trays In		Trays Out		Run Time		Extra Dry		Total	
		am pm		am pm		am pm			hrs		hrs		hrs
Start Date:		Customize	Temp	Time		Check Time:		am pm		am pm		am pm	Subtract Dry from Wet for Water Loss
End Date:		Freeze Dry				mTorr:							
Tray Contents Description:	Examples: Raw, Cooked, Thickness, Liquid, Spread			Pre-Frozen		Wet grams		Check 1 grams		Check 2 grams		Dry grams	
1				Y / N									
2				Y / N									
3				Y / N									
4				Y / N									
5				Y / N									
6				Y / N									
Notes						Chamber Cleaned:	Y / N	Oil Changed:	Y / N	Maint. Needed:	Y / N		

Batch #		Start Cooling		Trays In		Trays Out		Run Time		Extra Dry		Total	
		am pm		am pm		am pm			hrs		hrs		hrs
Start Date:		Customize	Temp	Time		Check Time:		am pm		am pm		am pm	Subtract Dry from Wet for Water Loss
End Date:		Freeze Dry				mTorr:							
Tray Contents Description:	Examples: Raw, Cooked, Thickness, Liquid, Spread			Pre-Frozen		Wet grams		Check 1 grams		Check 2 grams		Dry grams	
1				Y / N									
2				Y / N									
3				Y / N									
4				Y / N									
5				Y / N									
6				Y / N									
Notes						Chamber Cleaned:	Y / N	Oil Changed:	Y / N	Maint. Needed:	Y / N		

Batch #		Start Cooling		Trays In		Trays Out		Run Time		Extra Dry		Total	
		am pm		am pm		am pm			hrs		hrs		hrs
Start Date:		Customize	Temp	Time		Check Time:		am pm		am pm		am pm	Subtract Dry from Wet for Water Loss
End Date:		Freeze Dry				mTorr:							
Tray Contents Description:	Examples: Raw, Cooked, Thickness, Liquid, Spread			Pre-Frozen		Wet grams		Check 1 grams		Check 2 grams		Dry grams	
1				Y / N									
2				Y / N									
3				Y / N									
4				Y / N									
5				Y / N									
6				Y / N									
Notes						Chamber Cleaned:	Y / N	Oil Changed:	Y / N	Maint. Needed:	Y / N		

L   FREEZE-DRYER BATCH LOGS   PAGE#

Keep track of how the foods process in your freeze-dryer.

Batch #		Start Cooling	Trays In	Trays Out	Run Time	Extra Dry	Total
		am pm	am pm	am pm	hrs	hrs	hrs
Start Date:		Customize	Temp	Time	Check Time:	am pm	am pm	am pm	Subtract Dry from Wet for Water Loss
End Date:		Freeze Dry			mTorr:				
Tray Contents Description:	Examples: Raw, Cooked, Thickness, Liquid, Spread		Pre-Frozen	Wet grams	Check 1 grams	Check 2 grams	Dry grams	
1			Y / N					
2			Y / N					
3			Y / N					
4			Y / N					
5			Y / N					
Notes			Chamber Cleaned: Y / N	Oil Changed: Y / N	Maint. Needed: Y / N		

Batch #		Start Cooling	Trays In	Trays Out	Run Time	Extra Dry	Total
		am pm	am pm	am pm	hrs	hrs	hrs
Start Date:		Customize	Temp	Time	Check Time:	am pm	am pm	am pm	Subtract Dry from Wet for Water Loss
End Date:		Freeze Dry			mTorr:				
Tray Contents Description:	Examples: Raw, Cooked, Thickness, Liquid, Spread		Pre-Frozen	Wet grams	Check 1 grams	Check 2 grams	Dry grams	
1			Y / N					
2			Y / N					
3			Y / N					
4			Y / N					
5			Y / N					
Notes			Chamber Cleaned: Y / N	Oil Changed: Y / N	Maint. Needed: Y / N		

Batch #		Start Cooling	Trays In	Trays Out	Run Time	Extra Dry	Total
		am pm	am pm	am pm	hrs	hrs	hrs
Start Date:		Customize	Temp	Time	Check Time:	am pm	am pm	am pm	Subtract Dry from Wet for Water Loss
End Date:		Freeze Dry			mTorr:				
Tray Contents Description:	Examples: Raw, Cooked, Thickness, Liquid, Spread		Pre-Frozen	Wet grams	Check 1 grams	Check 2 grams	Dry grams	
1			Y / N					
2			Y / N					
3			Y / N					
4			Y / N					
5			Y / N					
Notes			Chamber Cleaned: Y / N	Oil Changed: Y / N	Maint. Needed: Y / N		

M   FREEZE-DRYER BATCH LOGS   PAGE#

Keep track of how the foods process in your freeze-dryer.

Batch #		Start Cooling	Trays In	Trays Out	Run Time	Extra Dry	Total
		am pm	am pm	am pm	hrs	hrs	hrs
Start Date:		Customize	Temp	Time	Check Time:	am pm	am pm	am pm	Subtract Dry from Wet for Water Loss
End Date:		Freeze							
		Dry			mTorr:				
Tray Contents Description:	Examples: Raw, Cooked, Thickness, Liquid, Spread		Pre-Frozen	Wet grams	Check 1 grams	Check 2 grams	Dry grams	
1			Y / N					
2			Y / N					
3			Y / N					
4			Y / N					
Notes			Chamber Cleaned: Y / N	Oil Changed: Y / N	Maint. Needed: Y / N		

Batch #		Start Cooling	Trays In	Trays Out	Run Time	Extra Dry	Total
		am pm	am pm	am pm	hrs	hrs	hrs
Start Date:		Customize	Temp	Time	Check Time:	am pm	am pm	am pm	Subtract Dry from Wet for Water Loss
End Date:		Freeze							
		Dry			mTorr:				
Tray Contents Description:	Examples: Raw, Cooked, Thickness, Liquid, Spread		Pre-Frozen	Wet grams	Check 1 grams	Check 2 grams	Dry grams	
1			Y / N					
2			Y / N					
3			Y / N					
4			Y / N					
Notes			Chamber Cleaned: Y / N	Oil Changed: Y / N	Maint. Needed: Y / N		

Batch #		Start Cooling	Trays In	Trays Out	Run Time	Extra Dry	Total
		am pm	am pm	am pm	hrs	hrs	hrs
Start Date:		Customize	Temp	Time	Check Time:	am pm	am pm	am pm	Subtract Dry from Wet for Water Loss
End Date:		Freeze							
		Dry			mTorr:				
Tray Contents Description:	Examples: Raw, Cooked, Thickness, Liquid, Spread		Pre-Frozen	Wet grams	Check 1 grams	Check 2 grams	Dry grams	
1			Y / N					
2			Y / N					
3			Y / N					
4			Y / N					
Notes			Chamber Cleaned: Y / N	Oil Changed: Y / N	Maint. Needed: Y / N		

S   FREEZE-DRYER BATCH LOGS   PAGE#

Keep track of how the foods process in your freeze-dryer.

Batch #		Start Cooling	Trays In	Trays Out	Run Time	Extra Dry	Total
		am pm	am pm	am pm	hrs	hrs	hrs
Start Date:		Customize	Temp	Time	Check Time:	am pm	am pm	am pm	Subtract Dry from Wet for Water Loss
		Freeze							
End Date:		Dry			mTorr:				
Tray Contents Description:	Examples: Raw, Cooked, Thickness, Liquid, Spread		Pre-Frozen	Wet grams	Check 1 grams	Check 2 grams	Dry grams	
1			Y / N					
2			Y / N					
3			Y / N					
Notes				Chamber Cleaned: Y/N	Oil Changed: Y/N	Maint. Needed: Y/N		

Batch #		Start Cooling	Trays In	Trays Out	Run Time	Extra Dry	Total
		am pm	am pm	am pm	hrs	hrs	hrs
Start Date:		Customize	Temp	Time	Check Time:	am pm	am pm	am pm	Subtract Dry from Wet for Water Loss
		Freeze							
End Date:		Dry			mTorr:				
Tray Contents Description:	Examples: Raw, Cooked, Thickness, Liquid, Spread		Pre-Frozen	Wet grams	Check 1 grams	Check 2 grams	Dry grams	
1			Y / N					
2			Y / N					
3			Y / N					
Notes				Chamber Cleaned: Y/N	Oil Changed: Y/N	Maint. Needed: Y/N		

Batch #		Start Cooling	Trays In	Trays Out	Run Time	Extra Dry	Total
		am pm	am pm	am pm	hrs	hrs	hrs
Start Date:		Customize	Temp	Time	Check Time:	am pm	am pm	am pm	Subtract Dry from Wet for Water Loss
		Freeze							
End Date:		Dry			mTorr:				
Tray Contents Description:	Examples: Raw, Cooked, Thickness, Liquid, Spread		Pre-Frozen	Wet grams	Check 1 grams	Check 2 grams	Dry grams	
1			Y / N					
2			Y / N					
3			Y / N					
Notes				Chamber Cleaned: Y/N	Oil Changed: Y/N	Maint. Needed: Y/N		

TROUBLESHOOTING

Harvest Right™ Customer Service

The phone number is 1-801-386-8960. The website is https://harvestright.com.

They have awesome customer service. They will work with you to make sure your freeze-dryer is working properly. If your machine is out of warranty they will help you get the info and parts you need so you can fix it.

The Freeze-dryer Problem Diagnosis Guide

This is the first step to getting help with your freeze-dryer when something is amiss. Here's a shortcut to the HarvestRight's website: FDHR.2MHE.COM or scan the QR Code.

On the website, go to the top right corner and click on Customer Support. Scroll down and pick a category from these options: Set Up & Basics, Vacuum Error, Refrigeration Issues, Drying Issues, Touchscreen Issues, Power Issues, and Software Versions.

From here the Diagnosis Guide will walk you through troubleshooting your particular issue. There is a lot of great help available for all kinds of issues. You can also search the customer support articles. If you don't get it worked out with the guide, then submit a ticket to get personal help. You can do that on the same page.

Facebook Groups & Pages

Join a few freeze-drying Facebook groups to connect with other people like you, check out recipe ideas and tips, and also get help troubleshooting your machine if the need arises. There are a lot of members with the information you may need and the compiled group knowledge is invaluable for getting helpful ideas quickly.

Micro-Homesteading Education's Freeze-Drying Facebook group is "Food Preservation with Freeze Drying." Connect with us! Scan the QR Code or use the shortcut: FDFB.2MHE.COM.

Contact Us:

Email: freeze-drying@micro-homesteading-education.com
Website: www.micro-homesteading-education.com
Facebook Group: www.facebook.com/groups/foodpreservationwithfreezedrying

MAINTENANCE LOG

Keep track of your freeze-dryer maintenance and repair expenses.

Date	Part/Service	Cost	Notes

MAINTENANCE LOG

Keep track of your freeze-dryer maintenance and repair expenses.

Date	Part/Service	Cost	Notes

IMPORTANT INFORMATION
ABOUT MY FREEZE-DRYER

Chosen Name

Size Option

Model Number

Serial Number

Purchase Date

Order Number

Software

Updates

Vacuum Pump

Oil Change Info

Preferred Oil

Customer Service

IMPORTANT INFORMATION
ABOUT MY FREEZE-DRYER

Chosen Name

Size Option

Model Number

Serial Number

Purchase Date

Order Number

Software

Updates

Vacuum Pump

Oil Change Info

Preferred Oil

Customer Service

NOTES

NOTES

GLOSSARY

A

Abrasive: Harsh or corrosive.

Accelerate: To speed up a process.

Accumulate: Increase gradually.

Additive: A substance added to food to increase its storage life.

Airtight: Impermeable to air.

Allergens: A common substance that has the ability to induce an allergy.

Altitude: Elevation above sea level.

Ambient temperature: Average temperature of an environment.

Artificial: Not natural. Man-made.

Automated: Operates without needing adjustment or instructions.

B

Bacteria: Single-celled microorganisms which can cause disease.

Batch: The quantity prepared during one operation.

Best if used by date: Recommended date to eat food before it loses its nutrients.

Blanch: Process of steaming food to remove its skin. Typically 3-5 minutes in boiling water.

Boil: Cook in boiling water.

Botulism: Acute food poisoning caused by bacteria.

C

Canning: Preserving food in jars by the use of heat.

Climate: Average weather condition of a place.

Commercial: Products designed for large markets.

Compress: Reduce in volume or size.

Consistency: Firmness or density of a substance.

Consume: To eat or use a substance.

Contaminated: Soiled from exposure to bacteria.

Conversion: To change from one measurement to another.

Coolant: Fluid used to cool the temperature in a machine.

Cycle: Interval of time from the beginning of a process to the end.

D

Debris: Waste materials such as lint, dirt, or dust.

Decay: Gradually decrease in quality.

Decibels: Unit for expressing sound.

Default: Pre-set setting that runs automatically.

Defrost: The process of melting ice.

Dehydrate: Remove water from food.

Deplete: To lessen, finish or empty a substance.

Desiccant: A substance that absorbs moisture from the surrounding environment. Not for use with freeze-dried foods.

Deteriorate: Decrease in quality.
Discoloration: Losing original coloration.
Distribute: To lay out a substance or weight evenly over a surface.
Drain line: Thin plastic tube used to drain water out of a machine.
Dry cycle: Interval of time in which drying takes place.

E
Edible: Safe to eat.

F
Food grade: A material that is safe for the storage of food products.
Freeze cycle: Interval of time in which freezing takes place.
Freeze-drying: The process of removing water from food through freezing, heating, and sublimation.
Freezer burn: The loss of moisture from frozen foods, leaving the food shriveled.

G
Gas: Vaporous state of a liquid or solid.
Gasket: A rubber seal used to make a joint airtight.

H
Humidity: Degree of moisture in the atmosphere.

I
Impulse sealer: A machine used to seal plastic using heat.

L
Life-sustaining shelf-life: The time until a food product is not safe to consume.
Lightweight: Less than average weight.
Liquid: Fluid state of a product.
Lubricant: Substance used to oil components to prevent friction.

M
Mercury: A liquid, heavy metallic element.
Microorganisms: Organisms invisible to the naked eye.
Minerals: Elements found on earth and in food essential for bodily health and growth.
Moisture: Small quantities of condensed liquid, typically water.
Molecules: A tiny particle of a substance composed of one or more atoms.
MTorr (T): A very small pressure unit used to measure vacuum pressure.
Mylar bags: Food-grade plastic bags used to store dry food.

N
Nutrition content: The number of healthy vitamins and minerals contained in food.

O
O-rings: Rubber rings used to seal fittings, making them airtight.
Outlet: Receptacle for an electronic plug.
Oxidize: To introduce oxygen.
Oxygen Absorbers: A sealed sachet that contains iron fillings used to absorb oxygen from sealed containers. Used for freeze-drying.

P
Predetermined: A direction or decision made before the process begins.
Pre-freezing: To freeze foods 24-48 hours before freezing them to a lower temperature in the freeze-dryer.

Preservation: The act of prolonging the life of food.
Pressure: The force exerted on a surface.
Proteins: A molecule made up of amino acids, enzymes, and antibodies.

R
Reconstitute: To restore food to its original condition by adding water.
Rehydrate: To add moisture back into a product.
Residual: The small amount of a substance that remains after most of it has been removed.
Retains: Holds in a substance.
Roast: Cook by exposing to surrounding heat, as in an oven.

S
Sauté: Fry food in a small amount of fat, water, or other liquid.
Sealer: A piece of machinery used to seal containers through a vacuum or heat.
Serving size: Recommended portion of food for a meal.
Shelf-life: Period of time in which a product can be stored and remain edible.
Silica Gel: A type of desiccant that is used to remove moisture from packaged items. Not for use with freeze-dried foods.
Silicone: A flexible water and heat-resistant substance that is used to create molds.
Solid: The hard state of a substance.
Spoil: To lose all valuable nutrients and quality.
Sublimation: The process of water passing directly from a solid to a vapor state, bypassing the liquid state.
Substitution: To replace one product with another similar product.
Suction: The act of removing a substance, such as air, from a container.

T
Tare: To adjust the scale to make the weight of the container 0.
Torr (t): A unit of pressure measured in millimeters of mercury.
Triple point: The temperature and pressure at which water can be a solid, liquid, or gas.

V
Vacuum pump: A machine that creates a low-pressure environment by removing air.
Valve: Mechanical device which stops or starts the flow of liquid or air.
Ventilation: Circulation of air.
Versatile: Something that can be used in many ways.
Vitamins: Organic compounds that are beneficial for growth and nutrition.
Volume: Measurement of liquid content.

W
Warp: Curving or bending of a straight surface.
Wicking: The process of absorbing or moving liquid by capillary action.

REFERENCES

Design of healthy snack based on Kiwifruit. (n.d.). PubMed Central (PMC).
   https://www.ncbi.nlm.nih.gov/pmc/articles/PMC7397248/

Freeze-drying technology in foods. (n.d.). PubMed Central (PMC).
   https://www.ncbi.nlm.nih.gov/pmc/articles/PMC7404989/

Fundamentals of freeze-drying. (n.d.). PubMed.

High efficient freeze-drying technology in food industry. (n.d.). Semantic Scholar |
   AI-Powered Research Tool.
   https://www.semanticscholar.org/paper/High-efficient-freeze-drying-technology-in-food-
   Liu-Zhang/2b40b2f06a339ca684a5b8da4d752d6314d7e123

Impact of three different dehydration methods on nutritional values and sensory quality of
   dried broccoli, oranges, and carrots. (n.d.). PubMed Central (PMC).
   https://www.ncbi.nlm.nih.gov/pmc/articles/PMC7602416/

Is freeze-dried food healthy? An expert weighs in. (2022, September 12). EZ-Prepping.
   https://ezprepping.com/freeze-dried-food-healthy/

Lang, A. (n.d.). freeze-drying: How it works, benefits, and how-to. Healthline.
   https://www.healthline.com/nutrition/freeze-drying

LeafSide Team. (2022, March 1). What is freeze-drying? Are freeze-dried foods safe and
   healthy? LeafSide.
   https://www.goleafside.com/faq-one/what-is-freeze-drying-are-freeze-dried-foods-safe-an
   d-healthy/

Primary Drying Optimization in Pharmaceutical Freeze-Drying: A Multivial Stochastic
   Modeling Framework. (2020, February 24). ACS Publications.
   https://pubs.acs.org/doi/10.1021/acs.iecr.9b06402

Should I eat freeze-dried fruits and vegetables? (2022, September 29). DrWeil.com.
   https://www.drweil.com/diet-nutrition/should-i-eat-freeze-dried-fruits-and-vegetables/

Images used with permission from Katilyn Prickett, Christina Jewell, Rob Prickett,
   Shutterstock, and Canva.

AUTHOR BIO

Micro-Homesteading Education's co-founders, Katilyn Prickett and Christina Jewell are sisters on a mission to help families achieve food stability. They focus on sharing simple sustainability by teaching practical skills anyone can learn.

Both of them own a freeze-dryer and have enjoyed consuming freeze-dried foods since 2015. They are excited about this state-of-the-art method of preserving food that is the way of the future and want to help others learn this art quickly.

The team working behind Micro-Homesteading Education has over 35 years of experience in gardening and food preservation, horticulture and animal husbandry. They want to help readers gain comfort from a full pantry without the overwhelm that comes from full-scale homesteading.

They teach about growing nutritious food, raising healthy animals, creating a micro-homestead, and preserving the harvest so you can regularly make healthy, mouth-watering meals from the storage pantry. They encourage others to start small and do what they can.

There are tremendous benefits from healthy eating and peace from growing and storing your own food. Micro-Homesteading Education wants others to experience the joy of seeing their plants and their pantry grow with nutrition.

The team is committed to sharing knowledge and takes extra care to provide information suitable for beginners while being thorough. Micro-Homesteading Education's mission is to create highly educational content that will support learning various homesteading skills. They are committed to alleviating the learning curve by teaching simple ways to gradually become capable of growing or raising food and then preserving it for use throughout the coming years.

Contact Us:

Email: contact@micro-homesteading-education.com

Website: www.micro-homesteading-education.com

Facebook Groups & Pages

www.facebook.com/microhomesteadingeducationcom

www.facebook.com/groups/foodpreservationwithfreezedrying

www.facebook.com/groups/funwithgardeningandhomesteading

Scan the QR code or visit the shortcut to Facebook Group: FDFB.2MHE.COM